The Ottoman Empire and Early Modern Europe

Despite the fact that its capital city and over one third of its territory were within the continent of Europe, the Ottoman Empire has consistently been regarded as a place apart, inextricably divided from the West by differences of culture and religion. A perception of its militarism, its barbarism, its tyranny, the sexual appetites of its rulers, and its pervasive exoticism has led historians to measure the Ottoman world against a western standard and find it lacking. In recent decades, a dynamic and convincing scholarship has emerged that seeks to comprehend and, in the process, to de-exoticize this enduring realm. Daniel Goffman provides a thorough introduction to the history and institutions of the Ottoman Empire from this new standpoint, and presents a claim for its inclusion in Europe. His lucid and engaging book – an important addition to New Approaches to European History – will be essential reading for undergraduates.

DANIEL GOFFMAN is Professor of History at Ball State University. His publications include *Izmir and the Levantine world, 1550–1650* (Seattle, WA, 1990), *Britons in the Ottoman Empire, 1642–1660* (Seattle, WA, 1998) and *The Ottoman City between East and West: Aleppo, Izmir, and Istanbul*, with Edhem Eldem and Bruce Masters (Cambridge, 1999). He is currently editor of the *Middle East Studies Association Bulletin*.

D0819357

New Approaches to European History

Series editors
WILLIAM BEIK *Emory University*
T. C. W. BLANNING *Sidney Sussex College, Cambridge*

New Approaches to European History is an important textbook series, which provides concise but authoritative surveys of major themes and problems in European history since the Renaissance. Written at a level and length accessible to advanced school students and undergraduates, each book in the series addresses topics or themes that students of European history encounter daily: the series embraces both some of the more "traditional" subjects of study, and those cultural and social issues to which increasing numbers of school and college courses are devoted. A particular effort is made to consider the wider international implications of the subject under scrutiny.

To aid the student reader scholarly apparatus and annotation is light, but each work has full supplementary bibliographies and notes for further reading: where appropriate chronologies, maps, diagrams and other illustrative material are also provided.

For a list of titles published in the series, please see end of book.

The Ottoman Empire
and Early Modern Europe

Daniel Goffman

Ball State University

CAMBRIDGE
UNIVERSITY PRESS

PUBLISHED BY THE PRESS SYNDICATE OF THE UNIVERSITY OF CAMBRIDGE
The Pitt Building, Trumpington Street, Cambridge, United Kingdom

CAMBRIDGE UNIVERSITY PRESS
The Edinburgh Building, Cambridge CB2 2RU, UK
40 West 20th Street, New York, NY 10011-4211, USA
477 Williamstown Road, Port Melbourne, VIC 3207, Australia
Ruiz de Alarcón 13, 28014 Madrid, Spain
Dock House, The Waterfront, Cape Town 8001, South Africa

http://www.cambridge.org

First published 2002
Fourth printing 2005

Printed in the United Kingdom at the University Press, Cambridge

Typeface Plantin 10/12 pt.   *System* LaTeX 2_ε [TB]

A catalogue record for this book is available from the British Library

Goffman, Daniel, 1954–
The Ottoman empire and early modern Europe / Daniel Goffman.
   p.   cm. – (New approaches to European history; 24)
Includes bibliographical references and index.
ISBN 0 521 45280 5 (hardback) – ISBN 0 521 45908 7 (paperback)
1. Turkey – History – Ottoman Empire, 1288–1918.   2. Turkey –
Relations – Europe.   3. Europe – Relations – Turkey.   4. Turkey –
Civilization – European influences.   I. Title.   II. Series.
DR486 .G62   2002
956.1′015 – dc21   2001043336

ISBN 0 521 45280 5 hardback
ISBN 0 521 45908 7 paperback

In Memoriam
Donald F. Lach
(1917–2000)

Contents

Illustrations

Maps

Preface

The writing of Ottoman history has changed dramatically, for the better I believe, in the past few decades. In part, a widening access to Ottoman source materials in Istanbul, Ankara, Jerusalem, Cairo, and elsewhere has supplemented and in some cases supplanted the Ottoman chronicles and western European correspondences and observations that previously had constituted the documentary backbone of our knowledge of the empire. Increasing reliance upon the views of the Ottomans about themselves in place of often hostile outside observers has allowed us to better imagine an Ottoman world from the inside. In addition, a growing appreciation for non-European societies and civilizations and the generation of new historical and literary analytical techniques have helped us take advantage of this plethora of documentation, while enlivening and making more sophisticated the historiography of the early modern Ottoman world.

One goal of *The Ottoman Empire and early modern Europe* is to help move some of these innovative and stimulating approaches toward Ottoman history out of monographic and article form and make them accessible to a general and student audience. The result may seem a hybrid between the new and the old, for developments within the field have been uneven, many gaps remain in our knowledge, and some of our interpretations still are speculative or rest on publications and approaches that are terribly outdated. For example, whereas recent studies provide thought-provoking insight into elite Ottoman households, our knowledge of gender relations outside of the privileged order remains thin. Similarly, we know much more about urban societies and economies in the Ottoman world than we do about their rural counterparts. This volume cannot help but reflect such strengths and weaknesses within the field of Ottoman studies. Indeed, I hope that a sense of these irregularities will help stimulate readers to explore our many empty historical spaces.

Perhaps unavoidably, this work also echoes its author's own attraction to certain aspects of Ottoman history, such as the rich and multi-layered world of the early modern eastern Mediterranean or the similarities and differences between western European and Ottoman treatment of religious minorities. Consequently, in the following pages the reader will find more on the Venetians than on the Austrians or Hungarians, and more on social organization than on diplomacy. Threaded through these topics and emphases, however, is a core belief that the early modern Ottoman Empire constituted an integral component of Europe, and that neither the Ottoman polity nor Europe makes a lot of sense without the other.

The Ottoman Empire and early modern Europe adopts a two-pronged approach toward investigating the dealings between the Ottoman Empire and the rest of Europe. The body of the text is broadly chronological, examining Ottoman political, religious, societal, diplomatic, and economic concerns, particularly in that empire's dealings with the balance of the European landmass. Since a principal intent is to look at Europe from the Ottoman perspective – an approach which demands some knowledge of the Ottoman world – Part One of the text gives considerable weight to Ottoman organizations and peoples. Part Two of the narrative then focuses on how such institutions and the personalities they produced co-existed with and influenced the Mediterranean and European worlds. Within this structure the book offers examinations of particular topics – such as the construction of an Ottoman imagined past, the Ottoman–Venetian conflicts, and the development and composition of commerce, diplomacy, the sultanate, the janissary corps, and other Ottoman pursuits and institutions. By this means the text undertakes to integrate much of the fresh and enterprising historiography of recent years into a broad examination of Ottoman events and issues.

Prefacing each chapter of this master narrative is one in a series of "vignettes" that venture to address a troubling quandary in Ottoman historiography. Although pre-modern Ottoman studies is blessed with a profusion of chronicles and administrative sources, it seems to me that a paucity of diaries, memoirs, letters, and similar writings has served to dampen scholarship in this potentially tantalizing discipline. In other words, despite the celebrated poetry of devotion that so displays the characters of Süleyman and his wife Hürrem, Evliya Çelebi's revealing comments about his patron Melek Ahmed Pasha and his wives, and a few other scattered revelatory tidbits,[1] there is an acute shortage of personality – which after all constitutes the sinew of historical narrative – in our sources on the early modern Ottoman world.

[1] See, on Süleyman and Hürrem, Leslie P. Peirce, *The imperial harem: Women and sovereignty in the Ottoman empire* (Oxford, 1993); and, on Melek Ahmed Pasha, Evliya Çelebi, *The intimate life of an Ottoman statesman: Melek Ahmed Pasha (1588–1661)*, intro. and trans. Robert Dankoff, historical commentary Rhoads Murphey (Albany, 1991).

These vignettes aim to follow the lead of historians and writers in other fields[2] to flesh out and personalize the historical record. My intent is not to concoct fables, but to conjecture on the basis of available information how a particular individual in a certain situation might have behaved, in order to recreate as realistically as possible the movements, associations, and dispositions of a person who was physically and culturally embedded in Ottoman civilization. Relatively extensive notes help mark the line where documented knowledge ends and supposition begins. It is hoped that the reader will gain from this method a richer and more empathetic understanding of an Ottoman world that many Westerners, inaccurately I believe, consider alien, profane, unknowable, and inconsequential. In turn, one purpose of the master narrative is to describe and explain the world in which Kubad Çavuş, the subject of the pseudo-biographical vignettes, lived.

[2] I have in mind such works as Maxime Hong Kingston, *The woman warrior* (New York, 1976); Jonathan D. Spence, *The death of woman Wang* (New York, 1978); Robert Darnton, *The Great Cat Massacre and other episodes in French cultural history* (New York, 1984); Simon Schama, *Dead certainties (unwarranted speculations)* (New York, 1992); and Amitav Ghosh, *In an antique land: history in the guise of a traveler's tale* (New York, 1992). The idea for the vignettes offered here also owes much to Selim Deringil, *The well protected domains: ideology and the legitimation of power in the Ottoman Empire, 1876–1909* (London, 1998); and Edhem Eldem, "Istanbul: from imperial to peripheral capital," in *The Ottoman city between East and West: Aleppo, Izmir, and Istanbul* ed. Edhem Eldem, Daniel Goffman, and Bruce Masters (Cambridge, 1999), pp. 135–207.

Acknowledgments

Several years ago, Richard Fisher of Cambridge University Press came to me with the suggestion that the Press would like to include a book on the Ottoman Empire in their series New Approaches to European History. This volume is one result of that proposal, and I thank him and Cambridge University Press for wishing to include the Ottoman world in this series. I also am grateful to my editors, Vicky Cuthill, Elizabeth Howard, and Sophie Read, for their diligence and patience with a project that took several detours and arrived at their offices rather late, and to my copy-editor, Leigh Mueller.

As with every such undertaking, this book owes a great deal to many people. Its first draft was sketched out during a rich and exciting year at Boğaziçi University in 1993–94. I thank the members of the department of history at that institution – particularly Selim Deringil, Edhem Eldem, Selçuk Esenbel, and Aptullah Kuran – for hosting me and serving as tireless sounding boards. I also thank my own institution, Ball State University, for providing me with time to write this volume, and my Department of History for its support and enthusiasm. Our faculty seminar has become a model of its kind, a sharp and constructive intellectual scalpel, and twice my colleagues – Larry Birken, Jim Connolly, Michael Doyle, Rene Marion, Chris Thompson, and several others – have read, critiqued, and helped shape chapters from this work. I have also twice presented versions of the Kubad Çavuş vignettes publicly, once in 1998 at a conference in Istanbul organized by Suraiya Faroqhi and a second time at New York University at the kind invitation of Ariel Salzmann. Each occasion was stimulating and encouraging, and I thank both the organizers and participants for the opportunities to present and for the lively discussions that followed.

The research and writing of this book relied upon a number of universities, archives, libraries, and endowments. At Ball State University, Ronald Johnstone (the Dean of Sciences and Humanities), Warren Vander Hill (the Provost), Ray White and John Barber (the chairs of the Department of History), and the staff of the Office of Research have generously supported me with time off for research and writing as well as with various matching monies. The principal archives I have made use of in this project are the Başbakanlık Osmanlı Arşivi in Istanbul and the Public Record Office in London. The staffs of both of these facilities are knowledgeable and exceptionally gracious. They have my profound thanks, as do the staffs of the Bodleian Library in Oxford, the British Library in London, the Library of Congress in Washington, and the Bracken Library in Muncie. The research and an early draft of this book were undertaken during a year in Istanbul. The National Endowment for the Humanities made that trip possible through its Fellowship for College Teachers and Independent Scholars, and I am deeply grateful to this endowment, which through the years has given so very much to the humanities. The Ball State Department of Geography is blessed with a wonderful cartographer, Connie McOmber, who prepared the maps (as she has done for me twice before) with uncommon patience, diligence, and expertise. Lori A. Sammons patiently helped me proofread the final version of this book.

The final drafts of this book benefited enormously from the scrutiny of several readers. First of all, Kevin Brooks, Mike Brown, Brett Calland, Brent Chapman, Eric Conderman, Chris Farr, Kirk Overstreet, and Julie Reitz, all students in my graduate course on the early modern eastern Mediterranean world, read, critiqued, and vastly improved it. In addition, Cambridge University Press itself provided three anonymous referees. Although I cannot thank them by name for their sometimes tough but always thoughtful comments, I am grateful nonetheless. I also asked three other colleagues to read the manuscript, which they did with care and energy. My deepest thanks, then, go to Ginny Aksan, Drew Cayton, and Carolyn Goffman. Without their critical input, this volume would have been much less than it is; without their keen and prudent support, it could not have been written at all. I used to thank my daughter and son for distracting me and reminding me about real values. More and more, however, I find myself marveling at and drawing upon their quick and critical minds. I thank Sam and Laura especially for providing this service, and pledge: the next one is for you!

The Ottoman Empire and early modern Europe is dedicated to the memory of Donald F. Lach, who died just months before its completion. For three years I worked as Donald's graduate assistant at the University of Chicago. His devotion to his scholarship was unrivaled, and his faith in my efforts more than anything else kept me going while a student at that university. Donald's vision of world history has been much in my thoughts the past few months as I have worked through the last stages of this manuscript, which is deeply inspired by his example and his monumental *Asia in the making of Europe*. I end these acknowledgments with a paraphrase from Donald Lach's own writings: the mistakes that exist in this book are my responsibility alone, and I only hope that they are funny and not fundamental.

Note on usage

There are many transliteration schemes for Arabic-script terms. In this text, I have kept such words to the minimum. Nevertheless, in those cases when they have seemed unavoidable, I have adopted modern Turkish orthography (except for words that have found their way into the English language, such as kadi or pasha). Several simple rules will allow the reader to pronounce these words with some accuracy:

> *c* sounds like the English *j*
> *ç* sounds like the English *ch*
> *ğ* is silent but lengthens any preceding vowel
> *ı* sounds like the *a* in *serial*
> *j* sounds like the French *j*
> *ö* sounds like the French *eu* in *peu*
> *ş* sounds like the English *sh*
> *ü* sounds like the French *u* in *lune*

Vocalization that stresses no syllable generally is the most faithful. Ottoman terms are contextually defined in the glossary and can be found with their Ottoman Turkish spellings in *The new Redhouse Turkish–English dictionary* (Istanbul, 1968).

Chronological table of events

1071	Battle of Manzikert; Seljuk Turks established in Asia Minor
1204	Fourth Crusaders capture Constantinople
c. 1300	Foundation of the Ottoman Empire
c. 1301	Osman defeats Byzantine force at Baphaeon
c. 1324	Death of Osman; succession of Orhan
c. 1326	Ottoman conquest of Bursa
c. 1345	Ottomans appropriate the emirate of Karasi
c. 1346	Orhan marries Theodora, daughter of John VI Cantacuzenus
c. 1352	Ottomans cross over into Europe by taking Tzympe
c. 1354	Ottomans take Gallipoli
1361	Conquest of Adrianople (Edirne)
1362	Death of Orhan; succession of Murad I
1389	First Battle of Kosovo; death of Murad I; succession of Bayezid I
1402	Defeat and death of Bayezid I at hands of Tamerlane
1402–13	Ottoman Interregnum
1413	Mehmed I proclaimed sultan
1420	Murad II accedes to the throne
1423–30	Ottoman–Venetian War
1444	Murad II abdicates in favor of his son Mehmed; Battle of Varna
1446	Murad II's second accession to the throne
1451	Mehmed II's second accession to the throne
1453	Ottoman conquest of Constantinople
1463–79	Ottoman–Venetian War
1470	Ottoman conquest of the island of Negroponte
1480	Ottoman landing at Otranto in Italy
1481	Death of Mehmed II and accession of Bayezid II
1498	Vasco da Gama brings Portuguese ships into the Indian Ocean

1499–1502	Ottoman–Venetian War
1512	Abdication of Bayezid II and accession of Selim I
1514	Battle of Çaldıran
1516–17	Ottoman conquest of Syria, Egypt, and the Hijaz
1517	Protestant Reformation
1520	Death of Selim I and accession of Süleyman I
1521	Ottoman conquest of Belgrade
1522	Ottoman conquest of Rhodes
1526	Battle of Mohács
1528	Luther publishes his "On War Against the Turk"
1529	Ottomans capture Buda; first Ottoman siege of Vienna
1533	Hayreddin Barbarossa becomes Ottoman grand admiral
1534	Ottoman conquest of Tabriz and Baghdad
1535	Grand vizier İbrahim Pasha executed
1537–39	Ottoman–Venetian War
1538	Naval battle at Préveza
1541	Ottomans annex Hungary
1543	Franco-Ottoman fleet take control of Nice
1551–52	Ottomans take control of Transylvania
1552	Prince Mustafa executed
1565	Ottoman siege of Malta
1566	Death of Süleyman and accession of Selim II
1569	French capitulations
1570–73	Ottoman–Venetian War
1570	Ottoman attack upon Cyprus
1571	Ottoman conquest of Cyprus and defeat in the naval battle of Lepanto
1574	Death of Selim II and accession of Murad III
1578–90	War with Persia
1580	English capitulations
1595	Death of Murad III and accession of Mehmed III
1603	Death of Mehmed III and accession of Ahmed I
1603–18	War with Persia
1606	Peace Treaty of Zsitva-Török
1612	Dutch capitulations
1617	Death of Ahmed I and first accession of Mustafa I
1618	Deposition of Mustafa I and accession of Osman II
1622	Assassination of Osman II and second accession of Mustafa I
1623	Death of Mustafa I and accession of Murad IV

The Ottoman House through 1687
(dates are regnant)

Osman (*c.* 1299–1324)
|
Orhan (*c.* 1324–62)
|
Murad I (1362–89)
|
Bayezid I (1389–1402)
|
Ottoman Civil War (1402–13)
|
Mehmed I (1413–20)
|
Murad II (1420–44, 1446–51)
|
Mehmed II (1444–46, 1451–81)
|
Bayezid II (1481–1512)
|
Selim I (1512–20)
|
Süleyman I (1520–66)
|
Selim II (1566–74)
|
Murad III (1574–95)
|
Mehmed III (1595–1603)
|
Ahmed I (1603–17)————Mustafa I (1617–18, 1622–23)
                                        |
Osman II (1618–22)————Murad IV (1623–40)————İbrahim (1640–48)
                                                            |
Mehmed IV (1648–87)

1 Introduction: Ottomancentrism and the West

One chapter in a recent history of the Ottomans begins with the assertion that "the Ottoman Empire lived for war."[1] This statement constitutes a concise précis of a damaging and misleading stereotype, long pervasive in both Europe and the United States. Pursuing this thesis of an acute Ottoman militancy, the author explains that "every governor in this empire was a general; every policeman was a janissary; every mountain pass had its guards, and every road a military destination." Not only were officials also soldiers, this account declares, but "even madmen had a regiment, the *deli*, or loons, Riskers of their Souls, who were used, since they did not object, as human battering rams, or human bridges." Indeed, according to this same writer, it was "outbreaks of peace [that] caused trouble at home, as men clamoured for the profit and the glory." Although these and similar observations strictly speaking may not be wholly false, they certainly are partial (*deli* in modern Turkish indeed suggests "loony" or "deranged"; in Ottoman Turkish, however, a more accurate translation would be "brave" or even "heroic"), dangerously credible, and confirm long-lived Western assumptions that the Ottoman state was thoroughly and relentlessly martial. Even more misleadingly, they imply that such militarism was somehow peculiarly foreign and contrary to Western norms.

The truth is that such portrayals not only privilege a single aspect of a rich and varied world, but also could describe virtually any state in early modern Europe. Did the early modern Habsburg state, the French state,

---

[1] Jason Goodwin, *Lords of the horizons: a history of the Ottoman Empire* (London, 1998), p. 65. In general, though, this is among the most readable and sympathetic of such texts. Indeed, at times it reads like an apologetic, a tone that makes Goodwin's stress on Ottoman militarism all the more salient. The notion stands at the very core of other books. In his *The Ottoman impact on Europe* (New York, 1968), p. 77, for example, Paul Coles writes: "From the point of their first entrance into history as a nomadic war-band, the Ottomans were carried from one triumph to the next by a ruthless dedication to conquest and predation. . . . The perpetual search, in Gibbon's phrase, for 'new enemies and new subjects' was not a policy, weighed against alternatives; it was a law of life, the principle that animated what had now become a large and complex society."

THE OTTOMAN EMPIRE
AS PART OF EUROPE

Map 1

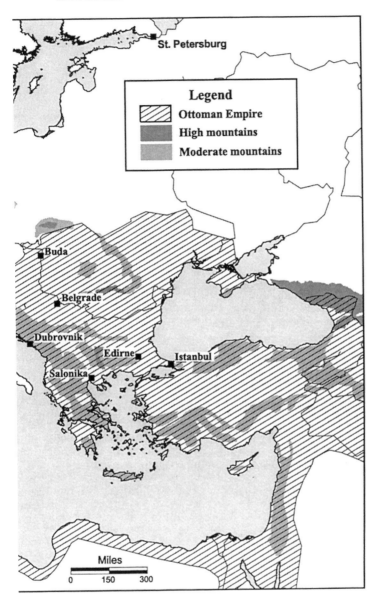

or the English state somehow *not* live for war? Were the sheriffs of England not also both policemen and soldiers? Were Peter the Hermit, who led a group of peasants against seasoned *delis*, others who led Christian children on suicidal crusades, and numerous Christian extremists not just as fanatically committed to their faith as were frenzied Ottoman soldiers? Bayezid I may or may not have proclaimed "For this was I born, to bear arms," as the same recent text avows.[2] Is it any less likely, however, that Bayezid's contemporaries in late feudal Europe would have uttered the same words? Many of the protagonists in William Shakespeare's history plays espouse soldierly virtues. Some, such as Coriolanus (even though his proud spirit in the end defeated him), certainly seemed born for war, and others, such as Henry V, seemed to become "kingly" only through the vehicle of war. Voltaire, perhaps cynically but certainly baldly, states that "the first who was king was a successful soldier. He who serves well his country has no need of ancestors," a sentiment that Sir Walter Scott seconds: "What can they see in the longest kingly line in Europe, save that it runs back to a successful soldier?"[3] Should we then believe that the Habsburg Charles V or the French Francis I were less bellicose than their Ottoman contemporary Süleyman (the Magnificent and Lawgiver)? The Ottoman state and society certainly was distinctive (what polity is not?). It was not, however, exceptional in its militarism, in its brutality, or, as others have claimed, in its misogyny or its sexual appetites, and it simply buys into Christian and Western legends to proclaim that such characteristics were somehow distinctly Ottoman.[4]

The existence of such Eurocentric mythologizing in scholarship is almost axiomatic.[5] Particularly in the last four centuries – the conventionally labeled ages of European exploration, European expansion, European imperialism, and European retreat – especially western Europe has imagined itself politically, philosophically, and geographically at the

---

[2] Goodwin, *Lords of the Horizons*, p. 66.

[3] François Marie Arouet de Voltaire, *Mérope, a tragedy*, by Aaron Hill, adapted for theatrical representation (London, 1795), Act I, sc. 3; and Sir Walter Scott, *Woodstock* (New York, 2001), Ch. 28.

[4] The idea of an innate Ottoman military prowess persists to the present day, in the United States as well as Europe. On which see John M. VanderLippe, "The 'Terrible Turk': the formulation and perpetuation of a stereotype in American foreign policy," *New Perspectives on Turkey* 17(1997): 39–57.

[5] On which see Thierry Hentsch, *Imagining the Middle East*, trans. Fred A. Reed (Montreal, 1992), pp. 1–48 and *passim*. The very idea of Eurocentrism also may be anachronistic for the early modern era, since Europe is a cultural and secular rather than a geographic notion and neither Christian nor Muslim imagined a "European" culture before the eighteenth century (see M. E. Yapp, "Europe in the Turkish mirror," *Past and Present* 137[1992]: 134–55). There is, of course, a strong tendency to associate Europe with Christianity.

center of the world. Europeans and neo-Europeans in America and else-where have routinely judged art, literature, religion, statecraft, and tech-nology according to their own authorities and criteria.[6] It remains to this day a common conviction that few have measured up to these stan-dards – certainly not the Ottomans with their menacing and seemingly "demonic religion" and "savage nomadic ways." The academy no less than governments and the press has reflected this condescension, a coali-tion of points of view that has led to an almost irresistible temptation to view the globe "downward" from Paris and London or more recently Washington and New York. In this schema the Ottoman Empire joins the ranks of the "others" – exotic, inexplicable, unchanging, and acted upon by the powers of ruling authorities in Europe.

Such an attitude has been aptly designated as "orientalist" and has pre-disposed some historians to consider not only the Ottoman Empire but also other societies and ideas deemed "non-western" as peripheral to the concert of European states and their cultural satellites. In the Ottoman case as in others, scholars have tended to emphasize those aspects of soci-ety that are distinct from Europe. They have stressed that the Ottomans' ethnicity, language, religion, and even organizational aptitude differed from the European standard. All too often, implicit in this fixation on divergence is an assumption of inferiority, of uncivilized savagery (such as the conventional if hackneyed argument that plunder was the exclu-sive stimulus for Ottoman empire-building). As Said has pointed out: "Not for nothing did Islam come to symbolize terror, devastation, the demonic, hordes of hated barbarians. For Europe, Islam was a lasting trauma." He perhaps too categorically specifies that "until the end of the seventeenth century the 'Ottoman peril' lurked alongside Europe to rep-resent for the whole of Christian civilization a constant danger, and in time European civilization incorporated that period and its lore, its great events, figures, virtues, and vices, as something woven into the fabric of life." This author further argues that "like Walter Scott's Saracens, the European representation of the Muslim, Ottoman, or Arab was always a way of controlling the redoubtable Orient, and to a certain extent the same is true of the methods of contemporary learned Orientalists."[7]

Certainly, as Said contends, many within European society grew to dread the Ottoman giant to its east. Nevertheless, this attitude was not fixed; nor did it ever become nearly as hegemonic as he suggests.[8] Not

---

[6] The British treatment of India is a celebrated case, on which see Jyotsna G. Singh, *Colonial narratives, cultural dialogues: "discoveries" of India in the languages of colonialism* (London and New York, 1996).

[7] Edward Said, *Orientalism* (New York, 1978), pp. 59–60.

[8] On which see Hentsch, *Imagining the Middle East*.

only must one generally differentiate the attitudes of northern from Mediterranean Europe, but those western Europeans who experienced the Ottoman Empire first-hand often regarded it with respect, albeit with some apprehension. Furthermore, political philosophers who read these travelers' thoughtful texts, such as Guillaume Postel and Jean Bodin, helped nourish an esteem for many Ottoman institutions through their own writings. Nevertheless, the proclivity of historians to envisage the Empire as ignoble and antithetical to "refined" Western standards undoubtedly has obscured the nuances of Ottoman civilization as well as the many common elements between it and the rest of Europe.

Europe viewed from afar

We are not compelled to view the world from such a western-European perspective. The physical world has neither apex nor nadir, and it makes just as much geographic sense, to take an equally arbitrary case, to study the Far West (western Europe) from the viewpoint of the Near West (the Ottoman Empire) as it does to foreground the successor states of Christendom. If we imagine Istanbul rather than Paris at the middle of the world, Ottoman relations with the rest of Europe assume a startling character.

Historians customarily describe the Turkoman incursions into Anatolia and the Balkans as barbarian plunderings; however, one can just as easily imagine them as the foundation for a new and liberating empire. The fall of Constantinople to the Ottomans is typically portrayed as a catastrophe for western civilization; however, one might as readily see in the change of regime the rebirth of a splendid city long severed from its life-giving hinterlands.[9] The Ottoman conquest of the Balkans is often imagined as a suspension of that region's history, the immobilization of a society imprisoned for several centuries in the "yoke" of an exogenous and ungodly conqueror. With a change of perspective, however, one might regard the societal commingling and cultural blending that accompanied the infusion of Ottoman civilization into Europe as an explosion of vigor and creativity. The Ottoman Empire conventionally has been seen as a persecutor of Christians, but one might judge it instead a

---

[9] The very nomenclature for this city is muddied by rival claims to it (most powerfully, Greek versus Turkish). We will here refer to Ottoman Constantinople (also sometimes called "Byzantium") as Istanbul, even though the Ottomans themselves seem to have continued to use the term "Constantinople," but in a rather specific meaning. They usually referred by it to the old city together with all its suburbs (Eyüb, Galata, and Üsküdar), and used "Istanbul" more in reference to the city within the Byzantine walls (on which see Daniel Goffman, *Britons in the Ottoman Empire, 1642–1660* [Seattle, WA, 1998], pp. 33–35). For the sake of simplicity, this book will call the city "Constantinople" when discussing its Byzantine period and "Istanbul" when discussing its Ottoman one.

haven for runaways from a fiercely intolerant Christian Europe. After all, whereas in the Ottoman world there were thousands of renegades from Christendom, one almost never discovers in Christian Europe converts from Islam.[10]

Such an Ottomancentric perspective would reveal a relationship in which the ideological walls that seemed to divide Christian Europe from the Ottoman Empire instead become the framework to a rich and intricate representation. This is not to deny that a chasm existed at the ideological level; at least at the societal level, there never has been an enduring rapprochement between the Christian and Islamic worldviews. Nevertheless, a host of common interests always counterbalanced this doctrinal abyss.

The great spiritual divide

The historiography of Ottoman relations with the rest of Europe typically features religion. This focus makes sense given the historical consciousnesses of the two civilizations. On the one hand the Ottoman rulers recast their state from a nomadic and frontier principality into the primary heir to a religious foundation that had raised its edifice on previously Byzantine and Latin territories. This ability to remake its ideology by drawing upon Islam's Arab and expansionist heritage helped to give the Ottoman Empire its celebrated resilience, flexibility, and longevity. In contrast, those states with which the Ottomans shared the early modern Mediterranean world – whether Byzantine, Latin, or Habsburg – used religious ideology to legitimize their own regimes and to mobilize their populations in their struggles against Islam.

It thus makes good sense to highlight religion as a fundamental building block of civilizations that predated the Ottoman, Venetian, and Habsburg hegemonies. After all, early modern Europe emerged from a Christian ecumene that had helped define and grant legitimacy to a medieval Europe that presided over several crusades against Islam. Although the transformations of the Renaissance and the Reformation shook that world to its core, Christian Europe – particularly in its relations with non-Christian societies – continued to cast its existence in terms of a "universal" faith. The most visible manifestation of this obsession was the late Crusades, which continued to sputter well into the fifteenth century ("holy" alliances endured even longer) and whose nemesis and anticipated final victim was meant to be the Ottoman polity.

---

[10] On this topic, see Peter Lamborn Wilson's intriguing *Pirate utopias: Moorish corsairs and European renegadoes* (Brooklyn, NY, 1995); and, for the specific example of England, Nabil Matar, *Turks, Moors, and Englishmen in the Age of Discovery* (New York, 1999).

The Ottoman Empire, meanwhile, surfaced as an amalgam of many cultures and traditions. Its legitimacy, however, also was rooted in a "universal" belief – the faith of Islam, which normatively at least came to condemn change (*bida'*) itself. Because the sultans conceived of themselves and their society as Muslim and of their state as Islamic, each monarch had to comply, or appear to comply, with the laws of his faith (the Shariah). Every innovation demanded a justification in terms of the doctrines of Islam. The strictures of the religion manifested themselves in myriad ways, guided the maturation of Ottoman society, and limited the direction of Ottoman expansion.

The early Ottomans for example may have considered themselves "*gazi*" warriors, who justified bloodshed through faith.[11] Such a self-image would have demanded an unrelenting onslaught against the infidel and at the same time made it awkward to attack even the most troublesome rival Islamic state unless the government could demonstrate clear and unambiguous cause. The actuality seems to differ from this reconstruction. While the *gazi* credo would have justified Ottoman strikes against Byzantine borderlands, the Ottoman conquests also produced a subject people who were more and more non-Muslim. The new state had to learn and practice tolerance in order to survive. It recast the Shariah as it did so.

The spiritual bases of Christian Europe and the Muslim Ottoman Empire were remarkably similar. Unlike other major religions such as Hinduism or Taoism, Islam and Christianity are rooted in essentially the same Near Eastern and unitary doctrine. It is thus not only reasonable – but quite fruitful – to conceive and study a "Greater Western World" which encompassed the followers of both Jesus and Muhammed. This similarity, however, does not connote harmony. Just as siblings often fight with appalling brutality, the very resemblance and historical proximity of the two faiths created a bitter rivalry. This hostility is depicted forcefully in Christian and Muslim representations of the biblical tale of Isaac and Ismael. In the Judeo-Christian version, God asks Abraham to sacrifice Isaac, his son by his wife Sarah, in order to prove his faith. In the Islamic version, however, it becomes Ismael, Abraham's elder son by his maid-servant Hagar, who is to be sacrificed. In other words, for Christians, the younger brother is the pivotal character in this story, but for Muslims the elder brother is the key figure.[12] It is not that Muslims repudiate the tradition that Isaac became the patriarch for the Hebrew people. The Qur'an

---

[11] This image is under attack, however, to the degree that a new synthesis may be emerging that largely repudiates it. See Chapter 2 below.
[12] See Carol L. Delaney, *Abraham on trial* (Princeton, 1998).

does insist, however, that Ismael serves a similar, and consequently historically central, role for the Arab people. Two branches of the same tree, the religions constituted aggressive monotheisms, and they fiercely repudiated, persecuted, and negated rival creeds, most particularly each other. It is through this prism of sanguine arrogance that scholarship has routinely viewed, portrayed, and artificially divided the Ottoman from the rest of the European world.

The Euro-Ottoman symbiosis

In some ways, then, Ottoman and other European communities were hostile to each other. This temperament is explicitly and vividly displayed in the battles of Kosovo and Varna, the investment of Constantinople, the assault against Malta, the sieges of Vienna, and countless other aggressions. In other ways, however, the two civilizations were more symbiotic, seeming almost to converge in some arenas. Such intersections of character and purpose have been too little studied. They are most visible, perhaps, in the economic sphere, in which trade within the Mediterranean basin served to bind the two worlds, operating not only through the "spices" that Europeans coveted and long could gain only from Ottoman cities, but also, and especially after the sixteenth century, through bulkier commodities such as dried fruits, cottons, and grains.

Although western Europeans were the more eager to sustain and develop commercial relations because the Islamic world distributed the desired goods of Asia, it was the Ottoman rendering of the role of the non-Muslims in an Islamic society that fashioned the link. Late medieval European Christians often managed relations with the "other," particularly the Jew and the Muslim, by vigorous persecution and expulsion. The Ottomans handled their "others" less violently by asserting a theoretical Muslim superiority – signified by a head-tax upon non-Muslims and certain often symbolic sumptuary restrictions – and simultaneously practicing a nearly absolute but effective disregard in which the various religions, ethnicities, and aliens within the empire co-existed and commingled virtually at will.

Paradoxically this cultural convergence, in which the Ottomans integrated non-Muslims into the economic life of the community, is best articulated along the political and commercial frontiers, where Ottoman warriors simultaneously engaged in endemic conflict with Byzantine, Hungarian, Venetian, and Habsburg forces and fraternized with fellow Christian inhabitants. Particularly upon the military marches that for centuries demarcated first Byzantine and Ottoman Anatolia and then the Catholic and Ottoman Balkans, each side accommodated and even

1 This frontispiece juxtaposes the Habsburg emperor with the Ottoman sultan. Unlike many such depictions, there is no suggestion here of nobility versus malevolence. Both monarchs look regal and carry emblems of office; the *matériel* of war illustrated in the upper corners – battle axe, drum, and pistol for the emperor's armies and scimitar, bow and arrow, and pistol for the sultan's – are both neutrally rendered. Boissard, *Vitae et icones sultanorum turcico*.

assimilated the other's techniques and cultures.[13] Societies promptly accommodated whichever state ruled over them, warriors crept back and forth across a divide that proved remarkably porous, and, surprisingly,

[13] Cemal Kafadar has cogently argued such a symbiosis in *Between two worlds: the construction of the Ottoman state* (Berkeley and Los Angeles, 1995), especially pp. 19–28. See also

that great segregator religion itself slipped into a latitudinarianism that facilitated borderland communication and even sometimes blurred the distinction between Christianity and Islam.

The Ottoman Empire itself originated as such a society. It was born in the fourteenth-century middle grounds between the Byzantine and Seljuk Empires where it was one of a throng of petty and semi-autonomous Turkoman emirates crowded into western Anatolia. Here, its leaders vied with the emirs of Karasi, Menteşeoğlu, Aydınoğlu, Saruhanoğlu, and others for lucre and fame, struggled against the Byzantine Empire and various Latin states to enlarge their frontiers, and almost indiscriminately snatched from the venerable domains that enveloped them the most useful doctrines, weapons, and political formations. More than any other quality, the responsive plasticity that emerged in this milieu explains the astonishing achievements of Osman, the eponymous Ottoman, and his heirs.

Associations between the Ottoman Empire and the other states of Europe extended beyond commercial exchange and military campaign. The territories, indeed the very institutions, of the Ottoman Empire were in some ways successors to the Byzantine Empire, which, as an heir to Rome, was the most revered of European states. Not only did both the Byzantine and Ottoman political entities utilize a religious ideology as the glue for a vast territory and a diverse population, but also the Ottomans came to rule over virtually the same domains and peoples as had Constantine's eastern Roman heirs 1,000 years before. Furthermore, the successor state adopted much of the Byzantine tax structure through the utilization of customary law, which the Ottomans blended into sultanic law as a complement to Islamic law.[14]

This is not to say that the Ottoman polity constituted no more than a superimposed image of its immediate predecessor. It did not. Not only did the empire rely upon traditions from its own central-Asian past, but it also embraced Persian (particularly financial and political) and Arab (particularly spiritual) legacies.[15] The Ottomans fused these heritages

Ahmet T. Karamustafa, *God's unruly friends: dervish groups in the Islamic later Middle Period, 1200–1550* (Salt Lake City, 1994).

[14] Halil İnalcık, "Suleiman the lawgiver and Ottoman law," *Archivum Ottomanicum* 1 (1969): 105–38, and chapter 3 below.

[15] On the controversy over the roots of Ottoman law, see Halil İnalcık, "The Ottoman succession and its relation to the Turkish concept of sovereignty," in *The Middle East and the Balkans under the Ottoman Empire: essays on economy and society* (Bloomington, IN, 1993), pp. 37–69. The question of Ottoman origins and legacy has been thoroughly politicized. On origins, see Herbert A. Gibbons, *The foundation of the Ottoman Empire* (Oxford, 1916); Fuat M. Köprülü, *The origins of the Ottoman Empire*, trans. and ed. Gary Leiser (Albany, NY, 1992); Paul Wittek, *The rise of the Ottoman Empire* (London, 1938); Rudi P. Lindner, *Nomads and Ottomans in medieval Anatolia* (Bloomington, IN, 1983); and Kafadar, *Between two worlds*; on legacy, see L. Carl Brown (ed.), *Imperial legacy: the Ottoman imprint on the Balkans and the Middle East* (New York, 1996).

together with the Byzantine one into a unique order that endured for half a millennium. The threads of Ottoman legitimacy thus converged from the east, from the south, and from the north. Nevertheless the chief impression, at least from the perspective of much of Europe, was that the Ottoman Empire was the Byzantine Empire reborn, even though this rebirth may have appeared misshapen. When viewed from the West the Ottoman polity seemed to have arisen like a monster out of the Byzantine ashes. Evil or not, as the successor to a major Christian and Mediterranean civilization, both European and Ottoman considered the new state very much a part of the European world. Although many western Europeans hated it on ideological grounds, most also acknowledged that the empire could not be ignored, and some even grasped that it could not easily be expunged. Ways were found to accommodate it.

Istanbul: the middle city

Constantinople (Ottoman Istanbul) epitomized this physical and emotional integration into Europe. With the temporary exceptions of Iberia under Islam and the Syrian coast under the crusader states, an oceanic barrier had long separated the Christian and Islamic worlds. This obstacle swept in a roughly diagonal arc across the Mediterranean Sea from the Straits of Gibraltar to the Straits of the Dardanelles. Since the time of Muhammed the northeastern foundation of this buttress had been the capital of the Byzantine Empire. Constantinople was Europe's "line in the sand." Boundaries between Christendom and Islam may have ebbed and flowed elsewhere (and chiefly in Iberia); here they remained fixed. With the conquest of that city in 1453 and the fall of Granada, the last Islamic state in Iberia, to the combined forces of Ferdinand and Isabella thirty-nine years later, the emotional nucleus of this cultural clash shifted from the southwestern to the southeastern European world.[16]

In European lore, Constantinople was the great successor to Rome. Its immense walls and access to both oversea and land-based hinterlands preserved Christendom during times of extreme danger. In the fourth and seventh centuries it had withstood the onslaughts of pagan Goths and Muslim Arabs and, despite succumbing to a ruinous Latin onslaught in the early thirteenth century, in the thirteenth and fourteenth centuries it had stood as a bastion against the Mongol and Turkoman nomadic groups pushing westward across eastern Europe and Asia Minor. Byzantine defenses to the south and east may have crumbled, the walls of Byzantium

---

[16] This, however, does not mean that fighting along the western borderlands ceased, on which see Andrew C. Hess, *The forgotten frontier: a history of the sixteenth-century Ibero-African frontier* (Chicago and London, 1978).

may have tottered, but time and again the city had weathered the attacks of its assailants. However estranged the western Latin and eastern Ortho-dox churches may have grown, one cannot overemphasize the physical and symbolic relevance of Byzantium to all of Christendom.

The city loomed almost as large in Islamic lore. Muhammed himself imagined it as the center of the world, and the Arab surges of the seventh and eighth centuries several times touched its walls. The first Umayyad Caliph Mu'awiyah in 670 led an assault that shattered against its walls; the yearlong siege of 716–17 proved no more successful. Thus the as-tonishing advance of Islam in its early years veered off toward India in the east and Iberia in the west. In the north, it faltered at Constantino-ple. That barricade held, the eastern Christian church survived, and two great monotheisms there faced each other – sometimes in hostility and sometimes in uneasy peace – for almost a millennium.

Constantinople was not only a religious symbol, however. Constantine had founded his capital on a finger of land that functioned almost as an isthmus at the intersection of two continents. As a geo-political fulcrum its location was strategic, its geographic position augmented its strength. Not only did the site control trade between the Black and Mediterranean Seas, and between Asia Minor and the Balkans, but it also could potentially rely upon a vast and sea borne provisioning zone stretching from the Crimean peninsula to Egypt and beyond. With its conquest Mehmed II (the Conqueror) not only fulfilled an Islamic aspiration but also liberated the imperial core of an empire that already encompassed much of that zone and enveloped most of the territory that formerly had been Byzantium.

Before 1453 it had been possible for Europeans to conceive the Turkic invaders – Seljuk as well as Ottoman – as a temporary setback, however prolonged, in the advance of Christendom. European states and peoples accommodated the troublesome nomads, even traded and made treaties with them. Few, however, accepted them as part of a fixed political land-scape. After 1453 this worldview was hard to sustain. The Byzantine Empire had exploited Constantinople's unparalleled strategic location and had endured 1,000 years. Why would the Ottoman Empire not do the same?

Converging communities

The fall of Byzantine Constantinople seemed a horrifying and decisive turning point to many Europeans, an interpretation that most historians embrace. Nevertheless, the event liberated that city from a smothering en-circlement. Somewhat paradoxically, it also inaugurated a merging of the Christian European and Ottoman worlds. Hostilities certainly continued.

PLVS TIBI QVAM NVLLI INDVLSIT FORTVNA SED OLIM
HÆSIT IN EPIRO LAVS TVA FACTA MINOR.

SVLTAN MVCHEMET CHAN

EVROPAM ATQVE ASIAM HIC FELICIB° OCCVPAT ARMIS
GRÆCVM ET BITHYNVM DVM RVIT IMPERIVM.

2 As with most portraits of the early Ottoman sultans, this one of
Sultan Mehmed Han, the conqueror of Constantinople, is highly styl-
ized. Nevertheless, perhaps because of models based upon Gentile
Bellini's work, this woodcut seems more realistic than most. Boissard,
Vitae et icones sultanorum turcico, p. 41.

One cannot ignore Süleyman's campaigns in Hungary and his sieges of
Vienna and Malta in the mid sixteenth century, or the explosive naval engagements that crested at Lepanto in 1571. Nevertheless, alliances, commerce, and the movements of peoples more and more institutionalized

and complicated relations between other European and Ottoman civiliza-
tions. In fact, in the economic, political, and even religious spheres the
Ottomans assumed many of the duties that previously had characterized
Byzantine relations with western Europe.

Before 1453, for example, Europe had usually taken the initiative in
commerce that involved the southern (Islamic) Mediterranean basin. It
had done so in part because, while it was virtually impossible for Muslims
to trade and reside in most Christian lands, European Christians could
live in many Islamic societies as "People of the Book," that is, as those
who heeded the sacred writings of Judaism, Christianity, or Islam.[17] In
the late medieval Mamluk Empire, for example, quarters for Venetian and
Genoese merchants existed in Alexandria, Aleppo, and elsewhere. More
importantly, Europe simply produced little of interest to the peoples of
the Islamic Middle East. Italian merchants who sought the silk, pepper,
cinnamon, and other spices that flowed through Syrian and Egyptian
ports had little other than bullion to offer in return. Although Muslims
certainly were involved in this trade, their businesses tended to be sta-
tionary. It was merchants from the northwest who traversed the trading
corridors of the Mediterranean.

Christian Europe did not suddenly begin drawing Muslim merchants
after 1453. Nevertheless, after that date the initiative in commerce began
to swing to the Ottoman Empire as Ottoman merchants began to venture into the European world. Those who did so, however, were rarely
Muslim. It was other subjects of the socially complex empire – Armenian
Christians, Greek Orthodox Christians, and Jews – who took advantage
of their opportunity simultaneously to traverse the Ottoman domain and
to organize trading networks across southern and western European port
cities.[18]

The commerce of the Armenian middlemen originated in Persia, found
in silk an eminently marketable commodity, and by the early seventeenth century had expanded to the farthest reaches of northern Europe
and eastern Asia. In the Ottoman Empire, the Armenians constituted a
Christian community to whom the government granted autonomy in religion, economic life, and even internal politics. Their religion also gave
them access to the lands of Christian Europe. Thus, they moved easily
in both societies.

The Ottoman polity served as the linchpin of this far-flung commercial
network, granting Armenian traders a reliable anchorage as they pursued

---

[17] Mark R. Cohen, *Under crescent and cross: the Jews in the Middle Ages* (Princeton, NJ,
1994).
[18] See on these networks Philip D. Curtin, *Cross-cultural trade in world history* (Cambridge,
1984).

their risky endeavors. Armenian peddlers, meanwhile, not only brought to the Ottomans knowledge of the East, but also helped couple the two religious segments of the Greater Western World. Armenians from Istanbul and Izmir journeyed to Venice, Livorno, Marseilles, even to Amsterdam and St. Petersburg. This trading network helped produce a uniform commercial method throughout the Mediterranean and European worlds, a technological and cultural interplay between the Ottoman Empire and the rest of Europe, and a new people – the Levantines – who eventually became the principal communicators between the two zones.

Such adaptable persons – those who can conform to two or more societies even as they remain distinct from each – have long been associated with international commerce, whose merchants must be polyglot and compliant in order to survive. Economically at least such marginality virtually defined the Jewish community as it existed in both Christian and Ottoman Europe.[19] In each situation, the Jews constituted a religious minority, politically dominated by a rival monotheism. As such, they had to be familiar with and willing to adjust to their hosts' societies, and they had to be conversant in their languages. The irony is that even as both Christians and Muslims exhibited much the same hostility toward the Jews as they felt toward each other, Jews – particularly as traders and especially during the great confrontations of the sixteenth century – became instrumental in bridging the ideological chasm that separated much of Europe and the Ottoman Empire.[20]

Repercussions from the conquest of Constantinople proved crucial in the development of trans-Mediterranean commerce. Before 1453, Mediterranean Jewry existed in at least three distinct communities – the Spanish-speaking Iberian, the Arab-speaking Egyptian and Syrian, and the Greek-speaking Byzantine. After 1453, these communal lines became blurred. First of all, Sultan Mehmed II's policy of resettling in Istanbul Jews from the Balkans and Anatolia created a new mix of Jews of Ashkenazic (German), Romaniot (Greek), and Karaite (heterodox) origin. Secondly, the Christian reconquest of Iberia and the resultant policy of repression (culminating in the Spanish expulsion of Jews in 1492) pushed thousands of Sephardic Jews into Ottoman domains. Thirdly, the conquests of Syria and Egypt in 1516–17 transferred the ancient Arab-Jewish community into Ottoman hands.[21]

By 1550 these communities had fused into an uneasy amalgam that drew upon the various civilizations of Europe as well as the Middle East to

[19] On which, see Cohen, *Under crescent and cross*.
[20] For the sixteenth century in particular, see Benjamin Arbel, *Trading nations: Jews and Venetians in the early modern eastern Mediterranean* (Leiden, 1995).
[21] Avigdor Levy, *The sephardim in the Ottoman Empire* (Princeton, NJ, 1992).

fashion a new society. Particularly its Sephardic elements helped adapt the Christian-European and Ottoman administrations and economies to each other's commercial norms. Through Jews residing in Venice, Bordeaux, Amsterdam, and London, Ottoman subjects for the first time recipro- cated the foreign settlements in Istanbul, Izmir, Aleppo, and Alexandria. Ottoman Jewish subjects made good use of the knowledge gained by direct exposure to southern and western Europe. They involved them- selves in Ottoman textile production and employed western-European commercial techniques to compete with western-European merchants. Jews also bought positions in Ottoman finances and negotiated with Venetian, French, English, and Dutch merchants over customs dues, and Jewish brokers, factors, and translators represented foreign merchants and diplomats in Ottoman towns and villages and before Ottoman offi- cials. Through their ventures – often in concert with Ottoman Arab Mus- lims, Armenian Christians, Orthodox Greeks, and Turkish Muslims – commercial relations became cultural ties. Englishmen, Frenchmen, and Ottomans involved themselves in these exchanges and built and crossed economic, cultural, and political bridges by doing so.

The heyday for Greek Orthodox commerce did not arrive until the eighteenth century, when the Phanariot of Istanbul linked up with co- religionists in Ottoman outports not only to dominate seaborne com- merce within the Ottoman Mediterranean world, but also to direct the government's fiscal procedures and even challenge the Atlantic seaboard states in their own entrepôts. Even earlier, however, Greek Orthodox merchants had managed the intra-imperial carrying trade, Greek bro- kers had controlled commercial exchanges in many Ottoman port towns, and it had been Greek sailors who helped found and long remained the backbone of Ottoman naval and merchant marines.[22]

Thus, even as Sultan Süleyman challenged Emperor Charles V on the Mediterranean Sea and in the Balkans militarily and ideologically, Ottoman subjects busily wove together the commercial and social fabrics of Ottoman and Christian Europe. Religious discord often collided with personal interests in the streets of Istanbul, Aleppo, and Salonika as well as among directors of trading companies and in the councils of state, especially the Sublime Porte. The Armenian, Greek Orthodox, Jewish, and even inchoate Muslim trading diasporas eased communication and encouraged among these circles a more cohesive outlook. If inter-relations between the states of southern Europe and the Ottoman Empire had been piecemeal and largely theoretical in the fifteenth century, by the end of the

---

[22] See, however, Palmira Brummett, *Ottoman seapower and Levantine diplomacy in the Age of Discovery* (Albany, NY, 1994) for a somewhat contrary view.

sixteenth century a wide gamut of interests had entwined the Ottomans into the European order of states and economies. The economic and social crises to come jarred this system. What emerged by 1700, however, was an almost universal perception of the Ottoman Empire as a European state.

A changing image in Europe

Modern historians, however, rarely imagine the Ottoman Empire even in this period as a part of Europe, an area that they associate with crisis, change, and improvement (the obverse of the fantasy of an immutable Orient). Virulent religious wars concluded the sixteenth century; the brutal Thirty Years War helped usher in the next lengthy conflict. Drastic transformations occurred in food production, demographics, global commerce, and governance. Commonwealths arose in England and the Netherlands; governments became more centralized. These mutations concocted a Europe that in 1700 looked radically different than it had in 1500, a transformation that some historians have interpreted teleologically as a climb toward modernity or some other stated or implied goal. Most of these changes touched the Ottoman Empire as much as they did the rest of Europe. Nevertheless, even when scholars do acknowledge these developments, in this "oriental" context the influences are said to have marked decay rather than signaled progress.

Such a conclusion is not unreasonable when one considers how dramatically the Ottoman Empire's relationship with the rest of Europe had changed. The military balance certainly had shifted decisively toward the West, and Christian Europeans no longer feared that the "Turk" would sweep westward, despoiling, plundering, enslaving, and converting. It is not tenable, however, to see in this new balance an absolute Ottoman decline. Just as Spain, Portugal, or the Italian states responded differently and less successfully to the seventeenth century crises than did England or France, so did the Ottoman Empire. In no case did these Mediterranean states become less a part of the Greater Western World; in no case were they abandoned or forgotten by the rest of Europe.

In the Ottoman instance, the advance toward integration in fact quickened during the seventeenth century. This circumstance has not often been noted, perhaps because it was not reflected in the policies of the Ottoman state, which sought to "reform" itself to past days of glory and did not begin emulating innovations in the rest of Europe until the following century. Rather than the government assuming the lead, Ottoman subjects and foreigners residing in Mediterranean port cities and along Balkan borderlands intensified their dialogues and carved out commercial

and social enclaves along the Ottoman frontiers. In these provincial mi-
lieus, Jews and Muslims began to lose their commercial pre-eminence as
cross-cultural communicators to others who were less dependent upon
the goodwill of the Ottoman central government.

This transfer of economic power from one Ottoman subject people to
another also helped weaken the Ottoman state (but perhaps not Ottoman
society), for, as one consequence of the new association between western
European and local Ottoman merchants and officials, Istanbul began to
lose control over customs and other revenues. The resulting economic
and political decentralization proved advantageous to many Ottoman
subjects, and helped further integrate the Ottoman economy with the
rest of Europe. Not only Armenians and Greek Orthodox Christians,
but also Englishmen, Dutchmen, and Frenchmen muscled aside Jewish
and Muslim middlemen and assumed dominant stations in the new
Levantine world being fashioned by their multiple alliances. The changes
simultaneously affecting both Ottoman and western European society facilitated the abilities of these Levantines to communicate. For example,
Englishmen fleeing the upheavals of their civil wars in the 1640s experienced and could exploit the similar disturbances contemporaneously
jarring the Ottoman world.[23]

It is probably accurate to imagine the Ottoman Empire as non-
European before the late 1400s. Although the two entities already shared
much, their ideological, political, military, economic, and historical dissimilarities remained overwhelming. Over the next centuries, however,
the Ottoman Empire and other parts of Europe learned from and more
and more resembled each other. Differences remained, particularly in the
ideological realm. Although few eighteenth-century western Europeans
referred any longer to the Ottomans as the terror of Europe, as had
Richard Knolles in the late sixteenth century,[24] the image that replaced
it – the sick man of Europe – was hardly any more positive and was more
inclusive only in a negative sense. Not respect or inclusion but contempt
replaced fear in the minds of many Christian Europeans.

Nevertheless, the dense reality simply did not fit this simple-minded
construct – expressed by contemporaries and twentieth-century historians alike – of a religious animosity that engendered almost complete
separation. However reluctantly, the rest of Europe learned to accept its
Ottoman slice as a successor to Byzantium. Dutch, English, French, and
Venetian ambassadors resided in Istanbul, and the Ottomans became

---

[23] Goffman, *Britons*.

[24] *The generall historie of the Turkes*, 2nd edn (London, 1610), "Introduction to the Christian reader," as quoted in Christine Woodhead, " 'The present terrour of the world'?
contemporary views of the Ottoman Empire c. 1600," *History* 72(1987): 20.

part – perhaps even the core – of the diplomatic system that had arisen out of Italy in the fifteenth and sixteenth centuries. Armenian, Greek Orthodox, and Jewish Ottoman merchants roamed Mediterranean and even Atlantic waters. Islam and Judaism were acknowledged (if not accepted) as part of the re-evaluation of the relationship between religion and society that accompanied the early modern collapse of the Catholic ecumene. Even ideologically, then, differences receded and the two societies more and more resembled each other. An examination of this state of affairs opens for the historian a new world of research and interpretation.

Part 1

State and society in the Ottoman world

Kubad's formative years

Even the infidel comes to the fold of the faithful, but not the heretic
  dervish; the infidel has receptivity but not him.
He is out of the sphere of hope while the infidel is in the circle of fear
  of God,
By God, the infidel is far superior to him.[1]

*The young boy Kubad had no memory of his mother.[2] He had only heard tales
and rumors: that she was a prostitute, a gypsy, a Tatar princess, and, most
extraordinary of all, that she had been a favorite of İbrahim Pasha, Sultan
Süleyman's powerful if ill-fated grand vizier who led Ottoman armies and
conquered Baghdad in 1634, only to be executed two years later by sultanic
decree.*

*Not that it really mattered to Kubad. The only mother he had ever known –
his "milk mother" – was the daughter of a venerated Shaykh of the Haydari
order of dervishes.[3] The boy spent his first years near the Ottoman frontier town
of Erzincan, in a rustic hamlet next to the* tekke, *or house of worship, of this
Shaykh. One of his earliest memories was of an elder reciting the strange words
inscribed on the door of this* tekke: *"he who wants to enter our religion should
live as we do, and preserve his chastity." Kubad was so familiar with those who
did join this devout order, that he thought nothing of their appearance. Other
than a drooping mustache and a long tuft of hair at their foreheads, the heads
of these worshipers were clean shaven. On all their limbs they wore heavy iron
rings, and on their heads were towering conical hats. Bells, suspended at their
sides, banged away as they danced about, chanting poems and praising God.
Only much later did the boy understand how deviating these customs were, that*

---

[1] Vahidi, *Menakib-i Hvoca-i Cihan ve Netice-i Canu*, fols. 52a–52n; as quoted in Karamustafa, *God's unruly friends*, p. 6.

[2] Most of our knowledge about Kubad comes from Venetian sources, which Arbel has
culled. Mentions of this *çavuş* (on which see "Cha'ush," *Encyclopedia of Islam*, 2nd edn
[Leiden, 1962–], hereafter referred to as *EI*) are scattered through the pages of his
Trading nations. We know nothing of Kubad's youth other than his name, which suggests
an association with the Kubad River in Circassia. What follows in this vignette on his
early years is pure speculation.

[3] This order is discussed in Karamustafa, *God's unruly friends*, pp. 67–70.

the iron rings reeked of animistic paganism, the prayers echoed infidel Christian ones, and the hats resembled the headgear of Shi'ite heretics.

At the age of eight or nine, Kubad's life suddenly veered when a troop of Ottoman cavalry swooped into his village and carried him off. Two weeks later, he found himself standing all alone and silent in a three-day vigil construed to initiate him into a refined if isolated existence at the Ottoman sultan's palace school for male pages.[4] After this exercise, the head eunuch declared that the youth had now entered the Ottoman governing elite. The young boy, still so impressionable and raw, soon had settled in at Topkapı Palace in the heart of the capital of the sultan Süleyman's empire, living a life profoundly more luxurious and also incomparably more restrictive than the one from which he had been torn.

There were first of all no dervishes in this tiny world. In fact, Kubad saw no one who even remotely resembled any of the inhabitants of the small village in which he had spent his young boyhood. Instead, he resided in the third and most interior and opulent courtyard of the Ottoman sultan's palace. Here, he was thrust as a novitiate into a rigidly hierarchal existence in a closely scheduled, spartan, jam-packed, and single-sex dormitory together with some 400 clean-shaven boys. Here, he was expected to uphold a strict code of behavior whose showpiece was absolute public silence. Kubad only later discovered that the boys' strange hand movements constituted a special language that the pages had developed over the years to make up for their compulsory voicelessness. Incorruptibly ruling over these boys were five imperial eunuchs, whose castration physically symbolized their distinct condition and their absolute devotion to and dependency upon the sultan and his household.

Kubad, in short, had become an imperial page, who was being trained to assume high position in the Ottoman administration. He settled into a routine of schooling that rigorously taught him the Ottoman language of the ruling class – so utterly richer and more refined than the Turkish vernacular with which he had grown up – and the urbane etiquette of the court, and instructed him along with the other boys in the ins and outs of Islamic doctrine. He also trained in the sports and crafts that distinguished the Ottoman elite, and learned absolute obedience to his master, the sultan.

Kubad entered puberty in this world, and gradually moved up through the hierarchy until he attained the rare honor of attending – silently, unobtrusively, and with constant vigil – upon Sultan Süleyman himself. Throughout, the royal eunuchs observed him closely, assessed his talents, and judged how this gifted youth best could serve the Ottoman state. The young man saw his older companions graduate from this "inner service" into the imperial "outer service" as kapıcıs, bostancıs, janissaries, *and other sorts of servants of the sultan. Once*

---

[4] The description of Kubad's life at the palace school relies upon Gülru Necipoğlu's exceptional reconstruction in *Architecture, ceremonial, and power: the Topkapı Palace in the fifteenth and sixteenth centuries* (Cambridge, MA, 1991), pp. 111–20; and "Ghulām," *EI*.

DIVAN-TCHAVOUSCH.   ALAI-TCHAVOUSCH.

IS KEMLE-AGHA.   COZ-BEKDJI-BASCHI.
                                              Porte - boccière

3 Two of these four servants of the Ottoman sultan in this early
nineteenth-century print are *çavuşes*, as was Kubad, the protagonist in
this book's vignettes. The figure on the upper left is a pursuivant of
the Imperial Divan; the one on the upper right is a serjeant-of-arms in
imperial processions. One of the bottom two officials carried the imperial footstool; the other assured that the sultan's thirst was promptly
quenched. D'Ohsson, *Tableau général de l'Empire othoman*, vol. III, 2nd
plate after p. 294.

gone, it was as if they had ceased to exist, for no graduate ever returned to this third and most interior courtyard of the palace.

Kubad's own graduation ceremony occurred in his eighteenth year. He along with several other pages stood before the sultan and one by one kissed his hand before receiving vestments, a turban, and some money. The new graduate then left the confines of the third courtyard for the first and last time, passed through the second courtyard amidst much fanfare and throwing of coinage, stopped in the first courtyard to pick up a horse at the imperial stables, and crossed into the government's outer service as a çavuş.

The young page overnight was reborn as an imperial pursuivant, and even his physical appearance soon had utterly altered as he donned the turban and allowed his facial hair to grow out into a full and impressive beard. His principal charge was to carry the Sublime Porte's decrees into the city of Istanbul as well as the farflung Ottoman provinces. He also was issued specific verbal instructions and granted the authority to make sure that these imperial commands were obeyed, and years of training and close observation guaranteed that his education and personality fitted him for the job. Kubad and his colleagues formed the principal means of communications between the Ottoman government and its subjects. They also constituted the closest organization the Ottomans had to a diplomatic corps. A çavuş might find himself in Isfahan or Venice, even in Paris or London or Delhi as an emissary – the official voice of the Ottoman Empire itself.

2 Fabricating the Ottoman state

> At that time [the reign of Murad I (1362–89)] the tax was low. Conditions were such that even the unbelievers were not oppressed. It was not the practice to seize their purse [clothes?] or their ox or their son or their daughter and sell them or hold them as pledges. At that time the rulers were not greedy. Whatever came into their hands they gave away again, and they did not know what a treasury was. But when Hayreddin Pasha came to the Gate [of the government] greedy scholars became the companions of the rulers. They began by displaying piety and then went on to issue rulings [*fetva*]. "He who is ruler must have a treasury," they said. At that time they won over the rulers and influenced them. Greed and oppression appeared. Indeed, where there is greed there must also be oppression. In our time it has increased. Whatever oppression and corruption there is in this country is due to scholars.[1]

We have no real record of the early Ottoman state. Other than a few architectural remains and coins, virtually everything we know about the first overlords (emirs), Osman, Orhan, and Murad, is second-hand. Some of our information derives from Byzantine, Genoese, and other outsider witnesses to the birth of this state; much of it comes from the histories of later Ottomans who reconstructed the past from the jumbled recollections of their elders in order to justify or condemn the Ottoman state as it existed in the fifteenth and sixteenth centuries. Such is certainly the case with the anonymous chronicler quoted at the beginning of this chapter, who used an undocumented tale of life under the emir Murad to critique the reign of Sultan Mehmed II and his band of fraudulent "scholars." This passage, more revealing about the discontented age in which the author lived than about how the Ottoman state was fashioned, is representative of a whole genre, whose principal concern was to concoct

---

[1] "Anonymous Ottoman Chronicle," pp. 25–26. Quoted in Bernard Lewis (ed. and trans.), *Islam from the Prophet Muhammad to the capture of Constantinople*, Vol. I: *Politics and war* (Oxford, 1987), p. 135.

an Ottoman past that either glorified or condemned (depending upon the writer's stance) the Ottoman present.[2]

The historian thus must sift through the fitful musings of fearful foreigners struggling against an expanding Islamic state as well as the self-serving reminiscences of representatives of an established world empire as he or she tries to reconstruct the origins of this world state. Some deem the undertaking quixotic and foolhardy, arguing that our sources are so politicized and their creators so intent on legitimizing the Ottoman dynasty that they are of use only in ascertaining what the Ottomans and their enemies wanted its foundation to have been, rather than what it actually was.[3] Others accept the words of Ottoman chronicles, written two or three generations after the events, almost at face value, seeming at times to take quite literally such legends as Osman's dream of a moon floating from a Sufi Shaykh into his navel, out of which a tree sprouted, whose shade encompassed the earth: representing, of course, the House of Osman's future world empire.[4]

It can even be argued that when modern historians have approached the early Ottoman state, they no less than Ottoman chroniclers have at times written more about their own times and selves than about their topic. The intent of one of the earliest such accounts, written by Gibbons, an American resident in Istanbul, and published during the First World War, certainly aimed to explain the origins of an empire tottering on the edge of demise.[5] In his allusions to the "Great War" and his uncritical adoption of the racist underpinnings of turn-of-the-century nationalism, the author juxtaposes the civilizing influences of the West against the barbarisms of the East to conclude that the Ottomans' glory had rested on Byzantine institutions; their incurable defect was that they carried a savage line in their blood.

This thesis stimulated a historiographical debate that threads its way through and beyond the twentieth century. Its principal argument concerns the roots of the Ottoman genius: was the Ottoman Empire a legacy of the Byzantines, the Arabs, or the Central Asians? This question, which

---

[2] A sharp discussion of Ottoman use of the past is Colin Imber, "Ideals and legitimation in early Ottoman history," in *Süleyman the Magnificent and his age: the Ottoman Empire in the early modern world*, ed. Metin Kunt and Christine Woodhead (Harlow, Essex, England, 1995), pp. 138–53.

[3] Colin Imber is the most forceful proponent of this view. See particularly his "Canon and Apocrypha in Early Ottoman History," in *Studies in Ottoman history in honour of Professor V. L. Ménage*, ed. Colin Heywood and Colin Imber (Istanbul, 1994), pp. 117–37.

[4] A story told by several Ottoman chroniclers, and repeated by virtually every historian of Ottoman origins since. For an incisive discussion of this tradition and its uses, see Kafadar, *Between two worlds*, pp. 8–9 and 132–33. Kafadar's book should be the starting point for any examination of the early Ottoman world.

[5] Gibbons, *Foundation*.

would have been almost meaningless to the Ottomans themselves, has raged in the twentieth century in part because the ideology of imperialism has justified itself by claiming that the West brings civilization to the Orient. Equally important is that the ideologies of the nationalisms of Ottoman successor states have demanded imagined pasts that centered the identities of their own nations at the expense of rival identities such as the Ottoman one.[6] This mixture of suspect sources and muddying agendas makes any rendering of Ottoman origins particularly speculative and perilous, and the discussion offered here merely presents probabilities by assessing what evidence exists in light of human psychology and comparable historical activities in the Middle East, America, and elsewhere.

Imagined beginnings

Religion permeated the Mediterranean world during the age of the Crusades (1097 – c. 1453). It helped produce the separation between West and East, and it justified and excused war, massacre, and murder. Both Catholicism and Sunni Islam jealously guarded their orthodoxies. These stubbornly conventional and monotheistic religions left little room for adaptation or revision. Indeed, Crusaders remain even today a symbol of religiously excused ruthlessness. Nevertheless, even in this ideological sphere the lines between the Islamic and Christian European worlds – especially along their frontiers – were porous and the contacts were often symbiotic. Islamic societies surrounded the small states that Crusaders established in Syria and Palestine, and these new settlers soon learned to coexist with their neighbors. The Arab chronicler Usamah explained the ignorance of newly arrived crusaders: "Everyone who is a fresh emigrant from the Frankish lands is ruder in character than those who have become acclimatized and have held long association with the Moslems." He then relates the following tale as evidence:

Whenever I visited Jerusalem I always entered the Aqsa Mosque, beside which stood a small mosque which the Franks had converted into a church. When I used to enter the Aqsa Mosque, which was occupied by the Templars, . . . who were my friends, the Templars would evacuate the little adjoining mosque so that I might pray in it. One day I entered this mosque, repeated the first formula, "Allah is great," and stood up in the act of praying, upon which one of the Franks rushed on me, got hold of me and turned my face eastward saying, "This is the way thou shouldst pray!" A group of Templars hastened to him, seized him and repelled

---

[6] On which see Benedict Anderson, *Imagined communities: reflections on the origin and spread of nationalism* (London, 1983).

him from me ... They apologized to me, saying, "This is a stranger who has only recently arrived from the land of the Franks and he has never before seen anyone praying except eastward."[7]

Usamah recounted this anecdote not only to express the ignorance of the crusaders, but also to show how thoroughly exposure to the Islamic world had changed (or, in his thinking, "civilized") the barbarians from the West. In other words, even in this brutal milieu personal contact refined and complicated perceptions of the "Other." Stereotypes based upon fear and ignorance dissipated through contact. In the process, the very characters of the conquering Crusaders as well as their local victims became altered.

Usamah concretely describes processes that typify frontier societies. However brutal the immediate effects of the Crusades may have been, some of their long-term consequences were to educate the adversaries about each other and to establish commercial and cultural relations between them. The American frontier has been portrayed similarly as a "middle ground."[8] Just as our memories of European history privilege the butcheries of the crusaders, such as the "rivers of blood" that flowed down the streets of Jerusalem after its capture in 1099, over other aspects of their sojourn in the Middle East, so do we tend to hark back to the wars and massacres that punctuated relations between native Americans and colonists, and forget the decades of coexistence, identity switching, and "engendering" that prefaced and even attended the demographic blitz of European colonization in the Americas.

The Turkoman push across Anatolia should be recalled similarly. The almost 400-year history of Turkoman–Byzantine relations between the Seljuk defeat of a Byzantine army at the Battle of Manzikert in 1071 and the Ottoman conquest of Constantinople in 1453 was more than a series of bloody military campaigns. It also was a period of compromise, accommodation, and mutual learning in which a frontier society in the process of formation endured and eventually flourished only by adapting to and assuming the structures and strategies of those civilizations that surrounded it.

The political system out of which the Ottoman state emerged certainly constituted such a frontier society. To its east lay the successor states of

---

[7] Usamah Ibn-Munidh, *An Arab-Syrian gentleman and warrior in the period of the Crusades*, trans. Philip K. Hitti (Princeton, NJ, 1987), pp. 163–64. Arab attitudes toward the Crusades are imaginatively recreated by Amin Maalouf, *The Crusades through Arab eyes* (New York, 1984). They are strongly fictionalized by Tariq Ali, *The book of Saladin: a novel* (New York, 1999).

[8] On which see Richard White, *The middle ground: Indians, empires, and republics in the Great Lakes region, 1650–1815* (Cambridge, 1989).

the Mongol wave that had crashed across the Middle East in the early thirteenth century; to its west lay the Byzantine Empire, whose eastern frontiers, now in western Anatolia, served, as they had for some 600 years, as a bastion against Islam. A series of semi-independent principalities lay nestled between these two behemoths. Their titular head was the Seljuks of Rum (weakened by defeat at the hands of the Mongols), whose capital was in Konya. Nevertheless, a series of relatively small emirates – among them the Menteşeoğlu, the Aydınoğlu, the Saruhanoğlu, the Karasioğlu, and of course the Osmanoğlu (the "Ottoman son") – had by the early fourteenth century emerged to challenge both Seljuk sovereignty over them and Byzantine control over western Anatolia.

This frontier was in many ways a military march between two civilizations: the Byzantine and the Islamic. Such borders, however, tend to be fixed and unbending, which this frontier emphatically was not. The presence of these buffer emirates created a sense of "middle ground," of a world whose propensities toward compromise, adaptation, and heterodoxy might give birth to innovative institutions and worldviews. It seems likely that the very foreignness of these "statelets" stimulated this condition. Their leaders were recent arrivals from Central Asia who were Turkic-speaking pastoralists. Some probably retained their animistic beliefs, but even those who were Muslim (or Christian) had converted only recently. Furthermore, their political as well as religious practices remained more central Asian than Middle Eastern. This actuality is most tellingly revealed in local customs of inheritance: rulers divided their realms among sons, brothers, and other relatives, a practice which may have worked in nomadic societies, but which now repeatedly led to the quick collapse of both Mongol and Turkoman states and to political fragmentation within the Anatolian frontier zone.[9]

The emergence of the Ottoman state is incomprehensible unless one understands that this frontier society must have engendered cultural as well as political fractures. An emirate such as the Aydınoğlus, for example, whose principality included the port town of Smyrna, quickly shrugged off its nomadic past, took to the seas, and became a naval power in the Aegean. It took the Ottomans, whose early state in Bithynia was landlocked, centuries to realize such a leading maritime presence. Similarly, a state such as the Ottoman one, which not only abutted Byzantium but also for long periods of time controlled the countrysides around Byzantine cities such as Nicaea and Bursa (and later Adrianople and Constantinople), must have been far more influenced by Christianity and the institutions of Byzantium than were the Aydınoğlus, who shared

---

[9] These characteristics are more fully explored in chapter 3.

4   This plate and the one that follows are both of Osman, the eponymous founder of the Ottoman line. Each was produced by western
European artists in the late sixteenth century, and each is utterly stylized. Lonicer's book focuses on Ottoman military exploits, an emphasis
that is reflected in this Osman's imperious gaze, menacing mustaches,
and sceptre and shield. Lonicer, *Chronicorum turcicorum*, vol. I (in one
binding), p. 9.

only the seas with the eastern Roman empire. In other words, although
these emirates probably all were originated by charismatic chieftains, the
particular qualities of their successors and their locations led them in
different directions and toward divergent values.

What lent these principalities legitimacy, drew followers to them, and propelled them to conquest? These questions have proven enigmatic and helped generate a fierce historiographical debate. Some have argued the centrality of Byzantine institutions, others of Turkoman customs, others of Islam, and still others of an inclusive tribalism.[10] The third of these hypotheses (popularly know as "the *gazi* thesis") has proven the most durable and accepted. It argues that the early Ottomans and other western-Anatolian Turkomans had converted to Islam at some time during their migrations across Central Asia, Persia, and Anatolia and had become dedicated, even fanatical, warriors on behalf of *gaza* (holy war). The ideology of these *gazis* thus lent impetus and legitimacy to their strivings against the Byzantine infidel. Others have questioned this attractively coherent thesis on various grounds: that it neglects the nomadic structure of Turkoman society, which tended to be ethnically and religiously inclusive rather than exclusive; that it cannot explain the presence of many non-Islamic, even Christian, institutions in these states; and that such newly converted groups – who evidence suggests regularly fell into and out of various forms of Christianity and Islam – could not have represented the normative, or orthodox, Islam that holy war required. It even has been asserted, with some logic, that Osman, the founder of the Ottoman dynasty, himself may not have been Muslim, or even Turkic!

A recent and sophisticated reworking of the *gazi* thesis answers many of these objections.[11] The author bases his argument upon a less rigid definition of *gazi* and suggests that in such a plastic and ever-shifting world (so different from the age of the nation-state), ideology also must have remained unsettled. He uses the term "bricolage" to describe how the early Ottomans (and, with less success, other emirates) must have piled up various traditions and beliefs and fused them into a new civilization. One centerpiece of the argument is that fanaticism does not demand orthodoxy. In other words, the newly converted, however heterodox and ignorant of the basic tenets of her or his faith, is often the most passionate of believers – even as he or she is also the most likely to abandon one faith for another. We all have watched such individuals, moving from Christianity to Judaism to Islam to Buddhism, searching for enlightenment, acting zealously on behalf of whatever faith they currently embrace, and ending up either as rigorous advocates of one or another orthodoxy or in some ecumenical faith like Baha'ism or Unitarianism. Why should the world of the emirates, in which neither a strong central authority nor an embedded cultural heritage existed to insist on a particular set of beliefs, have been any different? In western Anatolia during

---

[10] Gibbons in *Foundation* argues the first of these, Köprülü in *Origins* the second, Wittek in *Rise* the third, and Lindner in *Nomads* the fourth.
[11] Kafadar, *Between two worlds.*

the 1300s, vacillating Christians and Muslims routinely married each other, converted to each other's faiths, and borrowed from each other's social and political structures, even as they gave, sometimes literally, their lives to whichever of these faiths they at times fleetingly embraced.

The early Ottoman state

Historical context may help explain the existence, the ideologies, and the idiosyncrasies of these frontier principalities. It does not, however, make clear how a particular one of them transformed itself into a world empire. Indeed, it is tempting simply to turn to the "great man" theory, to ascribe to genius the particular decisions that the early Ottomans made regarding the structure of their state and their methods of warfare, to confess the political and military brilliance of the first Ottomans, Osman, Orhan, Murad, and Bayezid, and leave it at that. Certainly, greatness should not be discounted. As the above-mentioned historian insists: "the Ottomans were much more experimental in reshaping [conquered societies] to need, much more creative in their bricolage of different traditions, be they Turkic, Islamic, or Byzantine" than were their rivals.[12] Nevertheless, as the same author also argues, local conditions and accident conferred upon the nascent Ottoman state a number of benefits.

Historians ascribe Ottoman success to several providential factors. These included the frontier location of settlements, a seemingly endless supply of warriors displaced by a persistent Mongol pressure, a syncretic form of Islam that allowed for political and ideological elasticity, and a deterioration in the Byzantine system of defense. A comparison with another emirate helps demonstrate the effectiveness of this particular combination of circumstances. The Aydınoğlus shared with the Ottomans a syncretic ideology and abundant manpower; nevertheless, having reached the Anatolian coast, they soon lacked a common frontier with their enemy and thus seem to have found it difficult to draw warriors to their banner. In other words, the Aydınoğlus no longer could expand by land because of other emirates – the Saruhanoğlu to their north and the Menteşeoğlu to their south. The emirate resorted to alliance with the Byzantines against Latin forces, and in 1345 a crusading army crushed their House. Having reached the Marmara Sea, the Ottomans faced a similar dilemma, and overcame it by passing across the Dardanelles Straits and into Europe (which they were able to do only because of Byzantine assistance).

The early Ottoman state seems to have appeared on the Byzantine frontier at a particularly vulnerable time and place. In 1261, the emperor had moved his capital back to Constantinople after almost sixty years of

[12] Kafadar, *Between two worlds*, p. 121.

ISNICA TE ET NICÆA·TIMĒT BITHYNNAQ.PRVSA
CÆDE TAMĒ GVNDÏ ET QVÆ SARIGATIS OVAT.

OSMAN · ERTVCVLIS FIL·

EDEBALIS NATAM·THALAMIˢ ADIᵛGE TVIS·NĀ
PVLCHRA HAC DICERIS POSTERITATE PARĒS·

5 Osman's physiognomy in this depiction seems utterly transformed.
Not only has his nose softened, his eyes become more prominent, and
his facial hair grown out, but he seems far less intimidating and more
prudent and wise than does Lonicer's rendition. Boissard, *Vitae et icones
sultanorum turcico*, p. 4.

exile (as a result of the Fourth Crusade) across the Sea of Marmara in
Nicaea. This relocation prompted a refocus of Byzantine attention from
its Anatolian to its European provinces, and helped expose all of western
Anatolia to Turkoman incursions, which occurred with growing intensity

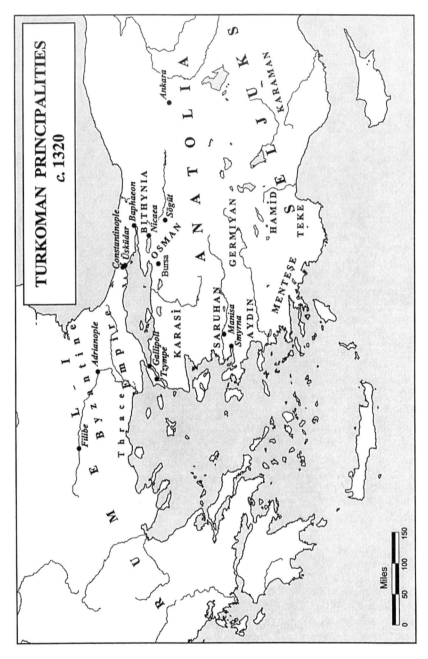

TURKOMAN PRINCIPALITIES
c. 1320

Map 2

because of flight from Mongol conquests in Central Asia, Persia, and eastern Anatolia. One such Turkoman group, the tribe to which Osman belonged according to Ottoman legend, established itself in the region of Bithynia near Nicaea and soon became a political and military force there. The embryonic state expanded quickly in the early fourteenth century. In about 1301 Osman defeated a small Byzantine force at Baphaeon, in 1326 his son captured Bursa, and in 1331 the former Byzantine capital Nicaea fell.[13] A decade or so later, Ottoman forces began appearing on the European side of the Dardanelles, and in the early 1350s that military presence became political with the capture of Tzympe and Gallipoli.

Osman and his successors thus took full advantage of their location, Byzantine weakness, and the continuous flow of Turkomans from the east. Doing so, however, called for a number of inspired strategies. First of all, the family's army could cross into Europe via the Dardanelles Straits only by first moving through the territory of another well-placed emirate, the Karasi, which Orhan's soldiers seem to have overrun and incorporated in the 1330s and 1340s, with some help from household feuds that spoiled that state's ability to resist. Orhan's successors only with difficulty were able to expunge the resulting animosity against their upstart state and its willingness to attack fellow *gazi* states (they seem to have done so in part by revising the history of this conquest). Secondly, because the Ottomans had no navy, they could not cross an army into Europe without foreign assistance. They secured such aid from the Byzantines themselves through a series of adroit military and marriage alliances with various pretenders to the Byzantine throne (Orhan married into the royal Cantacuzenus family in order to seal such a pact). The Ottomans and other so-called *gazis* evidently saw no contradiction between their values and alliance with Christians, even against states that shared their supposed enmity toward Byzantium.

The making of an imperial household

These immediate successes should have meant little in the long run, for the Mongol and Turkoman convention of multiparty heirship (polygeniture) in any case would have broken the unity of the state within a matter of generations. Such had been the fate of the Seljuks, Chengiz Khan's empire, and many lesser polities. The Ottomans perhaps were not the only emirate that did not succumb to this flaw in state building, but they were most successful at finding alternatives. In what seems to have been

[13] The very dates of these major events in early Ottoman history are speculative.

an inspired if brutal strategy, they moved to a system not of primogeniture, as became the norm in western Europe, but to one of unigeniture.[14] That is, when a chieftain (and later a monarch) died, one of his sons, rather than many of his brothers and sons, succeeded him. When, why, and how this guiding principle took over, we do not know, although some such scheme must have been in place as early as *c.* 1324, when Orhan succeeded his father despite the presence of several brothers.

Osman's declaration that his son should succeed him may have helped legitimize Orhan's triumph, although it does not sufficiently explain it. A father's wishes are rarely followed, and even in the Ottoman case favorite sons did not always inherit the throne. Nevertheless, despite some serious challenges, the Ottoman realm never was divided between heirs and no Ottoman ruler seems to have considered doing so, even after conquests in Europe might have made it seem logical to partition the kingdom at the Dardanelles Straits. Murad I (1362–89), Bayezid I (1389–1402), Mehmed I (1413–21), and Murad II (1421–44, 1446–51) all ruthlessly exterminated their brothers and other rivals rather than share (or lose) power. Finally, under Mehmed II (1444–46, 1451–81) the new principle was codified as the Ottoman law of fratricide.[15]

Despite such signs of intentionality, the road toward unigeniture remained rocky, its institutionalization a matter of luck as well as strategy. Bayezid, for example, probably was able to eliminate his competent elder brother Yakub with relative ease because it was Bayezid who in 1389 was on the battlefield at Kosovo when his father fell, who completed the rout of the crusading army which challenged Ottoman hegemony in the Balkans, and who had a Christian mother at a time when much of the Ottoman army also was Christian. Yakub, meanwhile, had the misfortune to be far away in Anatolia.

The fact that Bayezid was a younger son and that both he and Yakub led armies suggests a vital distinction between the Ottoman and other European monarchies: in the Ottoman case, no favorite legally existed until the succession actually occurred. In other words, all sons were groomed for the throne; all sons were expected to be capable to assume it even though only one would do so. The Ottoman choice to retain this particular element from their central Asian past while throwing off so many others was another example of genius (or luck), for by so doing the dynasty considerably improved its chances for an extended line of competent rulers. It also demonstrates how this frontier state picked through its various legacies and fused them into an innovative and prevailing totality.

[14] The specifics of this vital transformation remain a mystery, on which see Kafadar, *Between two worlds*, pp. 136–38.
[15] Discussed in chapter 3 below.

Ottoman modifications in laws governing the transfer of power did produce some difficulties. Civil war probably accompanied Orhan's and Murad's assumptions of power, and it certainly attended Bayezid's and Mehmed I's, with each victor ruthlessly having his rivals hunted down and murdered. Such violence may have consolidated power, for each regal death obviously ushered in a precarious moment for the Ottoman state, but it also gave a perception of barbarism and tended to produce resentment and pockets of resistance. After Yakub's assassination, for example, Bayezid began a long struggle against rival states in Anatolia who gained support even from Turkoman followers of the House of Osman, angry that their champion, Yakub, had lost the struggle for the Ottoman throne.

Of course, in capable hands the expunging of such threats could be turned to advantage. For example, the founding of a new army that would evolve into the janissary corps has often been attributed to Murad I's desire to counterbalance his most powerful cohorts (*beys*), who begrudged him his consolidation of power, his display of imperial trappings, and the loss of a sense of class solidarity that had characterized the emirates. Similarly, the drift toward orthodoxy that "began by displaying piety and then went on to issue rulings" (according to the anonymous chronicler quoted at the beginning of this chapter) has been explained as a reaction to the attractions of such charismatic and heterodox rivals as Shaykh Bedreddin. Active in 1416, just as Mehmed I struggled to consolidate his realm after an eleven-year civil war (1402–13), Bedreddin preached a social harmony between faiths that mightily appealed particularly to people (many important warriors among them) pining for the waning latitudinarian spirit of the frontier emirates. It surely is no coincidence that in the next decades Mehmed and his successors brought in scholars from the Islamic heartland and established prestigious theological seminaries (*medreses*) as they moved their developing state toward Islamic orthodoxy.

The detail that Yakub and Bayezid had different mothers highlights one of the domestic peculiarities of the Ottoman dynastic household – the existence of multiple wives and/or concubines and the expectation that each prince might have a different mother. This feature expresses a particularly Ottoman manifestation of both central Asian and Islamic legacies. In the nascent Ottoman state, a consort might be the offspring of a *bey* or spiritual guide, as in Osman's supposed marriages to Umur bey's daughter and to the daughter of the dervish shaykh Edebali. Or, the bride might come from a political rival, as with Orhan's marriages to the daughters of the Christian chieftain of Yarhisar and the Byzantine emperor John IV Cantacuzenus. Or she might have been taken in a raid, as probably was the case with Murad's concubine (and Bayezid's mother) Gülçiçek who seems previously to have been a wife of a prince of the House of Karasi. It is striking that in each case the consort was one of several, she almost always came from outside the tribe, her cultural background and religious beliefs mattered not at all, and it seems to have been inconsequential (in terms of legitimacy of offspring at least) whether she was a wife or a slave, light- or dark-skinned.[16]

This casual approach toward the personal histories of imperial companions probably derived in part from the fiercely patriarchic nature of the Ottoman concept of political culture and procreation. In other words, in terms of competence to inherit, the mother's pedigree was of no consequence; it was only germane that the father had been sultan. Nevertheless, the Ottomans did make rational choices and draw upon a number of traditions in establishing the imperial household. The legacy of acquiring women through "raids" most likely came directly from a central Asian tradition; the employment of polygyny, that is multiple wives, probably derived from Islamic sources; the Ottomans may have learned of concubinage from the Persians; and they may have adapted from the Byzantines the idea of securing alliance and treaty through marriages.

From wherever they received these structures, the manner in which the Ottomans cobbled them together granted the dynasty enormous flexibility, greatly enhanced its chances of prolonging itself, and guaranteed a steady entry of "new blood." The flexibility came from the state's ability to cement multiple alliances through marriage, as Osman, Orhan, and Murad all seemed to have done. The dynastic prolongation came from the imperial House's ability, through multiple partners, to secure an heir. (This is exactly the consequence that many European rulers – including most notoriously Henry VIII of England – found so difficult to produce, and precisely the one that has allowed the Japanese imperial house, which until the twentieth century relied on concubinage, to last for some 2,500 years.) The "new blood" occurred because the dynasty's exogamous reproduction precluded the type of inbreeding that so debilitated the Habsburgs and other European dynasties.

The Ottomans did not adopt all of these domestic approaches simultaneously. Rather, their strategy evolved along with their state. For example, the family contracted many marriages with rival dynasties in its early years; once it was established, however, it preferred the security of partnering with slaves to the possibility that an infidel or heretical wife or mother might taint the monarch's values and conduct (just as much of England feared Charles I's French Catholic wife was doing in the 1630s

---

[16] On these points, see especially Peirce, *Imperial harem*, pp. 32–42.

and 1640s). It is in fact likely that Murad was the last ruler whose mother was not a concubine. The Ottomans did not do away with marriage, but separated that institution from procreation. During the fifteenth and early sixteenth centuries not only did sultans always couple with concubines, but also an unwritten principle barred them from continuing sexual relations with the same woman once she had borne him a son.[17] This prohibition probably derived from a practical concern that the prince would become the focus of his mother's life. The aim was realized in two ways: first, the lack of a dowry or political power outside the Ottoman context made the concubine completely dependent upon the imperial household; second, the severing of intimate ties with the sultan forced her to focus exclusively upon the abilities of her only son (should he fail to win the throne, then she also would fail, and at best be condemned to isolated exile). We know neither the period during which such expediencies arose nor how unique they were to the Ottoman dynasty. Their effectiveness, however, is undeniable.

Early conquests and the redesign of Ottoman society

The pattern of early expansion is one indication that *gaza* early became a vital Ottoman principle, for with the sole exception of the principality of the Karasi, Ottoman conquests under the first three Ottoman emirs were generally of lands controlled by Christian states.[18] Osman seems to have spent most of his career working to surround and thus isolate Bursa, the most important Byzantine city in the region. By *c.* 1321, he had succeeded in doing so. Nevertheless, he probably never saw the fruits of his investment, for despite Bursa's isolation it did not fall to his son until *c.* 1326. Orhan made Bursa his capital and continued rounding out his territories, in the next fifteen years taking Nicaea and Üsküdar (just across the straits from Constantinople itself) and then the entire principality of Karasi. By the mid-1340s, Orhan could claim the entire northwestern tier of Anatolia.

The late 1340s was a critical period for the emerging Ottoman state. Not only was it now strong enough to proclaim political independence, but also it had to make a decision: whether to remain an Anatolian state (in which case it could expand only against fellow Turkoman-Islamic states), or cross over into Europe. At first glance, the espousal of a *gazi*

---

[17] Peirce, *Imperial harem*, deals with this progression brilliantly.

[18] Nevertheless, the Karasi exception could be generalized into an Ottoman readiness to attack other Islamic states. On how the Turkic idea of "raider"(*akinci*) may gradually have shifted into the Islamic idea of "holy warrior" (*gazi*), see Imber, "Ideals and legitimation," pp. 140–41.

ideology seems to have foreclosed any decision to turn on other Islamic states. Nevertheless, if it is accurate to suppose that the Ottomans were recent and still heterodox converts, they must have been as capable as were so many of their followers of identity switching, especially from one monotheistic faith to another. After all, not only were the inhabitants of their territory overwhelmingly Christian, but so also were many of their warriors and members of their households.

Furthermore, the style of Islam to which the early Ottomans were exposed was hardly conventional, at least in the sense that the mature Ottoman state would have defined it.[19] It is likely that Sufis first exposed the Ottomans and other Turkic groups to the religion. These were heterodox proselytizers who were able to communicate the basics of Islam in familiar if unauthoritative terms. For example, Shaykh Edebali, who may have been Osman's spiritual advisor and whose daughter – according to legend – he married, probably was a dervish disciple of a certain Baba Ilyas, a Turkoman rebel against Seljuk authority. In his doctrine, Baba Ilyas seems to have combined shamanistic with Islamic beliefs in a manner that most traditionally trained Islamic scholars would have deemed heretical but that found great appeal among Turkomans. This is not to say that the early Ottomans did not consider themselves "good" Muslims, that they were not strong, even devoted, believers in Islam and *gaza*, but only that no overarching political and religious infrastructure existed to define exactly what Islam was and how one might deviate from it. In other words, there was no one in a position of authority who could ostracize or "excommunicate" the heretic and thereby exclude him or her from society. The practical incentive to become and remain Muslim in that milieu was not social but political and military. It provided legitimacy for the formation of states and justification for marauding and other belligerencies.

The Ottoman state did not collapse in the mid fourteenth century; nor did it become integrated into larger states. Instead, it joined other emirates in sending armed forces into Europe at the behest of Byzantine factions eager for aid in the civil wars that distinguished imperial politics in that period. John IV Cantacuzenus appealed to Orhan, who in 1346 came to his assistance against John V Paleologues (who himself had appealed to the rival Karasi emirate for support). Then, in 1352 the Byzantine emperor gave Orhan the fortress of Tzympe, on the European side of the Dardanelles, and two years later his son Süleyman occupied the town of Gallipoli. With the establishment of this foothold, a radical change

---

[19] On which, see Kafadar, *Between two worlds*, pp. 74–77, and Karamustafa, *God's unruly friends*.

6 The conical hat and earthy and tattered clothing mark this man as a member of a socially deviant religious order. In a distinctly un-Islamic ritual, he seems to be reading the palm of the person on the right. Nicolay, *Le navigationi et viaggi nella Turchia*, p. 207.

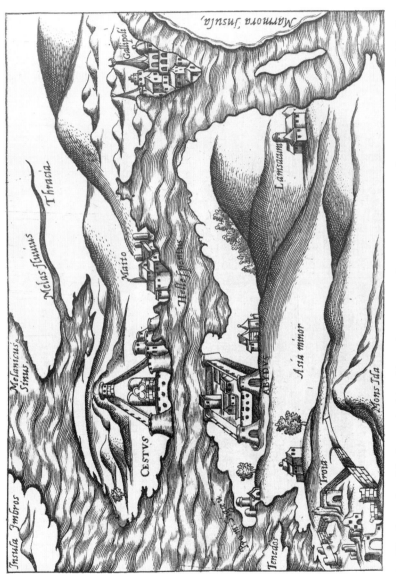

7 Clearly and strikingly marked in this early seventeenth-century map are the town of Gallipoli (the first important Ottoman conquest in Europe) as well as the two fortresses that controlled access into the Dardanelles Straits. Breuning, *Orientalische Reyss dess Edlen*, p. 42.

in ideology or religion became unthinkable. The prestige of being the first Islamic state since the first century after Muhammed to carry the war against the infidel into Europe secured the place of the House of Osman as the pre-eminent emirate. Ottoman achievements drew a flood of supporters, both Muslim and Christian, to its banner.

In the next half-century, Orhan's son and grandson, Murad and Bayezid, probably employed the idea of *gaza* more explicitly to press further into Europe. In 1361, Edirne (Adrianople) fell, to be followed by Filibe in 1363, which put all of Thrace under Ottoman rule. Murad spent much of the rest of his reign, which ended on the fields of Kosovo in 1389, in a three-pronged push up the Black Sea coast, up through Bulgaria into Serbia, and westward as far as Salonika. Ottoman territories also expanded in Anatolia, despite the fact that the *gaza* ideology may have made it tricky to justify aggression against other Islamic states. Murad at first acted diplomatically, by marrying his son Bayezid into the House of Germiyan and even buying some territories. In the end, however, he resorted to war, using Christian troops to defeat the Karamans before wheeling back toward Europe in 1389 to confront the crusading armies led by King Lazar of Serbia. Bayezid thus inherited a principality that encompassed virtually all of southeast Europe as well as western Anatolia.

The Ottoman state in 1389 may have been large, but it also was fragile. In Europe, not only did opposition remain in Macedonia, Constantinople, and elsewhere, but King Sigismund of Hungary also resisted Ottoman advances. In Anatolia, resentment against Ottoman aggression festered, and Bayezid was forced repeatedly to lead armies against rebellions and attacks on both fronts (hence his nickname "Thunderbolt"). Ottoman successes of course both attracted supporters and stirred rivals. The state not only had to contend with crusading armies, but also with a resurging threat from the east under the leadership of Tamerlane. It was his forces that near Ankara in 1402 defeated Bayezid's army, and he who captured, publicly humiliated, and executed the sultan, and dismantled the Ottoman state, sending it into an eleven-year interregnum (1402–13).

Creative social, political, and military adjustments had accompanied this rapid Ottoman expansion, cut short so humiliatingly in 1402. The principal catalyst for many of the social changes was demographic, for the society that the Ottomans fashioned and had to organize was overwhelmingly Christian, even though, especially in Anatolia, conversion and migration over time eroded the Christian majority.[20] This conquering

---

[20] On this process, the classic study is Speros Vryonis, *The decline of medieval hellenism in Asia Minor and the process of Islamization from the eleventh through the fifteenth century* (Berkeley, 1971).

Islamic state, then, had a principally Christian subject population, to which it accommodated itself in various ways. Meanwhile, a predictable Ottoman consolidation of power against the state's notable supporters stimulated rebellions by displaced military and political groups, which in turn inspired the authorities to create countervailing military and political institutions.

One immediate problem was of politically and socially integrating peoples accustomed to a Christian government and fearful of both Islam and the central-Asian warriors who were carrying it into Europe.[21] Such hurdles were less forbidding than they may seem today, for most of the regimes that the Ottomans displaced were essentially illegitimate and many were reviled. Not only had the Fourth Crusade of 1204 installed Latin and thus heretical lords in many of these Greek Orthodox lands, but also these rulers exploited their subjects through high taxes and onerous personal services (including the infamous corvée, by which the lord weekly demanded several days of personal service from his serfs). Such exploitation came even at the hands of the rulers of Byzantium who may have shared the faith of most of their subjects but whose desperate plight gave them little choice but to compromise with the Latins and heavily tax their peoples.

As a frontier principality with long experience of Byzantine conditions, the Ottomans understood how to exploit such instability. The justification for Ottoman conquest may have been religious – that is, the absorption of the "abode of war" (*dar al-harb*) into the "abode of Islam" (*dar al-Islam*) – but the techniques and resultant society were distinctly political. First of all, principalities were not always conquered directly. Instead, local Latin and Greek lords sometimes bought military aid (as John IV Cantacuzenus had done in the 1450s), or paid for titular self-rule through tributes. The Ottomans justified such arrangements through the concept of the "abode of the covenant" (*dar al-ahd*), a kind of halfway house into the Islamic world, and polities occasionally were able to stave off conquest for quite some time. Dubrovnik, Wallachia, and Chios long retained their autonomy by paying such tributes. Nevertheless, such measures generally were only a first step, to be followed by imperial sons being held in the Ottoman capital, ever-increasing tribute, and the forced contribution of troops to Ottoman campaigns.

The resentment of Greek Orthodox Christian subjects against existing Catholic regimes helped the Ottomans, under whose government non-Muslims prospered. It is true that, in accordance with Islamic law,

---

[21] On patterns of conquest, see İnalcık, "Ottoman methods of conquest" and, for a specific if much later case, his "Ottoman policy and administration in Cyprus after the conquest," reprinted in İnalcık, *The Ottoman Empire: conquest, organization and economy* (London, 1978), pp. 112–22 and article 8, respectively.

both Christians and Jews were liable to a special head tax (*cizye*). Never-theless, not only did a steep reduction in tithes and the abolition of the corvée more than offset this imposition, but also a particularly moderate reading of Islamic principles ameliorated even such religiously obligatory levies, which at first often were collected from communities as an under-valued lump sum (*maktu'*). Furthermore, payment of these dues ensured religious, cultural, and even a certain political autonomy. In other words, the Ottomans chose not to embrace the insularity of the Catholic and the Greek Orthodox worlds. Instead, they drew upon the egalitarianism and inclusive traditions of Central Asia and the relative tolerance of Islam to construct a society in which non-Muslim monotheists could live and work in relative freedom. Oppressed inhabitants of exclusionary Christian states found such an alternative enormously attractive.

Of course, not all Ottoman subjects approved of their government's centralizing and accommodating strategies. Many Turkomans, for exam-ple, not only resented the loss of status that accompanied the trappings of monarchy, but also disapproved of the state's drift toward Sunni or-thodoxy. Whether because of loss of power, or because of heterodoxy, or because of exposure to Shi'ism, chronic rebellion plagued the eastern Ottoman frontiers in the late fourteenth and fifteenth centuries. Although never able to resolve this difficulty, the state did manage to ameliorate it by resettling tribesmen in Ottoman Europe (*sürgün*). Not only did this policy remove a fractious people from its natural environment, but it also injected an effective military force into the frontier marches and helped establish Islam in the overwhelmingly Christian Balkans. Ironically, then, at the very time that the Catholic reconquest of Iberia was removing Islam as an element in the making of southwestern Europe, the Ottomans in-troduced it in the southeast.

Tribal chiefs with whom the Ottomans had shared power in their early days also lost influence during this process of consolidation, and as lead-ing warriors their discontent was a serious threat. Bayezid, for example, confronted such malcontents twice: in 1391–92, he defeated an assem-blage by recruiting Christian troops; in 1402, they helped defeat him through the agency of Tamerlane. Bayezid's experiences suggest that, if the Ottomans wanted to construct a stable Islamic state, the recruitment of non-Muslims or the hiring of mercenaries could only be stopgaps. The regime's long-term solution was to create a new army (the janissaries) as a countervailing force to the Turkoman cavalry.

According to Ottoman tradition, it was Murad I who, with the help of a certain scholar named Kara Rüstem from Karaman, established the corps. As ruler and in accordance with Islamic law, he not only began collecting a tax upon prisoners, but also claimed one out of every five of them. Not only did the state collect these "young men," but they

8 Another whimsical depiction of an Ottoman sultan; this fuming and stern warrior is meant to be Murad I. Lonicer, *Chronicorum turcicorum*, vol. I (in one binding), p. 11.

then gave them "to the Turks in the provinces so that they should learn Turkish . . . After a few years they brought them to the Porte and made them janissaries, giving them the name *yeni çeri* [new troops]."[22] We need not take at face value this explanation of the invention of the janissary

[22] F. Giese (ed.), *Tevarih-i Al-i Osman (Die altosmanischen anonymen Chroniken)* (Breslau, 1922), as quoted in Lewis (ed.), *Politics and war*, pp. 226–27.

corps. Nevertheless, implicit in it is the logical proposal that the idea for it came from the Islamic heartland, where slave armies were long established, and that the Ottomans creatively modified it. The end product was an army (and eventually a government as well) that was owned by the ruler, that was exclusively composed of converts to Islam, that was recruited not only from captives but also from human tithes against Christian populations in the Ottoman Balkans, and whose troops were educated into a particularly Ottoman high culture.[23]

Fashioning a new civilization

However responsible Murad may have been for its shape, it is certain that the janissary corps was decisive in the reinvention of the Ottoman state after the Interregnum of 1402–13. After defeating Bayezid, Tamerlane did not consume his territories. Instead, he reconstituted the Anatolia emirates that Murad and Bayezid had destroyed and left the Ottomans in control of those lands they had conquered from the Byzantines. In the end, then, the first decade of the fifteenth century became more an extended civil war between Bayezid's sons and a few other pretenders than a true interregnum. The recovery came about in part because the approach toward imperial succession that the Ottomans had shaped over the previous century meant that each of these potential heirs was competent and determined. Equally important was that a geographic heartland remained in Europe, and that an administrative and military infrastructure existed. The Ottoman land-tenure system gave cavalrymen land in return for service (the *timar* system) and a janissary corps gave the state a superlative armed force.

The monarchy's awareness of the value of these new institutions helped distinguish the empire that re-emerged after 1413 from its previous incarnation. During the next fifty years, the land-tenure system was expanded and standardized, both Christian and Muslim lords were rewarded for service with large grants of land, the religious identities within Ottoman society were institutionalized, the process of moving Turkomans from Anatolia to the Balkans was accelerated, orthodox Sunnism was more and more embraced as the ruling ideology of the state, and the janissary corps was acknowledged as the backbone of the Ottoman army. These innovations, which in many ways were a consequence of living on the western-Anatolian frontier, helped consolidate the Ottoman state even as it stabilized and made more orthodox Ottoman society. They

---

[23] One of the only sustained sources we have on the janissaries is Konstantin Mihailovich, *Memoirs of a janissary* (Ann Arbor, 1975).

also allowed the empire more smoothly to absorb both succession disputes and the civilizational shifts that accompanied the conquest of Constantinople (1453) and the integration of vast Arab lands into the empire (1516–17).

The restoration did not come easily. Mehmed I spent most of his reign battling brothers, pretenders, and rival states, and his son Murad II devoted his first years to fending off his uncle, his brother, and various Balkan and Anatolian states and former rulers eager to dismantle his principality. Both rulers became aware that their survival depended upon specifically Ottoman institutions, especially the cavalry whose prestige depended upon Ottoman control of their landholdings, and the bureaucrats and army whom the imperial family owned. These institutions granted the Ottomans a decisive advantage over their rivals, and by the time Mehmed II came to the throne (for the second time) in 1451, the janissaries constituted the mainstay of the army and the *timariot* was the principal organizing institution of Ottoman lands.[24]

Even though the "classical age" in Ottoman history is said to have begun under Mehmed II, who conquered Constantinople, it was under his father that many of that period's most momentous battles were won and its most vital institutions perfected. When Murad II came to the throne in 1421, he was faced first with an uncle, Mustafa, who, upon his release from Byzantine captivity, proceeded to lead an army of frontier *beys* against the new sultan; then, he confronted a brother (again named Mustafa) who rose against him at the instigation of western-Anatolian principalities. Having defeated these rivals, Murad spent much of the next twenty years in a series of campaigns against the Venetians that ended with the Ottoman reconquest of Salonika in 1430, and against the Hungarians under John Hunyadi, who successfully opposed Murad in the early 1440s. In 1444, the Ottoman sultan, apparently exhausted after twenty years of almost constant warfare, signed treaties with his rivals in both Anatolia and Europe, and handed the monarchy over to his twelve-year-old son Mehmed.

By abdicating, which was unprecedented, Murad perhaps hoped not only to be left with time to write and meditate, but also to avoid the bloody conflicts that had accompanied the deaths of earlier sultans and to establish a pattern of peaceful succession. These objectives were thwarted, however, by the immediate rise of several enemies, the most threatening of which was a coalition of European powers – Hungary, Wallachia, and Venice – that the Ottomans defeated only by recalling Murad, who smashed a crusading army at Varna in November 1444. Mehmed II ruled

---

[24] These and other institutions of the mature Ottoman state are discussed more fully in chapter 3 below.

for two more years, until in 1446 a janissary revolt again brought Murad II out of retirement, and he remained in power until his death in 1451.

Murad's recurrent conflicts accelerated existing tendencies in the development of the Ottoman military and bureaucracy. Not only did he expand the janissary corps, but he also built a navy with which to confront Venetian sea power in the Aegean and Black seas. It also was under Murad II that the Ottomans adopted gunpowder, both arming their infantry with muskets and employing large cannon in sieges. Accompanying and making possible these innovations were economic growth that increased income and led to an expansion of the Ottoman bureaucracy and ruling class. Consequently, when Mehmed II assumed the throne for the second time in 1451, the extent of his kingdom – stretching from the Danube to central Anatolia – and his resources far surpassed those of his predecessors.

A maturing sense of self accompanied the physical expansion of the Ottoman realm. The civilizations of Central Asia, Persia, Arabia, Islam, and Byzantium all had helped fashion the empire's ruling class; their blending generated a mores that has been termed Ottoman. It was distinguished by a language that was grammatically Turkic but enriched with sophisticated Persian and Arabic poetic and narrative traditions and vocabularies, and was restricted to a small ruling elite in Istanbul and in other principal Ottoman cities. This privileged class had no basis in ethnicity, race, or religion. Its members included individuals of Arab, Greek, Italian, Jewish, Slavic, sub-Saharan African, Turkish, and myriad other extractions. The manner in which it carefully distinguished itself from all over whom it ruled – Muslims as well as Christians and Jews – was through the expression of a fastidious and urbane culture.

Creating an imperial center: the winning of Constantinople

The new sultan, however, had no shortage of problems in 1451. A pretender to the throne – Orhan – lived ensconced and menacing in the "Turkish" quarter of Constantinople. Even worse, Çandarlı Halil, the high Ottoman official whom Mehmed held responsible for recalling his father in 1444 and staging the janissary revolt that had deposed him in 1446, five years later remained in power as grand vizier, as representative of powerful frontier lords and the religious elite (*ulema*), and as the principal advocate for peace with the Byzantines and other European powers. For Mehmed, it seems, Halil was also a reminder of his shameful deposition and the almost universal perception that he would be an ineffective and unthreatening ruler. The opportunity simultaneously to remove

the danger of Orhan, to show himself an effective and devout commander, and to bring down a powerful and intimidating Ottoman statesman
(as well as the pseudo-aristocracy that he represented) decided Mehmed
finally to realize for Islam the conquest of Constantinople.

The story of Byzantium's fall has been told many times,[25] for it, more
than any other event in Ottoman history, was also a major episode in
European history. Indeed, it is even considered by many a pivotal event,
as the moment when the medieval European world ended and the modern one began. There is a certain irony in this assessment. First, the city
had been taken and pillaged before, by the Fourth Crusaders in 1204,
when the blind Venetian doge Dandolo led a zealous and brutal army
against it. It was then and not in 1453 that most of the artwork and
wealth of Constantinople vanished – into Venetian and other palaces and
public buildings – and that most cultural artifacts were destroyed; it was
in 1204 and not in 1453 that the Great Library was destroyed. Second,
little of the fabulous wealth for which Byzantium was known remained
in 1453. Not only had the city already been ransacked two and a half
centuries earlier, but also the Byzantines had never regained a hinterland
that could have financed a significant renaissance. Latin and Turkic lords
held most Byzantine lands, and those that remained were swallowed up
by the Ottomans during the fourteenth and early fifteenth centuries. The
fact that there were only some 8,500 men to defend the city against an
Ottoman army of some 50,000 reveals not only the self-sacrificing futil-
ity of the effort, but also how inconsequential the Byzantine entity had
become. In other words, Constantinople was significant to Christendom
mainly as an emblematic bulwark against Islam and various hordes –
whether Mongol or Turkic. The immediate consequences of its fall were
symbolic. Its practical significance lay in the future rather than in the
present, for control of the city was eventually to bring the Ottoman dynasty enormous wealth, prestige, and power.

Although Mehmed II certainly was aware of the symbolic centrality
of the city for Europe, his motivation for its conquest was as much domestic as international. Factionalism divided his administration. On one
hand, a "peace party," represented by Çandarlı Halil and other *ulema*
officials and inherited by Mehmed from his father, advised caution and
consolidation; on the other, a "war party" led by the sultan's warrior-
tutor Zaganos, advocated conflict. Mehmed's intimacy with his tutor as

---

[25] For the Byzantine perspective, the best study is Steven Runciman, *The fall of Constantinople, 1453* (Cambridge, 1991). For Ottoman policies toward the city immediately after
the conquest, see Halil İnalcık, "The policy of Mehmed II toward the Greek population
of Istanbul and the Byzantine buildings of the city," *Dumbarton Oaks Papers* 23(1970):
213–49.

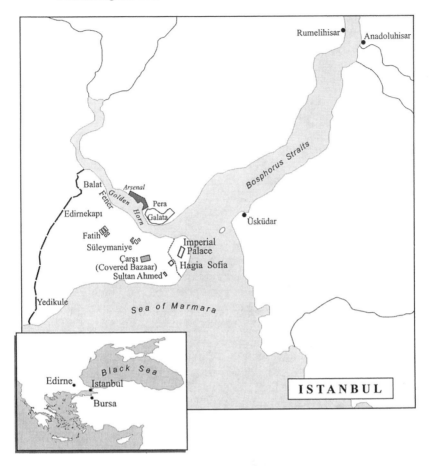

Map 3

well as his bitterness against the man who had engineered his ousting in
1446 must have influenced his decision to act aggressively. Nevertheless,
the attack upon the grand but weakened city also made political and ideological sense, especially for a sultan who was almost universally perceived
as indecisive and ineffective.

The young sultan's principal threat came not from the Byzantines
themselves, but from potential allies, and especially the Genoese and
Venetians whose powerful navies could relieve the siege by sea. So, his
first move was to build a castle just across the Bosphorus Straits from
Anadoluhisar, which his great-grandfather Bayezid had constructed half
a century before. Within a year after his succession, Rumelihisar had been

completed, and cannons placed in the two fortresses effectively sealed the sea passage from the Black Sea. This maneuver diminished the likelihood of reinforcements; moreover, the declared neutrality of the Genoese colony in Galata, the capacity to shift a fleet over land and launch it into the Golden Horn, the casting and deployment of massive cannon against the city's land walls, the doggedness especially of the janissary corps, and a dispirited sense of inescapability among the defenders – heightened perhaps by the preference of a large segment of the city's Greek population for Ottoman over Latin government – secured Constantinople for the Ottomans in May 1453 after a 54-day siege. With news arriving that same month that Venetian and Hungarian troops were on their way, the defenders probably never learned how nearly the Ottomans, fearing an attack from their rear, came to raising the siege just before the final assault.

As the city had been taken by assault, Mehmed was legally obliged to let his troops seize Constantinople's goods and enslave its inhabitants, and a good deal of plundering occurred. Nevertheless, perhaps because the population of the city was already destitute and many of its districts virtually abandoned, the scale of destruction paled in comparison to the sack of 1204. Furthermore, Mehmed II intended to turn this city into his capital and did not want to inherit an empty husk. Consequently, he limited the plundering to one day, protected several important structures from it (including the great church Hagia Sofia, which he consecrated as a mosque), and immediately proclaimed the city his new capital.[26]

With the capture of Constantinople the Ottoman Empire gained a hub. Ideologically, the monarchy now considered itself a great conquering Islamic dynasty that by reducing Byzantium inherited also the legacy of Rome. Militarily, the city's formidable defenses at the center of an enormous territory granted the state a sense of security and a launching point for further conquests. Economically, the new capital's control of extensive hinterlands in the Balkans and western Anatolia, as well as seaborne access to the goods of the known world, would turn it into a principal financial and commercial gathering place and bring great wealth to its inhabitants and the imperial treasury. Socially, the city's depopulated state in 1453 provided an opportunity for the Ottomans to re-form it in their image, and, at first by force and then by preference, Armenian, Greek, Jewish, foreign, and Muslim Turkish settlers soon had constructed a polylingual, polyethnic, and polyreligious metropolis that existed and thrived in striking contrast to non-Ottoman cities in the Mediterranean and European worlds.

[26] See İnalcık, "Policy of Mehmed II."

Kubad in Istanbul

Be damned, O Emperor, be thrice damned
For the evil you have done and the evil you do.
You catch and shackle the old and the archpriests
In order to take the children as Janissaries.
Their parents weep and their sisters and brothers too
And I cry until it pains me;
As long as I live I shall cry,
For last year it was my son and this year my brother.[1]

The çavuş Kubad, journeying from Istanbul to the most Christian Serenissima as a representative of his sultan, felt uneasy. His visit to Christendom seemed an eerie adventure, but he was unsure why. It was not dread of the infidel creed. Some of his closest acquaintances had been claimed by the devşirme*: snatched from their Christian towns and villages in the Ottoman Balkans, declared His Most Imperial Majesty's personal property, persuaded as boys to convert to Islam, and trained to become Ottoman soldiers and bureaucrats. Indeed, such had been the career path of his own grand vizier, Sokollu Mehmed Pasha, who had grown up a Christian on the Ottoman borderlands of Bosnia, been "tithed" into imperial service and converted, worked his way brilliantly up the administrative ladder in the imperial palace, served as the recently deceased Süleyman's last grand vizier, became also an imperial grandson-in-law by marrying İsmihan sultan, that padishah's favorite granddaughter, and now, as both grand vizier and son-in-law to the new Sultan Selim II, was arguably the most influential person in the entire realm.[2] Rumor had it that Mehmed Pasha maintained personal and financial ties with his Bosnian-Christian relatives, and even had established a religious endowment in his home town; Kubad,*

---

[1] As quoted in Apostolos E. Vakalopoulos, *The Greek nation, 1453–1669: the cultural and economic background of modern Greek Society*, trans. Ian Moles and Pharia Moles (New Brunswick, NJ, 1976), p. 37.

[2] On career paths and identity, see İ. Metin Kunt, "Ethnic-regional (*cins*) solidarity in the seventeenth-century Ottoman establishment," *International Journal of Middle East Studies* 5(1974): 233–39; and Cornell H. Fleischer, *Bureaucrat and intellectual in the Ottoman Empire: the historian Mustafa Âli (1541–1600)* (Princeton, NJ, 1986). On sons-in-law in the imperial household, see Peirce, *Imperial harem*.

along with countless others, certainly had beheld him attend and pray at the Grand Patriarch's church in the Greek quarter of Fener (Phanar) whenever his illustrious brother, himself a patriarch in Bosnia, visited the Sublime Capital.

Kubad's own tale differed little from his vizier's (even though he had been born a Muslim), having been yanked from beyond the eastern borders of the Empire. He was of Circassian descent, and had been named after the river that flows through his Caucasian homeland. Although his professional achievements certainly could not match Mehmed Pasha's, the envoy was proud to be a senior courier, responsible not only for protecting His Imperial Majesty during public functions, but also for bearing imperial decrees to the furthest corners of the Empire and beyond and seeing that they were entirely fulfilled.

So it was not distant travel that the envoy found disconcerting. Nor was it the close proximity to or even the sheer mass of Christians that he would find in Venice. He almost daily jostled, bargained, celebrated, and quarreled with Christian subjects on the streets of Istanbul. Such was the milieu of the multi-layered Ottoman capital.[3] *The urgency of trade and the diversity of citizenry in the teeming city easily bridged the doctrinal chasm that separated the Muslim envoy from the tens of thousands of Christian and Jewish subjects who lived and toiled there.*

In the political sphere in which Kubad labored, attachments could become especially close and intense. One needed merely to board a caique, savor the ten-minute cruise as its sturdy oarsmen whisked one across the Golden Horn with its spectacular views of the imperial residence, the Byzantine-built Hagia Sofia, the Genoese-raised Galata Tower, and Mimar Sinan's almost-completed contender for dominance of the Stamboul skyline – the glorious Süleymaniye mosque – and disembark at the pier at the bottom of Galata to plunge upward into a world dominated by diplomatic, commercial, and religious representatives from Christian Europe.[4]

Kubad had often undertaken that short passage to deliver imperial rescripts and admonitions from the Ottoman government to Venetian, Genoese, Habsburg, and French envoys resident in Galata. Only months earlier he had accompanied the Venetian bailo, Soranzo, to the court of the kadi, the Muslim magistrate in charge of judicial and social matters in Galata.[5] *There he had helped negotiate an agreement over Venetian liability for some wares owned by*

---

[3] On which see Eldem, "Istanbul," in *Ottoman city*; and Philip Mansel, *Constantinople: city of the world's desire, 1453–1924* (New York, 1996).

[4] All of these monuments, representing almost 1,000 years of history, still stand. Hilary Sumner-Boyd and John Freely, *Strolling through Istanbul* (Istanbul, 1972) remains unsurpassed as a leisurely armchair tour of the city's architecture. On water-borne transport, see Cengiz Orhonlu, "Boat transportation in Istanbul: an historical survey," *Turkish Studies Association Bulletin* 13.1(1989): 1–21.

[5] The events that follow occurred (see Arbel, *Trading nations*, pp. 95–168); we do not know whether Kubad or some other *çavuş* was involved. Except when noted, the descriptions of Kubad's activities are documented; his thoughts are not.

the sultan and recently "misplaced" by a certain Hayyim Saruq, a Jewish merchant resident in Venice, with whom the di Seguras, an eminent Jewish family of Istanbul with personal and commercial alliances throughout the Mediterranean world and more vitally with the Ottoman imperial family, frequently exchanged. Saruq had recently declared bankruptcy and seemed unable to compensate the di Seguras for recent loans, including a supply of alum entrusted for sale to leather tanners on the Venetian terra firma.[6]

The çavuş had been astonished at the willingness of the Venetian representative to put himself (and his state) in the hands of Ottoman justice, agreeing to be judged six months hence by this very kadi if the sultan's alum had not yet been recovered. Kubad knew from long experience that the Venetians and other foreigners feared, however irrationally, the kadi's legal courts, and carefully wrote into their capitulations exemption from the Ottoman system of justice.[7] *Despite this fear, the bailo had allowed the registration of the affair in the kadi's official register (*sicil*) and had accepted and signed the agreement that legally bound him to the Shariah.*[8] *The envoy could only surmise that Soranzo knew that the Venetian rulers would ensure that the padishah would be compensated for his alum before the six-month period of grace had passed.*

After these proceedings Kubad had lingered, as he so often did, to imbibe the beverages for which Galata was deservedly famed. He even had spent a rowdy and tipsy evening bouncing from tavern to tavern up the Golden Horn and into the environs of the Sweet Waters of Europe in the company of several subjects of the recently enthroned Elizabeth of England.[9] *From these exotic comrades he had gleaned much about the great schism within Christendom, and about that island's recent and bloody restoration to Protestantism. He had awakened the next morning at home in the old city, his head aching and pondering what indiscretions might have passed his lips the previous evening.*

Even while dipping into the sins of Galata, Kubad remained within the well-protected domains of the Ottoman padishah, the Shadow of God on earth. To actually enter the dar al-harb, *the lands of misbelievers who were not yet*

---

[6] This dispute between two Jewish merchants is fully examined in Arbel, *Trading nations, passim.* On Ottoman alum production, see Marie Louise Heers, "Les Génois et le commerce de l'alun à la fin du moyen-âge," *Revue d'Histoire Economique et Sociale* 32(1954): 31–53; and Kate Fleet, *European and Islamic trade in the early Ottoman state: the merchants of Genoa and Turkey* (Cambridge, 1999), pp. 80–94.

[7] İnalcık, "Imtiyāzāt," *EI.*

[8] On the kadi's courts in Istanbul, Galata, and Üsküdar see Yvonne Seng, "The şer'iye sicilleri of the Istanbul müftülüğü as a source for the study of everyday life," *Turkish Studies Association Bulletin* 15.2(1991): 307–25.

[9] Although England did not establish formal commercial relations with the Ottoman Empire until the 1580s (on which see Susan A. Skilliter, *William Harborne and the trade with Turkey, 1578–1582: a documentary study of the first Anglo-Ottoman relations* [London, 1977]), Britons had traveled and traded in the empire for decades. They and other western sojourners certainly conveyed valuable details to the Ottoman government about western Europe, sometimes through çavuşes such as Kubad.

sheltered under God's shade, was something altogether different.[10] *He appreciated how less common it was for Ottoman subjects, particularly Muslim Ottoman subjects, to visit Christian Europe than it was for Venetian and Habsburg Catholics to enter Ottoman domains. With a visit to Venice not only would he step outside the radiant protection of the most powerful realm in the Mediterranean world, but also he would penetrate to the mother city of one of the sultan's most tenacious, cunning, and implacable foes.*[11]

[10] The Ottoman monarch ordinarily portrayed himself most sensationally. Mehmed II, for one, ordained himself: "the Sultan of the Two Continents and the Emperor of the Two Seas, the Shadow of God in this world and the next, the favorite of God on the Two Horizons, the Monarch of the Terraqueous Orb, the Conqueror of the Castle of Constantinople, the Father of Conquest Sultan Mehmed Khan . . . may God make eternal his empire and exalt his residence above the brightest stars of the firmament." Süleyman described himself even more illustriously. To leave these luminous lands (the *dar al-Islam*, or Abode of Believers) was to abandon God's country for the dim and tainted world of misbelievers (the *dar al-harb* or Abode of War).

[11] The tangled Ottoman–Venetian relationship, including Cypriot affairs, is discussed in chapter 5 below.

3 A seasoned polity

> The government of the Ottomans is completely despotic: for the
> Grand Turk is so much the master of all things contained within the
> bounds of his dominions, that the inhabitants account themselves his
> slaves, not his subjects; no man is master of himself, or of the house in
> which he lives, or of the fields he tills, except certain families of
> Constantinople whom Mohamet II has chosen and privileged; and
> there is no personage so great that he stands secure in his life or in his
> estate unless it so please the Grand Signor. He maintains such
> absolute power in two ways: by disowning his subjects and by turning
> everything over to the Renegados, whom he has taken in their
> childhood as tithes from his states.[1]

In the fourteenth and early fifteenth centuries the Ottoman polity was in
the process of invention, and was thus quite malleable. Its beginnings are
shrouded in myth and we probably never will be certain of its foundations. Nevertheless, as we have seen, the early Ottoman state did seem
endowed with the ability to shrug off those props that appeared not to
work, to knead out the flaws of others, and to create new formations as
needed. This facility helped the state survive crises of succession, jealous
rivals, civil wars, even defeat, dismemberment, and other vicissitudes of
fortune.

In the years after the reconstitution of the Ottoman state in 1413 the
principal constructions of Ottoman government and society began to
crystallize. By the time Mehmed II conquered Constantinople many institutions and ways of conduct had been established. Historians have
tagged such organizations with names such as the imperial household,
the *timar* system, the *kapıkulu* system, the janissary corps, and the *çifthane*
system. Modern scholars have also sometimes joined their early modern
Ottoman predecessors in a search for ideal manifestations of these edifices to which the empire had aspired and from which it had subsequently
sunk. Late sixteenth- and seventeenth-century Ottoman commentators

---

[1] Giovanni Botero, *Relationi universali*, as quoted in Lucette Valensi, *The birth of the despot:
Venice and the Sublime Porte*, trans. Arthur Denner (Ithaca and London, 1993), pp. 95–96.

believed that they had discovered such quixotic models in the Süleymanic [handwritten: whimsical vague] Golden Age, when, it was argued, these social and political structures had become immutably complete.[2]

Such institutions, of course, were neither comprehensive nor static by the sixteenth century, and a chief defect of some Ottoman historiography has been to imagine that they were. This act of constructing ideals, whether by statesmen or by historians, in fact precludes the possibility of envisaging progress beyond such standards. Instead, the framework forces one to imagine everything that followed the sixteenth century as deterioration, a vision that at second thought seems absurd. To reject such a model, however, is not to insist that important institutions did not reach maturity in the sixteenth century, that some were not instrumental in the empire's success, or that the idea of a golden age, however partial and flawed, has not generated a sophisticated understanding of many key Ottoman constructs. Several, about which we know a great deal, certainly had evolved in ways that helped organize and sustain the maturing polity.

The imperial household

The imperial household – that is, the collection of individuals who enjoyed personal contact, a familial, or a "possessed" relationship with the ruler – constitutes an important institution in any monarchy.[3] In the Ottoman case, the household was of particular political significance because, principally as a result of the *kapıkulu* organization, it was so intertwined with the military and bureaucracy, many of whose members served a dual political and personal role. However elaborate the Ottoman state became, most high Ottoman officials were servants of the sultan, who in fact owned them; they consequently were also, in theory at least, members of the imperial household. [handwritten: slaves ← play major role]

Such personal ties need not imply that the design of the ruler's household remained fixed through time, or that it was moving toward or falling away from some Ottoman ideal. Rather, the institution bounced along a string of jarring changes as it adjusted to dramatic growth, to a sedentary existence, and to the personalities of its principals. For example, in the early decades of Ottoman rule the monarch married and bore children by the princesses of such rival realms as Byzantium and Karaman. By the mid fifteenth century, however, the sultans not only had grown wary of letting foreign influences seep into the imperial household via their wives

---

[2] These matters are related to the hoary issue of Ottoman periodization, on which see Jane Hathaway, "Problems of periodization in Ottoman history: the fifteenth through the eighteenth centuries," *Turkish Studies Association Bulletin* 20.2(1996): 25–31.

[3] Peirce, *Imperial harem*, is the most vital work on this institution.

and offspring but also came to believe that the royal family of no other
state was worthy of the Ottoman ruler. Consequently, the monarchy severed the institution of marriage from procreation and for the latter turned
to concubinage. This seemingly unnatural disunion not only secured the
Ottoman dynasty from outside political and religious influences, but also
effectively prevented inbreeding.

concubinage

Probably the household's most fundamental transformation took place
after the empire's acquisition of Constantinople. Whereas the family, servants, and supporters of a fourteenth-century Turkoman emir such as
Orhan or Murad followed their patron from settlement to settlement and
even from campaign to campaign, by the early fifteenth century the core
of the household remained behind in the Ottoman capital (then Edirne).
After 1453 the imperial household settled in Istanbul along with other
ruling institutions. Mehmed II moved the female members of his family into what later became known as the "old" palace near the center of
the city. Here they lived in isolation and under the care of eunuchs who
had been enslaved and castrated at sites in France, Central Asia, and
elsewhere outside the Abode of Islam (where castration was religiously
proscribed).

Nomadic vs. Imperial way of life

Mehmed II simultaneously began building a new palace – Topkapı
Sarayı – at the confluence of the Golden Horn and the Marmara Sea.
This edifice went up quickly, and by the end of the 1450s boasted three
large and resplendent courtyards. Public business transpired in the first
or outer courtyard of this palace; the sultan's high officials gathered in the
second or middle courtyard; and young male members of his personal
household resided, observed, and trained to govern in the third or inner
courtyard.

Division of courtyards

Innovation did not end here. By inhabiting two palaces, Mehmed II
managed to distinguish between his private and public, his female and
male, worlds. This seclusion not only followed the practice of Islam in
Persia and elsewhere, but also reflected the Turkoman division between
the familial and political spheres. The ruler perhaps realized that it had
become increasingly difficult to maintain the traditional categories as
rapid expansion and influences from rival states transformed his society.
The splendor of the sultan's palace may have been in emulation of Middle
Eastern and European monarchies; the horizontal layout of his abode,
however, reflected the customs of his nomadic forefathers.

Layout of palaces

Public vs Private

Under Mehmed II's successors these spheres gradually merged, most
dramatically under Süleyman who used the prestige of presiding over a
mature empire to manipulate, revolutionize, even "westernize" his relations with his household. Already Mehmed II had begun settling his
favorite wives with him in the third courtyard of the new palace. Under

9 Imperial viziers smoke, drink coffee, and unwind in this spacious and sun-drenched chamber located in the second courtyard of the imperial palace. D'Ohsson, *Tableau général de l'Empire othoman*, vol. II, before p. 129.

Bayezid II and Selim I this drift toward a physical merging of the political and personal spheres continued. Süleyman concluded it through the building of an imperial harem in Topkapı Palace, settling there all the sultan's wives, concubines, and children together with their staffs – several hundred individuals in all. Whereas previously the families of deceased sultans and lateral lines had been exiled to Edirne, now imperial widows and the families of the sultan's brothers lived confined behind the cold walls of the old palace.

Suleyman merges political w/ familial

Süleyman's prestige allowed him to thoroughly undermine the rules of personal behavior that had evolved under his predecessors. Perhaps the most peculiarly Ottoman of these was the custom that separated imperial wives from imperial mothers. Whereas the first sultans had married for political expediency as well as procreation, around the end of the fourteenth century the monarch began making celibate marriages and restricting his sexual relations to slave concubines. The intent of this radical innovation probably was to sever the Ottoman state from foreign sympathies and protect princes from heresy. However callous such a practice might seem, it was just such tendencies toward religious and political deviance, passed through the persons of foreign wives and mothers, that bedeviled the early modern English, French, Spanish, and other European states. At about the same time the Ottomans also limited to one the number of male offspring each concubine could produce, and institutionalized the practice of fratricide, through which a newly enthroned monarch was expected to have his brothers executed. The first of these practices ensured that each mother would concentrate exclusively upon the welfare of, and prepare for governance, her one princely son; the second helped secure the state against the recurrence of civil wars such as those that had almost brought down the realm in 1389, in 1402–13, and again in 1481.

Marriage ≠ procreation

Male offspring 1

Through the person of Hürrem (known in the west as Roxelana) – a slave concubine whom he fell in love with, scandalously married, and conceived several sons by – Süleyman dismantled this remarkable order. His impetuous act, however, did not restore imperial reproductive patterns to Turkoman or early Ottoman norms. In fact, Süleyman's decision to marry his concubine was radically innovative and helped spawn yet another mutation in the administration of empire. Whereas whatever authority early Ottoman imperial wives could muster derived from their links with non-Ottoman states as well as reproduction, the authority of Hürrem and succeeding wives and imperial mothers (*valide sultans*) derived almost exclusively from their positions in the imperial household.

Suleyman innovation, marries concubine

Hürrem herself, for example, formed alliances with the grand vizier and other powerful Ottoman statesmen. Such combinations carried the influence of women in the imperial harem far beyond the palace walls and made the physical isolation of imperial consorts and daughters less and less a reflection of their real power. The consequent factionalism tended also to splinter and diffuse even male power, for another new trend was to marry off imperial daughters to men of state who thus became imperial consorts (*damads*), and through their spouses gained entrance into the sultan's household. Even though the fiction of imperial authority remained throughout the sixteenth and seventeenth centuries, such alliances probably tended to decrease the dependence of statesmen upon the person of the sultan, to isolate the ruler even from his own harem, and especially to decrease the sultan's ability to act independently.

Later Ottoman observers condemned such innovations in the workings of the imperial household as a principal cause for the enfeeblement of their state. More recently, historians have perceived them as a symptom rather than a direct cause of Ottoman decline. Either of these interpretations may be valid if one accepts that the only Ottoman principality that could thrive was one that was centralized, despotic, and aggressively expanding. Success, however, can be measured in other ways. In their diffusing of authority, these late sixteenth-century changes also removed power from the hands of a single man who was as likely to be inept as skilled. They also tended to bureaucratize governance, which helped shield the Ottoman state and society from the vagaries of personality, from a changing world trade, from the growing strength of rival states, and from shifting relationships within Ottoman society.

These transformations in the private lives of the imperial family also considerably facilitated Ottoman integration into Europe (indeed, the Süleymanic innovations may have been meant to emulate other European dynasts), for a monarch who married and had several children by the same woman seemed conventional and thus comfortingly explicable to Venetian, French, and English diplomats. In other words, in both their governance and their personal behavior, the Ottoman and western European elites were moving closer to each other. In addition, the factionalism and infighting that characterized the new system closely reflected royal courts in Europe. Diplomats from the subcontinent moved more easily into this less strange world where secrets could be bought, alliances made, and intrigue seemed a way of life.

The Ottoman slave culture

In the sixteenth century, the culture as well as the institutions of Ottoman governance drifted closer to European standards. The bond deepened despite the fact that the foundations of Ottoman society seemed so Asiatic

(Turkoman, Persianate, and Arab). A seemingly exotic type of slavery, so different from the chattel slaves of Europe and the Americas, is one example of such differences. This institution had emerged as a decisive component of a particular set of beliefs, behaviors, and education that defined membership in the Ottoman elite. What made Ottoman slavery seem so strange to the rest of Europe was not so much that the select of society owned slaves (although they certainly did) as that they *themselves* often were slaves: that is, members of the imperial family legally owned those very same viziers and pashas who administered the realm.

The Ottoman elite had not always been slaves of the sultan. Indeed, as we have seen, under Osman, Orhan, and Murad, Turkoman companions to the emirs had acted as military, administrative, and religious leaders. Such comrades often resented and occasionally defied Ottoman rule, and helped produce an unstable regime. In the late fourteenth century, the Ottoman ruling house adapted, perhaps from the Seljuk example, the idea of using captured slaves as the backbone of a new army or janissary corps. Removed from their native cultures and presented with power through the person of their master the sultan, these foot soldiers acted domestically to neutralize the Turkoman cavalry and internationally to neutralize European innovations in military technology. Under Bayezid I, Mehmed I, Murad II, and Mehmed II, Ottoman authority rested more and more in the hands of the monarch himself through the power of his infantry troops.

The janissary corps was only one component of the _kapıkulu_, or "slaves of the Porte," which came to encompass also much of the Ottoman bureaucracy. After Mehmed II, most of the highest men of state, including almost every grand vizier from Mehmed II's Mahmud Pasha (r.1453–66) to the Köprülü triumvirate of viziers (r.1656–83) who served under Mehmed IV, were *kuls*. Indeed, by the reign of Mehmed II's great-grandson Süleyman, not only had being a *kul* become a virtual prerequisite to advancement, but also a new social class had emerged around the concept. If no Ottoman aristocracy ever issued in the style of the blood of European noble houses, the conceit of imperial slavery became a peculiarly analogous and equally powerful unifying factor. Blood played some role in this quasi-aristocracy, as the Köprülü case suggests; however, even more than lineage, possession of one human being by another marked this elite and made it seem somewhat misleadingly exotic to Europeans. In other words, possession more than ethnicity, language, geography, or any other element identified this pseudo-aristocracy. The requirement that these *kuls* become Ottoman – that is, that they develop linguistic and cultural homogeneity and exclusivity – grew out of this peculiar status.

GIANNIZ-
ZERO.

SOLDA-
TO.

Ddd 2

10 The janissary was often depicted as daunting in European works, even those that do not deal directly with the Ottomans. This volume on costumes includes a classic portrayal, complete with moustaches, high conical hat, firearm, and scimitar. Vecellio, *Habiti antichi*, f. 386r.

The roots of this slave culture lay in the Islamic creed, and especially in the stricture against enslaving fellow believers. This rule combined with the presence of a seemingly boundless sea of pagan nomads to the northeast of Arab lands had led to the development of a new form of slavery. As the Arabs pushed into Central Asia in the eighth and ninth centuries under the Abbasid dynasty, they confronted, traded with, fought, and converted Turkic-speaking nomads. The Arab leaders also began both to hire these steppe people as mercenaries and to choose for training as soldiers and scribes the most fit and most talented of those enslaved on the battlefield. By the tenth century, this tendency had evolved into a system, the *ghulam*, by which non-Muslim Turks were enslaved, converted, and trained to become warriors and statesmen.[4] Many late-medieval Middle Eastern dynasties adopted this procedure, most notoriously in Egypt where the servants toppled the rulers and established the Mamluk Empire, a regime of former slaves. Probably beginning with Murad in the late fourteenth century, the Ottomans also adopted the *ghulam*, using it to build a loyal army and administration to stand in opposition to rival *gazi* warriors who might challenge the Ottoman house.

The Ottomans not only took up this practice that the Seljukid and other Turkic dynasties had introduced into Asia Minor, but also adapted it. As the expansion of their empire slowed, and with it their ability to capture persons and thus rejuvenate their army and ruling class as a consequence of conquest, the state began more and more to purchase (and sometimes have castrated) non-Muslims along its Empire's northeastern and southern frontiers. It also initiated the more sustainable if problematic program of drawing from the millions of non-Muslim inhabitants of the Empire itself. In a process known as *devşirme*, state officials went especially into the upcountry towns and villages of today's Serbia, Bosnia, and Croatia and took a human "tithe" of young Christian boys to become the sultan's servants.

Contemporary western Europeans (and many today) counted this practice as one of the most heathen and non-European of Ottoman innovations. Not only did the *devşirme* rip young boys away from their families and homelands, but it also forced upon them an exotic culture and religion perceived as profoundly hostile to their own. They were taught to believe in Islam rather than Christianity, to speak Turkish rather than Serbo-Croatian, and to affirm a binding loyalty to the Ottoman sultan, their new master (and family head). For loving parents and for those proud of their religious, ethnic, and linguistic identities (and especially

---

[4] On which see "Ghulām," *EI*; and Matthew Gordon, *The breaking of a thousand swords: a history of the Turkish military of Samara. 200–275 AH/815–889 CE* (Albany, NY, 2001).

for the modern nationalist), the forfeiture of these young boys constituted a bitter defeat and shame.[5] There were, however, compensations.

First, their sons were lifted out of provincial, impoverished, and oppressed surroundings into the ruling class of arguably the most powerful and refined polity in the world. At worst, they would become infantrymen in the celebrated Ottoman legions; at best, they might become powerful statesmen such as the *kapudanpaşa*, Piyâle Pasha, who began life as a Christian Hungarian, or the grand vizier, Sokollu Mehmed Pasha, who was born a Christian Bosnian.

Second, despite the insistence of many national historiographies that such personal fortune was attained only through the utter obliteration of heritage, evidence has recently emerged that the Ottomans were not always so insistent that these boys discard their birthrights. Sokollu Mehmed Pasha was only the most prominent of those selected by the *devşirme* who maintained contact with, protected, and even lent monetary assistance to parent, sibling, relative, and region.[6] Consequently, these levies may not only have replenished a perpetually depleted elite, but also have served to bind Christian provinces to this Islamic state through a system of personal ties and favors. The outcome if not the method of this process resembled systems of provincial advocacy concurrently developing in southern and western Europe. Furthermore, the targets of these levies understood such compensations so well that some parents even implored and paid off officials to conscript their son rather than someone else's.

During the sixteenth century, a grand vizier stood at the pinnacle of the quasi-aristocracy that developed out of this arrangement. It was not a strictly vertical hierarchy, however, for this "slave culture" became diffused across the Ottoman ruling estate and through the imperial household. Servants, for example, had servants, most curiously and nefariously the eunuchs who oversaw not only the imperial household, but also the intimate worlds of other notables' harems. The sultan's servants also developed political networks of their own through artifice, patronage, payoffs, and matrimony. One result was the late sixteenth-century formation of political cliques, usually created through the union of a princess and a statesman and often including an imperial eunuch, whose power derived from his unique ability to pass easily between the sultan's private and public domains.

Despite Qur'anic admonitions to treat slaves kindly and manumit them whenever possible, the early modern Ottomans did not forbid more

---

[5] The epigram that begins this chapter's vignette, damning the sultan for enslaving Greek children, is only one of many reflections of this attitude.

[6] For a more modest example, see Cemal Kafadar, "On the purity and corruption of the janissaries," *Turkish Studies Association Bulletin* 15.2(1991): 273–80.

powerless forms of household slavery, or even plantation slavery of the sort that became so notorious in the Americas during the eighteenth and nineteenth centuries. Most lamentable perhaps was the Ottoman exploitation of captives for the cultivation of rice, which the imperial court fancied. Since there was no ideological logic that proscribed plantation-style slavery, the principal reason it remained secondary was geographical and institutional: rice, cotton, and other crops appropriate for the intensive agriculture in which slavery tended to thrive developed only on a few littoral fringes of the Empire. In short, the *kul* system, which seemed so exotic to the western European mind, looked less and less strange with time. Indeed, within the order lay the potential for both a pseudo-aristocracy and a system of plantation-style slavery.[7] That the first rather than the second of these options developed was little more than happenstance.

Religious elites

A range of professions and social groupings existed between those *kuls* who stood at the pinnacle of early modern Ottoman society and those slaves who were at its bottom. Most prominent in this hierarchy were the religious elite – the *ulema* – and the cavalrymen known as *sipahis* who had inherited the privileges and obligations of those *gazi* warriors who had fought with Osman, Orhan, and Murad, the founding fathers of the Ottoman polity. These groups represented radically different aspects of Ottoman rule: broadly speaking, the *ulema* served to legitimize the state and the *sipahis* served to enforce its rule. Nevertheless, ideology bound the two elites; they shared a commitment not only to high Ottoman culture but also to a belief in the Hanafi school of Islamic jurisprudence.[8]

The *ulema* became the chief custodians of Islam in the Ottoman Empire, just as they were in other Islamic states. They did not attain their position overnight, however. Early indigenous religious consultants to Ottoman emirs – men such as Shaykh Edebali, Osman's presumed spiritual guide, were notoriously heterodox. Those who were more orthodox – such as Kara Rüstem, who, or so legend proclaims, brought to the Ottomans from the Islamic heartland the principle of *ghulam* – were usually outsiders. Although many educators never completely abandoned

---

[7] Most works on Ottoman slavery deal with the late period, on which see Y. Hakan Erdem, *Slavery in the Ottoman empire and its demise* (Oxford, 1997); and Ehud R. Toledano, *Slavery and abolition in the Ottoman Middle East* (Seattle, WA, 1998). On the earlier period, there is Shaun Elizabeth Marmon (ed.), *Slavery in the Islamic Middle East* (Princeton, 1999).

[8] For a short and clear discussion of Islamic law and the four accepted schools of Sunni jurisprudence, see Fazlur Rahman, *Islam*, 2nd edn (Chicago, 1979), pp. 68–84.

their deviating roots, they did tend to become more orthodox, more locally educated, and more powerful as Ottoman state-building proceeded.

The religious elite received its training in schools (*medreses*) that typically were parts of the complexes attached to important mosques, along with markets and soup kitchens. Although Orhan probably opened the first such Ottoman institution in İznik (Nicaea) in 1331, the Ottoman state continued drawing higher *ulema* from the Islamic heartlands until well into the following century. It was only in the late fifteenth century, upon the establishment of Istanbul as the Ottoman capital and the consequent declaration that the Ottomans had become a world-class empire, that eight *medreses* built around Mehmed the Conqueror's mosque provided a viable alternative to schools in Baghdad, Cairo, and elsewhere. From this time, the state drew even the highest *ulema* from these establishments and, after the mid sixteenth century, from students who graduated from the six *medreses* attached to Süleyman's grand mosque. The preparation and abilities of these graduates rivaled those of any other academy.

The mosques to which such *medreses* and lower schools were attached dominated and gave focus to the social life of Muslims in Ottoman cities, just as churches and synagogues did for Christians and Jews. One of Mehmed II's first moves after the conquest of Constantinople, for example, was to direct his principal viziers to subsidize the construction of mosques in various parts of the city. Residential quarters (*mahalles*) soon emerged in the vicinities of these complexes, whose upkeep, and the salaries of staff, were supported by endowments (*evkaf*) given by members of the imperial household (both male and female) and Ottoman statesmen, as well as by revenue from markets and other commercial services.

There were two categories of *ulema* in the empire (even though there was considerable overlap between them): those who interpreted Islamic law (the *müftis*) and those who administered Islamic and other laws (the kadis). On the one hand, *müftis*, who presided over mosques and *medreses*, enjoyed relative independence from the government and occasionally even functioned as centers of opposition to its policies. On the other, kadis more and more became hierarchically ranked appointees of the state. At the bottom were assistant kadis (*naibs*), who serviced the Ottoman countryside and villages and seconded kadis in major towns. Next in rank were kadis stationed in towns and small cities; then came the kadis of the eight major cities in the empire. Placed at the pinnacle of the hierarchy were two *kadiaskers*, one in charge of "Rumeli" (European provinces) and the second in charge of "Anatolia" (Asian provinces). The two *kadiaskers*, as well as the *şeyhülislam*, all sat on the sultan's imperial council.

CADIL ESCHIER

Ccc 4

11 The artist's emphasis here is on clothing, the figure's rich outer-garments and fabulous headgear. The *kadiasker* (or *kazasker*) was a high-ranking member of the Ottoman judiciary. Vecellio, *Habiti antichi*, f. 380r.

In a reflection of the theoretical basis of Islam, which denies the existence of a priestly class and insists upon religious law as the basis for political and social laws, the *ulema* had less influence over the individual believer and more influence upon Islamic society and government than did their priestly counterparts in Christian lands. For example, a *müfti* not only taught Islamic jurisprudence, but also interpreted Islamic law (which was the law of the state). Consequently, an important religious figure on the one hand could enjoy an influence in society and government that rivaled, for instance, the U.S. Supreme Court. On the other hand, the Qur'an specifically forbade him, or anyone else, from serving as a spiritual conduit who could forgive sins or "save" an individual believer.

The kadi, even more than the *müfti*, has no parallel in the Christian world. Perhaps his closest analogy would be not a priest or a clergy man, but a magistrate, for the kadi was an appointee of the state and presided over the social and judicial life of his city, town, or region. In his court he heard cases dealing with matters both public – loans, property, robbery, and murder – and private – divorce, rape, and child custody. Although he was expected to draw upon sultanic law and local customs in his judgments, the underpinning of his decisions had always to be Islamic law – the Shariah. As a functionary of the state, the kadi was also expected to forward petitions to Istanbul and act upon imperial responses and other decrees.

Theoretically at least, anyone, subject or foreign, could petition a kadi, who often dealt with such claims in his own court. In certain instances, however, the petitioner asked that the complaint be forwarded to the imperial government, or even traveled to Istanbul in person in order to register a complaint with the divan. In such cases, an Ottoman official known as a *çavuş* often carried and was authorized to help implement the imperial decision. His ability to do so both helped define and impose the authority and power of the central state, and circumscribed the authority and power of the kadi.

In short, the kadi's decisionmaking powers depended upon his personality and his posting as much as upon his training. On the one hand, the proximity of the imperial government and foreign ambassadors tended to curtail the authority of the kadi in districts of Istanbul like Fatih or Galata, even as their presence increased his implicit power. On the other, distance from the imperial core lent kadis in towns such as Aleppo or Temesvar increased authority as a representative of the state even as regional political and commercial networks, local customs, and the presence of powerful Ottoman military commanders weakened his power. Wherever his appointment, however, the kadi was expected not only to implement Islamic law but also to represent the Ottoman state and its supplemental laws (*kanun*).

The Ottoman government granted primacy to Islamic law. Nevertheless, the Shariah was not the only structure of adjudication in the empire. Ottoman Armenian, Greek Orthodox, and Jewish communities all established courts that judged their peoples according to their own religious laws, and Genoese, Venetian, Dutch, English, and French residents also founded self-governing courts in the major trading cities of the empire. The hearings of all cross-communal cases in the kadi's court, however, signified the privileges of this judicial system over all others. Paradoxically this prerogative in fact probably helped sustain communal autonomy, for patriarchic, rabbinic, and foreign records all urgently repeat warnings against commercial and personal dealings with Muslims, for fear of loss of control through lawsuits in the kadi's courts.

Even within the Muslim population, however, *müftis* and kadis did not constitute the exclusive religious authority in the Ottoman world. It is true that the conquest of most Arab lands in 1516–17 compelled the Ottoman state to exhibit itself as the protector of orthodoxy. Nevertheless, the heterodoxy that had constituted the ideological mainstay of early Ottoman expansion did not die when it became a world empire. Indeed, by embracing the Hanafi school – the most accommodating of the four schools of Islamic law – and drawing upon all four in its law-making, the state exhibited maximum flexibility within the limits of Islamic tradition, thereby helping to placate its disparate population of Christians, Jews, and followers of different schools within Sunni Islam. Furthermore, by institutionalizing various systems of sufism (Islamic mysticism) within its urban economies and military organizations, the state essentially sanctioned nonconformity.

The latitudinarianism of Ottoman state policy derived largely from the religious and cultural syncretism that had characterized Anatolian marches during the fourteenth and fifteenth centuries. During these formative years, spiritual as well as profane leaders, warriors, and wanderers found their way to the Anatolian frontiers. Some of these holy men became spiritual intimates of Ottoman emirs and other frontier lords. Others organized themselves into sufi orders (*tarikahs*), or wandered as vagabonds and exemplars of pious behavior.[9]

Such dervish orders, spawned by the chaos of cultural and physical frontiers that accompanied the waves of Turkoman migrations, existed in bewildering variety. According to the Spanish traveler Ruy Gonzales de Clavijo, for example, the followers of a certain Barak Baba "shave their beards and their heads and go almost naked. They pass through the street,

---

[9] See Mehmed Fuad Köprülü, *Islam in Anatolia after the Turkish invasion (prolegomena)*, trans., ed., intro. Gary Leiser (Salt Lake City, 1993), pp. 25–31.

whether in the cold or in the heat, eating as they go, and all the clothing they wear is bits of rag of the torn stuff that they can pick up. As they walk along night and day with their tambourines they chant hymns."[10] These disciples of Barak Baba represented an important strand within the Islamic world. Such fraternities could represent spiritual retreat, spiritual rebellion, personal strivings to be one with God, or exceptional sensibility to political and social injustices. Such followers of Barak Baba were only one of countless such organizations, often called collectively the Abdals of Rum, who formed an extensive Ottoman network of deviant Sufis.

Mysticism developed in different ways in the Ottoman world. Some Sufi orders withered away as frontiers hardened and opportunities for syncretism diminished. Others flourished under the new regime. One case was the Abdals, who never fully abandoned their deviance, as defined by societal norms and Islamic orthodoxy. Another case concerned those who followed the teachings of Haci Bektaş Veli. This Bektaşi order came late, perhaps not before the late fifteenth century, as a relatively minor popular religious order. It both quickly became institutionalized (that is, mainstreamed) within the Ottoman system and sometimes served as a focus for opposition to it. Its initial popularity may have been among Turkoman tribesmen; however, it seems to have been influenced by the frontier ideologies that arose during the Ottoman conquests in the Balkans and to have appropriated much of the syncretism of that ever-mutating borderlands. Whether because the frontier naturally produced religious plasticity or because so many members of the janissary corps hailed from the Christian Balkans through the *devşirme*, by the sixteenth century, and perhaps much earlier, the janissary corps had embraced the Bektaşi order as its official *tarikah*, an association that persisted for over three centuries. Much as, in the nineteenth-century Jewish community of eastern Europe, the opposition of the unorthodox hasidim to the enlightened *maskalim* helped others to perceive the hasidic Jew more and more as mainstream rather than deviant, so did the Bektaşi–janissary alliance encourage the order simultaneously to retain much of its aberrant ideology and to become doctrinally conventional.

Such institutionalization of nonconformism in some ways paralleled the establishment and ordering of mendicant orders (Franciscans and Dominicans) in Catholic Europe.[11] Whereas the mendicants remained

---

[10] Quoted in Karamustafa, *God's unruly friends*, p. 8.

[11] On which see Karamustafa, *God's unruly friends*, especially p. 101. A closer parallel might be with Jewish mysticism (Kabbalah), which through its Lurianic form in the seventeenth century almost brought down orthodoxy through Sabbatarianism, a potent theosophical movement (on which, see chapter 4 below), and by the late eighteenth century had been fully integrated into the Jewish world through Hasidism.

separated from the larger society by particular rules, celibacy, and monasticism, however, Ottoman orders became fully integrated. Not only did most sultans have Sufi connections, not only could a janissary also become a Bektaşi, but other military, economic, and social groups also joined and organized themselves around various religious orders. Thus did myriad unofficial religious communities develop in the Ottoman world, and occasionally became centers of opposition to the Ottoman state and its policies, as happened in 1416 when the Shaykh Bedreddin used his erudition, charisma, and a particularly expansive reading of Islam to gather a wide range of disgruntled Ottoman subjects into a massive rebellion against Mehmed I's fragile regime. More often, however, such religious versatility – often through orders such as the Nakşibendi and the Mevlevis – helped the state to defeat its rivals, to integrate diverse peoples, and to provide Ottoman society with religious and social resiliency and adaptability.

As the empire expanded first into southeastern Europe and subsequently into eastern Anatolia and the Arab lands, then, it incorporated a diversity of peoples, cultures, and legal traditions. Faced with such variety and wanting to integrate regions into the empire as smoothly as possible, the state chose not to impose a uniform and rigid legal system upon its territories. Instead, by compiling a series of provincial lawbooks (*kanunname*) that incorporated many local customs and statutes, in the fifteenth century the government used the concept of sultanic law to construct a flexible system of jurisprudence at the local level. In other words, "custom, modified through administrative practice and Sultanic decree" rather than strict adherence to a particular school of Islamic jurisprudence constituted the bases for provincial law.[12]

Such local codes often dealt with personal law and revenue, and thus complemented rather than displaced religious law. For example, one section of the lawbook compiled in 1528–29 for the western Anatolian town of Izmir and its surroundings explains that whereas the customs duty at Izmir and other regional ports "is taken on agricultural yields, from grains, fruits, and other goods, the customs on the silk and similar goods coming through Chios and Europe is under the jurisdiction of the agents and collectors of the port of Çeşme."[13] It is difficult to locate any Islamic law in such a declaration; rather, the passage replicates western Anatolian political and commercial realities before its conquest by Ottoman arms. At that time, the island of Chios and its sister port Çeşme had served

---

[12] Colin Imber, *Ebu's-su'ud: the Islamic legal tradition* (Stanford, CA, 1997), p. 44.
[13] Daniel Goffman, "Izmir as a commercial center: the impact of Western trade on an Ottoman port, 1570–1650" (University of Chicago: Ph.D. diss., 1985), p. 24. A facsimile of this legal code is on pp. 394–97.

as entrepôts for international trade, and Izmir had been a small town that traded almost exclusively in foodstuffs. The statutes of this Ottoman *kanunname* simply verified and sanctioned this state of affairs.

Ottoman jurisprudence did not remain frozen in this fragmented and decentralized form. Over the course of the late fifteenth and sixteenth centuries, various *ulema* compiled general lawbooks of sultanic law. These codifications gradually subsumed and replaced the many local ones that had accompanied occupation of territories, until by the middle of the reign of Süleyman (1520–66), sultanic law had been largely regularized and systematized. The process did not end here, however. During the first century or so of Ottoman rule in the Balkans and Anatolia, Islamic and sultanic legal usage had developed largely in parallel. In the process, many contradictions had arisen between them. It was left to Ebu's-Su'ud, who presided as the *şeyhülislam* during the last decades of Süleyman's reign and the first eight years of his son Selim II's, to identify and resolve the inconsistencies and ambiguities between the two systems of law.[14]

This *müfti*, whose father was himself both a scholar and a foremost dervish under Bayezid II, as a boy received exceptional tutoring. He furthered his education in one of the prestigious eight colleges attached to Mehmed II's mosque, and then rose rapidly after 1520 through the patronage and friendship of Sultan Süleyman. In 1527–28, Ebu's-Su'ud became a professor at one of those same eight schools. He then moved swiftly up the hierarchy, becoming kadi of Bursa, then of Istanbul, then *kadiasker*, and finally, in 1545, the *şeyhülislam*. He relinquished this highest post in the Ottoman religious career ladder only with his death in 1574.

The instrument through which Ebu's-Su'ud contrived to integrate Islamic and sultanic law was the *fetva*, a proclamation issued by a qualified religious authority in response to questions of law and usage. Obviously, such a pronouncement produced by the *şeyhülislam* would have particular weight, and Edu's-Su'ud used his authority to bring "the laws of mankind into harmony with divine law."[15] According to one modern authority, he did so in three principal areas. First, he shaped the diverse corpus of laws dealing with land and taxes into a form that Ottoman society came to accept as sanctified. Second, by routinely adding the caliphal title to the long list of Süleyman's honorifics, he affirmed that the sovereign was not only the head of the Ottoman state, but also the guide for the community of all Muslims, an invented tradition that helped validate sultanic law. Third, and most controversially, he justified, in accordance with Hanafi law, the use of endowments (*evkaf*) in the lending of money and the

---

[14] A lucid treatment of this effort and the man who undertook it is in Imber, *Ebu's-su'ud*, especially pp. 40–58.

[15] Imber, *Ebu's-su'ud*, p. 269.

generation of wealth.[16] In short, Ebu's-Su'ud and other Ottoman religious officials not only actively codified and standardized Ottoman law,
but also did so in a way that allowed the state to project itself as orthodox
even as it continued to respond creatively and with flexibility to challenges
both domestic and external.

Other elites

Military innovation as well as religious flexibility helped consolidate the
Ottoman state. As we have seen, Murad I and his successors checked
the claims of potential tribal rivals in part by introducing a countervailing *kul*-based administration and loyal infantry, artillery, mining,
road-bridge-building, and other corps. They not only founded competing
organizations, but they also strove to blend these warriors into Ottoman
society by granting the most successful of them land-holdings within the
expanding domains.

Just as the modern state conducts censuses for political and social ends
and in order to tax and conscript more systematically, so did the fifteenth-
and sixteenth-century Ottoman state survey its conquered territories in
order to ascertain their worth and where and how much land to grant
its warriors.[17] Such cadastral surveys (*tapu-tahrirs*) proved expensive and
complex. Despite this difficulty, administrators at first undertook them
systematically and exhaustively. The government first appointed an administrator (*emin*) who, accompanied by a clerk (*kâtip*) and the regional
kadi, collected available documentation about land and building ownership and local taxes. This information was written up and codified in a
narrative (*kanunname*) that sought to mediate and resolve contradictions
especially between those two non-Islamic legal traditions – local or customary and imperial – upon which the Ottomans based their dominion.
Although these statutes served as legal guidebooks for kadis and *naibs*,
they did not at first attempt to settle conflicts between imperial and religious jurisprudence. As we have seen, such a synthesis was left to the
jurisconsults of the mature Ottoman state.

These officials next consulted with local grandees and proceeded from
village to village and from town to town to inspect and evaluate land and
other holdings. They finally drew up the results of their survey in a register, prefaced by the *kanunname*, that listed the names of the towns and
villages, their populations, what they produced, and expected revenues.

---

[16] Imber, *Ebu's-su'ud, passim*.
[17] Halil İnalcık (ed.), *Hicri 835 tarihli suret-i defter-i sancak-i Arvanid* (Ankara, 1954) is the
classic study. But see also the same author's "Ottoman methods of conquest," *Studia
Islamica* 2(1954): 107–12.

12   Whereas the janissaries were the core of the early modern Ottoman infantry, the *sipahis* were the army's cavalry. Perhaps drawing a horse was beyond the capacities of this artist, for only the bow and arrows suggest a mounted existence in this uncluttered depiction. Helffrich, *Kurtzer und warhafftiger Bericht.*

13   The dignified bearing of this mounted figure announces his power.
Indeed, he is the military commander of Anatolia and served as a vizier
in the Imperial Divan. Happel, *Thesaurus exoticorum*, sec. 2, p. 16.

It was on the basis of these registers that the government distributed land
and villages to warriors, who thus became *sipahis* presiding over *timars*.

The government appointed over these *sipahis* (who were also termed
beys) *sancakbeyis*, who were responsible for a sub-province (a *sancak*).

14 Two janissaries proceed and two *sipahis* follow a figure who appears to be a high Ottoman official, perhaps a *kadiasker*, in this early seventeenth-century print. The janissaries, with their smoldering tapers, seem particularly ready for trouble. Breuning, *Orientalische Reyss dess Edlen*, p. 157.

Over the *sancakbeyis* Istanbul also appointed a *beylerbeyi*, or provincial governor. At first, these governors were usually Ottoman princes who established courts in places like Manisa and Ankara. Eventually, however, important Ottoman military commanders and powerful figures out of favor at the imperial court dominated these positions as governors. The government empowered the *sipahi* and his commanders to implement but not to promulgate punishment, which was the jurisdiction of the local kadi and the imperial authorities. This partition between power and authority became a mainstay of Ottoman governance.

On the surface, this system seems similar to European feudalism. It decentralized military power and resolved the dilemma of having to maintain a large army in a polity with a limited tax base and insufficient coinage. In fact, it was profoundly different. First of all, not only did the land upon which the *sipahi* lived remain the government's, but also it could not be inherited. The state, theoretically at least, lent it to the cavalryman for his lifetime only. This process made it difficult for the *sipahi* to identify strongly with the local community, and almost impossible for this class to translate decentralized military power into decentralizing political power and/or authority (which does not mean that the state was necessarily centralized and despotic, but simply that centrifugal potential lay elsewhere).

Secondly, the *sipahis* came together only during the campaign season. Although the time of year varied according to the target (Vienna or Isfahan, Kefe or Cairo) and the type of military operation (naval or ground, battle or siege), in the Balkans and Mediterranean, at least, the season normally lasted from May until September. At other times, the *sipahi* retreated to his *timar* where he acted as overlord – taxing, rewarding, punishing, and visibly representing the state. The state recruited these soldiers from various origins (even Christian warriors were at first granted *timars*) and never provided them with the type of standardized training and education that produced a sense of camaraderie among janissaries. These cavalrymen simply never had an opportunity to develop the strong awareness of community and purpose, either with each other or with their region, which might have given them a coherent political agenda and consequent clout.

Finally, the connection between sultan and *sipahi* was utterly different from the relationship between feudal king and lord. Whereas western European ruling classes lived in, and the monarchy had to live with, an inherited world of ritual, obligation, privilege, and birthright, the Ottoman military class was born with the Ottoman state, cobbled together from central Asian, Persian, Arab, and Byzantine traditions in a creative merging of exigencies. Furthermore, the kadi rather than the *sipahi* was the principal source of imperial authority in the provinces. Nor was the *sipahi* even the chief enforcer of the monarch's will, at least in urban settings, where the sultan's government more and more stationed autonomous garrisons of janissaries.

In short, the two wings of the Ottoman army contrasted profoundly in derivation and features. Whereas the janissaries were owned infantrymen who lived together in barracks, received salaries, contrived through the Bektaşi religious order a unique system of belief, and thereby developed an almost unparalleled sense of camaraderie, the *sipahis* were free cavalrymen who dwelt in relative isolation, lived off of their land holdings, tended toward a relative religious orthodoxy, and fraternized only during the military campaign season.

The *sipahi*, then, served an administrative as well as military function. He was the principal managerial deputy of the state in its core provinces, where he collected revenue (typically in-kind) and administered imperial justice. Nevertheless, his tax-collecting function was not a centralizing operation, as in a modern bureaucracy. The *sipahi* received no salary and his primary function was military rather than civic. Nor was the *timar* system designed to funnel resources to the imperial center. It did little to augment the state's treasury or the government's ability to gather and monopolize data.

Although the Ottomans never achieved (or even aspired to) the bloated and intrusive type of bureaucracy that marks almost every modern state, its administrative wing did mature and rival those of other early modern European states. The viziers who sat in the Imperial Divan headed this organization. Under them worked a gamut of individuals, some *kuls* and some not, devoted to receiving the innumerable complaints and problems that the vast and diverse Ottoman domains generated, and to recording and implementing an incessant flow of imperial decisions. Kadis and *sipahis* were a part of this system as appointees of the state as well as detached from it as legal authorities and military men. Pursuivants (*çavuşes*) and scribes (*kâtips*), as salaried employees of the government, were more representative of the state than were either the military or religious elites.

The *çavuş* classically was a slave of the sultan. His ceremonial responsibility was to accompany and protect his lord and retinue in public spectacles. His administrative function was more practical, however, for it was this official who appeared on behalf of the sultan before foreign representatives and traveled to foreign governments with communiqués. Furthermore, he carried imperial orders to local Ottoman officials and worked with them to ensure their implementation. Such orders usually rendered little of substance, but briefly instructed kadis and/or *beylerbeyis* to carry out a certain command. It was left to the *çavuş* to negotiate the thicket of local authorities and factions that irrepressibly worked to undermine such decrees. In short, *the çavuş*'s administrative function was vital, for he was the imperial voice and authority in the provinces and overseas.

The scribal class (*kâtips*) – usually *medrese*-trained – were the true bureaucrats of the Ottoman world.[18] They helped compose and record those decrees that the Imperial Divan produced and the *çavuşes* delivered. As we have seen, a scribe also accompanied other officials (*emins*) across the empire to record information on population and production for purposes of taxation and military mobilization. They also were the collectors and recorders of taxes.

Non-elites

In the Empire's formative decades and reflective of the Ottoman genius for accommodation and compromise, talented Christians as well as Muslims served within the Ottoman military and administrative elites. By the reign of Mehmed II, however, such men seem to have melted into Islamo-Ottoman culture. There were no longer exceptions to the rule that members of the sultan's household, the religious class, and the administration were Muslim. Over time, there also were fewer and fewer non-Muslims serving in the military. Outside of these cadres, however, there were few professions within the empire that imposed such religious limitations. In profound contrast to the rest of the European world, agriculturists, merchants, bankers, mariners, herders, and hawkers might be Muslim, or Armenian, Greek Orthodox, or Jewish.

This variety was reflected in urban demographics. In spite of the difficulty of characterizing the Ottoman city,[19] commercial districts did tend to be variegated, a concentrated blend of tongues, attire, cultures, and especially spiritual beliefs, and western European visitors to Istanbul, Aleppo, Konya, or Edirne marveled at and usually condemned what was for them an exotic and shocking mix. Even residential quarters were not nearly as segregated as is often supposed. While it is true that Ottoman cities comprised neighborhoods deemed Christian, Jewish, or Muslim and sometimes named after the inhabitants' places of origin, they were not wholly exclusive. The presence of Muslim households in ostensibly Jewish and Christian neighborhoods, and vice versa, belies the view of an Ottoman world that may have been integrated commercially but socially remained rigorously segregated.

---

[18] On the scribes, see Linda T. Darling, *Revenue raising and legitimacy: tax collection and finance administration in the Ottoman Empire, 1560–1660* (Leiden and New York, 1996).

[19] On which see Eldem, Goffman, and Masters, *Ottoman city*, introduction.

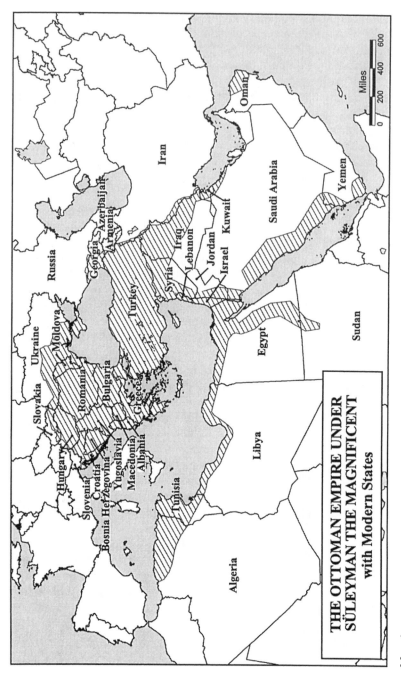

THE OTTOMAN EMPIRE UNDER
SÜLEYMAN THE MAGNIFICENT
with Modern States

Map 4

Which is not to say that particular religions did not dominate particular neighborhoods. The Phanariot Greeks took their name from the district in Istanbul known as Fener, where the Greek Orthodox patriarch resided and the Greeks certainly dominated, as did Jews in Balat and Muslims in Fatih. Nevertheless, a sprinkling of Muslims always inhabited Balat, some Jews lived in Fener and a sizeable number of Greeks resided in Fatih. This situation was replicated in cities as dissimilar as the old imperial capital of Bursa, the interior Antep, and the worldly Izmir.

Certain religions also controlled certain professions. Most pastoralists, for example, were Muslim (if sometimes deviant ones). Many mariners were Greek, Armenians tended to dominate international trade and brokerage, and textile manufacturers often were Jewish. The principal causes for such specialization, however, were not state-imposed restrictions upon non-Muslim employment or societal stereotyping of the sort so common in the Western world (Greeks as "natural" fishermen; Jews as "instinctive" bankers). Rather, it was nothing more than the legacies of the civilizations that the Ottomans inherited combined with the specifics of immigrant talents and employment opportunities that led to such specialization.

Greek Orthodox association with the Ottoman navy is a case in point. As Turkomans pushed to the north, west, and south across Anatolia they soon faced water – the Black, the Marmara, the Aegean, and the Mediterranean seas. These steppe people had had little experience with negotiating such bodies of water, and principalities such as Aydınoğlu and Karasi hired Byzantine ships and Greek shipbuilders and sailors to help them cross and navigate them. Ottomans of Turkoman ancestry did quickly learn about the sea and fully participated in commerce and expansion into the Black, Mediterranean, and even Red seas. Nevertheless, Ottoman Greeks early secured this economic niche in the Ottoman world, and disproportionate numbers of Ottoman Greeks continued to labor as oarsmen, sailors, and fishermen until the 1920s. It was western European travelers and Greek nationalists who in the eighteenth and nineteenth centuries observed this dominance and helped fabricate the fictions of an innate Greek aptitude for and an innate Turkish antipathy toward the sea.

Ottoman Armenians achieved a similar association with the commerce in silks and precious stones, and Jews with the Ottoman textile industry. Again, imperialists, racists, and nationalists have sometimes perceived these lines of work as inherently apt. In fact, they had nothing to do with supposed racially or ethnically innate characteristics. Rather, the historic development and diasporic nature of both the Armenian and Jewish civilizations put them in unique positions to serve as middle communities between the Ottoman and other worlds.

15   Three Armenian priests. Helffrich, *Kurtzer und warhafftiger Bericht*.

The ancient Armenian homeland, for example, was landlocked, which seems to argue against an involvement in international and overseas commerce. The condition, however, produced a series of Armenian colonies in India, Anatolia, the Crimea, and elsewhere that usually eventually melted into their dominant cultures but also generated sweeping commercial networks. Long before the Ottoman period, Armenian traders had ranged across the Persian Gulf, the Indian Ocean, and the Caspian, Black, and Mediterranean seas.[20] The simultaneous emergence of the Sunni Ottoman and Shi'a Safavid empires provided Armenians, who as neither Sunni nor Shi'a could live in both domains, an opportunity to serve as an unthreatening commercial link between these mutually hostile polities.

The vicissitudes of Ottoman–Safavid warfare at the turn of the seventeenth century produced an Armenian association with silks. After a dormant period in the early sixteenth century, under Shah Abbas (1587–1629) Persia again moved aggressively against the Ottomans. Abbas abandoned the old Safavid capital at Tabriz and built a new one at Isfahan, in a suburb of which – New Julfa – he resettled large numbers of Armenians who had been dispossessed in 1605 during devastating Ottoman-Safavid warfare in their homeland. This Armenian colony, established at the heart of Persia's silk-producing region, became the hub of a vast commercial network. Armenian merchants used their virtual monopoly over trade in Persian silks to establish satellite communities in several Ottoman cities, including Aleppo, Izmir, Bursa, Istanbul, and Edirne. In Ottoman as well as Safavid lands many learned to identify the Armenian community with this luxury commodity.

In the pre-Ottoman eastern Mediterranean world, Jews also were renowned international traders.[21] Ironically, the community's other principal association was with "dirty" occupations such as leather tanning and state execution. During the Ottoman period, however, manufacturing supplemented and to an extent superseded these associations, principally because of Sephardic migration from Spain, Portugal, and other western European countries. The capital and skills that these refugees brought into the empire produced vigorous, if short-lived, textile establishments in Istanbul, in Palestine, and especially in Salonika.[22] Whereas virtually no Jews had lived in this last city before the late fifteenth-century

---

[20] Curtin, *Cross-cultural trade*, pp. 182–86.
[21] The classic study on this community is S. D. Goitein, *A Mediterranean society: an abridgement in one volume*, ed. Jacob Lassner (Berkeley, 2000). But see also Ghosh's vivid *In an antique land*.
[22] See Benjamin Braude, "International competition and domestic cloth in the Ottoman Empire, 1500–1650," *Review* 1(1979): 437–54.

16 "Frank" woman dressed fashionably. Nicolay, *Le navigationi et viaggi nella Turchia.*

expulsions from Iberia, by the mid sixteenth century the settlement of thousands of Spaniards had granted the Jews a majority and turned Salonika into perhaps the principal Jewish cultural and economic center in the world.

Both contemporary and historical association of Ottoman Greek Orthodox, Armenian, and Jewish communities is with urban employment and metropolitan lifestyles. Nevertheless, such impressions are misleading. It was simply that such professions tended to be particularly visible to those most likely to disseminate information about these groups – travelers, diplomats, writers and bureaucrats. As with other early modern societies, the Ottoman polity remained demographically rural and economically agricultural. Just as many Ottoman fishermen were not Greek Orthodox, there were also Ottoman silk merchants who were not Armenian; and just as not all Ottoman industrialists were Jewish, so not all agriculturists were Muslim. Even though one or another community may have dominated farming regionally, in the empire as a whole every religio-ethnic community engaged in this basic occupation.

The Ottoman state was Islamic. Consequently, theoretically at least, Muslims were the most privileged of non-elite Ottoman subjects, and it is certain that in this intensely agrarian society, in which the basic unit of production remained the family farm and perhaps 90 percent of its inhabitants were farmers, Muslims were prominent as agriculturalists. Indeed, some argue that the *çift* – the amount of land plowable by two oxen in one day – constitutes a fundamental institution in the Ottoman world, and that the dominance of Muslims in this profession defines the polity as an Islamic one. Furthermore, as one historian explains, "the most important pre-requisite for the continuity of such a system appears to have been centralist state control over land possession and family labor."[23] In other words, it was the Ottoman government that both protected these small farms from notables anxious to consolidate and expand their holdings, and constrained and taxed the farmer's production. The state's principal tool in these endeavors to both safeguard and levy was the systematic and repeated surveying and registration of land and inhabitants.

Muslims labored in almost every sector of the Ottoman economy. Not only did they dominate the military and bureaucracy almost exclusively, but they also were represented – in varying proportions according to time, place, and occupation – in virtually every other of the myriad urban professions as well. Evliya Çelebi makes clear the bewildering diversity of urban employment in the best-known passages of his multivolume travelogue, a lengthy description of a three-day parade ordered by Murad IV in 1638 of "all the guilds of the city of Constantinople, both great and small."[24] Within these pages, that make up one-third of a volume, are mentioned 735 guilds, including carpenters, builders, woodcutters,

---

[23] Halil İnalcık, *An economic and social history of the Ottoman Empire, 1300–1914* (Cambridge, 1994), p. 145.

[24] John Freely presents an extensive description of the parade in his *Istanbul: the imperial city* (London, 1996), pp. 229–36.

sawyers, masons, chalk-makers, toy-makers, bakers, butchers, ship captains, fish-cooks, confectioners, gravediggers, thieves, pimps, beggars,
physicians, tavern-keepers, and others. The author provides only hints
of the religious composition of these "guilds" (perhaps a better translation would be "associations of artisans"), a silence which itself suggests
that, in the workplace at least, religion meant little to the early modern
Ottoman. Other sources confirm that virtually all of these urban organizations consisted of religiously mixed workers.

It probably is futile even to attempt guesses about which careers Muslims dominated. For example, and surprisingly, over half of the craftsmen
who built Süleyman's great mosque were Christian. Nor were Muslims
absent from professions one might associate with other religions. For example, some 20 percent of surgeons operating in Istanbul in 1700 were
Muslim.[25] In short, representatives of this religious community toiled
alongside Christians and Jews as peddler, fisherman, shipbuilder, construction worker, artisan, and every sort of urban and rural worker. In
striking contrast to many other parts of Europe, in the Ottoman economy
the success of the Muslim, as with the Christian and the Jew, depended
not upon policies of restriction and exclusion but upon talent, traditional
expertise, and practice.

This variety of worshipers in every urban employment suggests a complex identity in the Ottoman world. Religion, it seems, constituted only
one face of a subject's sense of self. At workplaces in the cities, there was
little segregation between Muslims and non-Muslims; although more religious homogeneity existed in residential districts, even here exclusively
Christian, Jewish, or Muslim neighborhoods were rare. This urban topography suggests that employment and economic level may have been
even more important than religion in the Ottoman subject's personal
identity.

The Ottoman Muslim presence was just as vital in trade and mer-
chandising as it was in other employments. Here again its position had
much to do with historical precedent and geographic distribution. In
most Arab lands, for example, Muslims were active in, but did not always control, both local economies and caravan commerce, just as they
had done for centuries. Muslim traders connected Aleppo, Damascus,
Baghdad, Cairo, and other cities with the essential produce of their rural
hinterlands.[26] They also dominated the caravan and seaborne commerce
that linked the cities of Aleppo and Cairo to the peppers, cloves, and

[25] Mansel, *Constantinople*, p. 124.
[26] One of the strongest statements on these activities is in Bruce Masters, *The origins of
Western economic dominance in the Middle East: mercantilism and the Islamic economy in
Aleppo, 1600–1750* (New York, 1988), especially pp. 47–68.

other spices of the East and their markets in the Middle East and Europe. Muslims were less dominant, but still present, in the local economies in other parts of the empire. Non-Muslims were a much stronger presence especially along the Anatolian and southeast European trading corridors. This difference again can be explained historically and demographically. First of all, in these lands the Ottomans had superimposed their political system upon Christian rather than Islamic economies. Consequently, non-Muslim communities such as Armenians, Jews, and Ragusan Catholics managed to establish themselves within the Anatolian and Balkan economies.

They also carved out positions as "middle merchants" between Ottoman domains and the West, and in the process helped freeze Ottoman Muslims out of these trading corridors. In fact, of all economic endeavors within the Ottoman world, it was only direct trade with the rest of Europe from which Muslims were virtually barred. This exclusion derived only in part from the ability of other groups to construct communal and familial trading diasporas. Also essential was that Catholic Europeans who settled in Ottoman port towns proved reluctant to deal directly with Muslims, and that, most crucial of all, bans against non-Christian settlement in many European port towns proscribed Muslim Ottomans from constructing their own commercial networks to rival Armenian, Greek, Jewish, and western European ones.

A world governed by exceptions

The Ottomans certainly used terms such as *kul, ulema, sipahi, askeri,* and *reaya,* and conceived them as types. Nevertheless, they were not in fact airtight categories. Considerable variation in the memberships and meanings of these groupings existed both spatially and chronologically. The functions of the janissary in Aleppo differed markedly from his counterpart in Istanbul; the path of acceptance into and promotion within the janissary corps was not the same in the fifteenth and seventeenth centuries. The same can be said of the *sipahi,* who hardly existed in Arab lands and whose prestige plummeted between the conquests of Constantinople (1453) and of Crete (1669), and the Jewish merchant, who by the end of the seventeenth century had seen the collapse of his impressive trading diaspora and its manufacturing foundation. Even the importance of being Muslim changed between and within the military, political, social, and economic spheres, as well as over time and place.

This implicit adaptability is one key to understanding the Ottoman world. The secret to Ottoman longevity and the empire's ability to rule over a vast and mixed collection of territories was not its legendary military, its loyal bureaucracy, its series of competent rulers, or a particular system of land tenure. Rather, it was simply its flexibility in dealing with this diverse society. Even as some western European states drifted toward concepts of constitutionality and citizenship – in the process at times establishing legal codes that granted each subject equal rights and opened for them a gamut of undreamed-of opportunities, and at other times demanding from them an unprecedented uniformity even as they condemned and expelled their rivals first in belief, and later in ethnicity, race, and even class – the Ottoman Empire moved in a different direction. It fashioned a society defined by diversity (although certainly not equality) of population and flexibility in governance.

Kubad at the Sublime Porte

There is, at the end of a secret gallery, a small square window which serves as a listening post. It is a wicker-work grille, with a curtain of crape or black taffeta, and is called the "dangerous window," because the prince may, whenever he wishes, listen to and see all that takes place, without being seen.[1]

Before embarking for Venice, Kubad had to appear before the Imperial Divan to receive his documentation and verbal instructions.[2] On a gloomy and drizzly morning in early September 1567, then, he rode from his home in Fatih, the quarter erected around the rather squat mosque of Mehmed II the Conqueror,[3] nudging his mount along the slippery and uneven cobbled roads that twisted up and down the hilly city and across the grounds of the ancient Byzantine hippodrome. He circled to the right of the Hagia Sofia mosque and through the Imperial Gate into the first and most public of the three courtyards of Topkapı, the imperial palace. Here he dismounted and left his steed to be dried and fed at the imperial stables. As Kubad hurried along, he unconsciously noted his surroundings: to his left lay the ancient Byzantine church, Hagia Irene, as well as the mint, the hospital, and the imperial stables; and to his right towered the high wall that marked out the entire palace grounds.[4] The imperial official, however, walked straight ahead, toward a second portal, the Gate of Salutation.

No guard had challenged his entry into the first courtyard, for all were allowed here. The area bustled with every type of person, both subject and foreigner. Some waited to present petitions to scribes who forwarded them to appropriate imperial

---

[1] *Illustrations de B. de Vigenère Bourbonnois sur l'histoire de Chalcocondyle athénien*, in *Histoire de la décadence de l'empire grec et l'éstablissement de celuy des turcs* (Rouen, 1660), p. 19; quoted in İnalcık, *Ottoman Empire*, p. 90.

[2] We have no information about how Kubad received his instructions. He certainly went to Topkapı Palace in order to do so, however. The best, indeed the definitive, work on this structure is Necipoğlu, *Architecture, ceremonial, and power*. See also Godfrey Goodwin, *Topkapi Palace: an illustrated guide to its life and personalities* (London, 2000).

[3] On this mosque and its district, see Sumner-Boyd and Freely, *Strolling through Istanbul*, pp. 253–69.

[4] Any visitor to the palace today can visit all of these landmarks, many of them restored.

93

17 Military and musical performances were a vital ingredient in imperial display. These often took place in the second courtyard of the palace, as when boys moved out of the imperial school and into public service. In this representation, the imperial guards circle with their horses in the center foreground as on the center left a band performs. The sultan watches all of this at the Gate of Felicity in the center background. D'Ohsson, *Tableau général de l'Empire othoman*, vol. II, after p. 16.

agencies, others were there to escape the city's grime and congestion, and a few morbid bystanders had come simply to examine the stuffed heads of disobedient high officials that grotesquely ornamented the first courtyard's marble pillars – a coarse and cruel barometer of Ottoman politics.[5] *At the second gate, however, began the sultan's private domain. No horse other than the monarch's own passed through its portal; the* bostancıs *who guarded it checked all pedestrians who demanded the right of entry.*[6]

As an imperial pursuivant, Kubad easily passed through the gates and into a capacious garden. Neither stately citadel nor commemorative statuary rose before his eyes. Indeed, the only lofty structures within the palace grounds were the smoldering chimneys of the imperial kitchens that stretched along the wall to his right and the only artwork was fountains. In front of him were well-kept gardens, fountains, and a series of pavilions that speckled the grounds like randomly raised tents, a landscape that faintly echoed Kubad's pastoral youth.[7] *He knew that this nomadic past resonated more strongly in the third courtyard that lay directly before him through a third gate, the High Gate, for he had spent much of his youth there. Nevertheless, he had not since passed into this* enderun-i hümayûn *(imperial interior) or imperial harem, which was strictly off-limits to anyone but members of the sultan's household, several hundred boys (among whom he had once been included) and girls being trained for imperial service, and eunuchs. The pursuivant swerved to his left away from this forbidden quarter, toward a square-shaped pavilion where the Imperial Council routinely met.*

As Kubad approached the building, he heard a clamor of angry voices and then saw the Venetian representative Soranzo emerge, red-faced, clearly flustered, and accompanied by an edgy dragoman and about a dozen retainers. The bailo *rushed out of the audience room, brushed by him with nothing more than an angry glare, and strode away toward the Gate of Salutation. The* çavuş *rightly guessed that Soranzo now recognized his error in having agreed to bind his community to the kadi's court six months hence and had just petitioned*

---

[5] Eldem presents a vivid reminder of this brutal side to high Ottoman politics in "Istanbul," pp. 164–74.

[6] On *bostancı*, see "Bostāndjı," *EI*.

[7] Some have made much of this faint echo of a nomadic past. John Keegan for example draws upon the palace's flatness to argue the persistent nomadic outlook of Ottoman civilization: "The persistence of the nomadic ethos is nowhere better caught than in the Topkapi at Istanbul, palace of the Ottoman Turkish sultans, where, until the beginning of the nineteenth century, the rulers of an empire that stretched from the Danube River to the Indian Ocean spent their days as they might have done on the steppe, seated on cushions on carpeted floors of makeshift pavilions set up in the palace gardens, dressed in the horseman's kaftan and loose trousers, and having as their principal regalia the mounted warrior's quivers, bow cases and archer's thumb rings. Planted though it was in the capital city of the eastern Roman empire, the Topkapi remained a nomadic camp, where the horsetail standards of battle were processed before great men, and stables stood at the door" (*A history of warfare* [New York, 1994], pp. 181–82).

the Imperial Council to request that they amend the settlement. His ire in part derived from that assembly's refusal to do so. What Kubad did not know, however, was that the newly appointed Ottoman grand admiral Piyâle Pasha had also protested in fiercely menacing tones against Christian pirates who darted out of the many small havens along the shoreline of Venetian-held Cyprus, attacked Ottoman vessels carrying grains from Egypt to Istanbul, and then, often with the Ottoman navy in hot pursuit, retreated to the protection of Venetian cannons.

Kubad paused for a few moments outside the pavilion, waiting for a bostancı *to usher him in for his audience. As he entered the room, he saw seated before him the viziers of the Council, including the head scribe Ebu al-Fazl Mehmed Çelebi, the grand admiral Piyâle Pasha, the revered* şeyhülislam *Ebu's-Su'ud Efendi, the long-lasting grand vizier Sokollu Mehmed Pasha, Selim II's trusted lâlâ Mustafa Pasha, and several others.[8] The recently installed Sultan Selim II of course was not among those assembled, although it was possible that he secretly watched the proceedings from behind the screen in a window that pierced one wall of the pavilion.*

It was clear that the just-concluded meeting had exasperated members of the Council as well as the Venetian representative. The grand vizier was speaking with soft force to Piyâle Pasha even as Kubad walked in, and the usually serene admiral seemed agitated. As soon as the pursuivant entered, however, Mehmed Pasha stopped talking and turned toward him. "As you know," he began, "the Venetian Jew Hayyim Saruq has reneged upon his obligations to some of our Jewish subjects and our sovereign padishah. *Carrying these documents," with which he motioned to an attending scribe who passed Kubad a sealed sachet, "you are to accompany to Venice the son of our cherished Joseph di Segura, where you will present our grievances to the doge and demand recompense for our losses. We authorize you to threaten dire consequences should he refuse."*

Kubad was startled by a sudden thud to his right, and out of the corner of his eye he saw the grand admiral jerk forward. "How insubstantial," he exclaimed. "Surely his most majestic damad *could recommend a more tangible threat!" The voice of lâlâ Mustafa, Selim II's influential tutor, seconded Piyâle's objection: "Just as my friend has recently removed the last Genoese outpost on Chios from the Aegean,[9] let us exploit this snub as a pretext to take control of Cyprus and in this manner also wipe the Venetian scourge from our seas."*

The grand vizier raised his hand for silence and then contemplated his colleagues. Finally he spoke: "I too would like to see an Ottoman Cyprus. But I

---

[8] On these and other Ottoman high officials, see İsmail Hâmi Danişmend, *Osmanlı Devlet Erkânı*, vol. v of *İzahlı Osmanlı Tarihi Kronolojisi* (Istanbul, 1971). Several of these men appear in the text below.

[9] On which, see Daniel Goffman, *Izmir and the Levantine world, 1550–1650* (Seattle, WA, 1990), pp. 61–62.

also much fear that such an attack would end the squabbling between Venice and other Catholic states and stimulate a grand alliance against us. Let us exercise some caution. Çavuş, say nothing of such matters. Soranzo knows that Cyprus is threatened and must already be warning his Senate of such. The implied danger will suffice to ease your negotiations."[10] *With these words, Kubad was dismissed.*

As he withdrew through the outer courtyards of the palace, he thought about the fractured Imperial Council. The political strife that put Sultan Süleyman's last grand vizier, struggling to retain his position under the new padishah, at odds with Selim II's personal favorites was plain. Perhaps Sokollu Mehmed's greatest burden was that the sultan had inherited him from his father and certainly must be tempted to replace him with his own man. This liability was only partially offset by his marriage to Selim's daughter İsmihan sultan, for others also had such ties to the imperial household. Piyâle Pasha for one had recently gained a vizierate only in part because of his conquest of Chios. The grand admiral's own wife was Gevherhan sultan, İsmihan's sister.[11] *As Kubad walked through the gates of the outer courtyard, he wondered if Mehmed Pasha would share the destiny of his predecessor Çandarlı Halil, who had conspired to depose Mehmed II after his father's abdication, had opposed the great sultan's attack upon Constantinople, and soon after the city's conquest had paid the price for his resistance with his head.*

[10] This dialogue is wholly invented, but reflects the likely positions of the principals.
[11] On these domestic politics, see Peirce, *Imperial harem*, pp. 65–79.

4 Factionalism and insurrection

The *reaya* no longer obeyed the sovereign's command; the soldiers turned against the sultan. There was no respect for the authorities and they were attacked not by words but blows. All acted as they pleased. As tyranny and injustice increased, people in the provinces began to flee to Istanbul. The old order and harmony departed. When these have finally collapsed, catastrophe will surely follow.[1]

This, also, is not concealed from the heart of the truth-seeker: in the Sublime State, in every period, the influence of speech and free action has fallen to the share of one group [or another]. And then until the time when, divine will permitting, influence and control pass from that corps to another corps, it is no more than natural for each group to vaunt itself foolishly while it has the royal favor and to rejoice in receiving profits to its heart's content. But one must add at least this much: those who attain to glory and favor through especial fortune of this sort must, no matter who they are, behave with good sense, and must not fail to observe the limits which the rights of God and of the people constitute.[2]

However invincible the Ottoman military machine seemed through much of the sixteenth century, however coherent Ottoman society seems to have become, and however much money poured into the state coffers, as a monarchy the empire remained dependent upon the abilities of a single man. Even though fortune, and prudent and inventive principles of succession brought a series of competent sultans to the throne, any despotism, reliant as it is upon whims and fancies as well as discretion and wisdom, is inherently unstable. Süleyman (1520–66) ruled during the supposed Ottoman golden age and exhibited all of these traits, both positive and negative. He was both a conqueror and the slayer of his chief lieutenant and his son, both a romantic poet and the spoiler of the Ottoman blueprint for imperial succession. He both benefited from a

[1] Selânikî Mustafa Efendi, *Tarih-i Selânikî*: as quoted in İnalcık, *Ottoman Empire*, p. 46.
[2] Naima, *Tarih-i Naima*, as quoted in Lewis V. Thomas, *A study of Naima*, ed. Norman Itzkowitz (New York, 1971), p. 101.

mature state and laid the seeds for the transformations that many insist ushered in Ottoman decline.

Süleyman as personifier of empire

Süleyman's father Selim was a great conquering sultan. With his defeat of the Safavids at the Battle of Çaldıran in 1514 and his conquest of much of the Arab world in 1516–17, Selim not only again proved the strength of Ottoman arms, but also transformed the empire's very ideological and strategic focus. Until that time and despite the Islamic nature of the state, the government had ruled over at least as many Christians as Muslims, and had contended with chiefly Catholic foes. With first the confrontation with the Shi'ite Safavid state, followed immediately thereafter by the capture of Aleppo and Cairo, Mecca and Medina, the Ottomans now became responsible not only for upholding Sunni orthodoxy against a potent opposing form of Islam, but also for the upkeep of the holiest cities in Islam and for the safe passage of pilgrims embarking upon the hajj.[3] Furthermore, the Ottomans also inherited not only the overwhelmingly Muslim Arab people, but also their strong sense of self, their long history, and their pride as the direct descendants of Abraham's elder son Ismael and Muhammed. Finally, Selim's conquests exposed the Ottomans, more directly than ever, to powerful empires. In the Red Sea, Persian Gulf, and Indian Ocean, they now faced an uncompromisingly Catholic Portuguese presence; in Mesopotamia and eastern Anatolia they now had to compete with an aggressively Shi'ite Safavid empire; and in the Mediterranean Sea and the Balkans, they were soon to confront a Holy Roman Empire united under the leadership of Charles V. The empire that Süleyman inherited in 1520 faced greater rivals than had existed earlier. It also was as potent as any European polity that had existed since Rome. It encompassed the Balkans, Anatolia, much of the Fertile Crescent, and Egypt, and stretched from the Danube River to the Red Sea and from the Caspian Sea to the Morean peninsula. Nor, unusually, did the new sultan have brothers to battle for the throne, but enjoyed the luxury of assuming the sultanate unopposed.

Consequently, Süleyman was well placed to continue the expansion of his empire, and did so with the capture in 1521 of the Hungarian city of Belgrade, which controlled access to the Habsburg capital of Vienna, and with the taking in 1522 of the island of Rhodes, which had been the base for the Knights of St. John, a crusading fraternity that preyed especially

---

[3] On which, see Suraiya Faroqhi, *Pilgrims and sultans: the hajj under the Ottomans* (London, 1996).

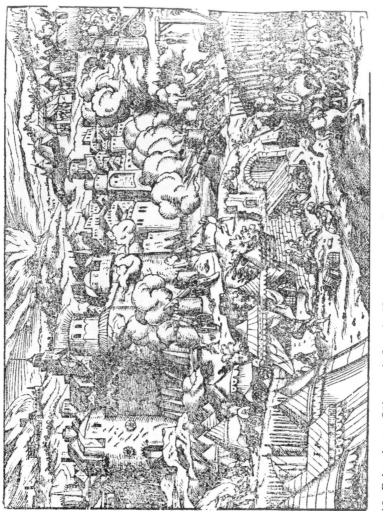

18 Belgrade was Süleyman's first significant conquest. Cannon and the mining of city walls that marked Ottoman sieges are notable in this busy woodcut. The figure on the white horse in the foreground is presumably the young sultan himself. Lonicer, *Chronicorum Turcicorum*, vol. II (in one binding), p. 22.

upon Ottoman ships carrying provisions and monies between Egypt and Istanbul. Through these two conquests, Süleyman not only rounded out his realm in Europe and the Mediterranean, but also legitimized his reign and asserted himself as a conqueror. Nevertheless, the international scene had changed. Whereas Mehmed II had faced little more than an enfeebled Byzantine city state and Selim had conquered an unstable Mamluk realm (after deploying firearms to defeat the Safavid Shah Ismael at the Battle of Çaldıran), Süleyman confronted two young and aggressive foes: in the Mediterranean world there was the Habsburg Empire, which under Charles V included almost all of Catholic Europe, and in the Indian Ocean was the seaborne Portuguese Empire, which was busily striving to establish presences throughout the region, particularly in the Persian Gulf and Red Sea. The Ottoman Empire may have been stronger and better placed than either of these realms, but Süleyman faced the prospect of having simultaneously to confront both.

He did so with great vigor, if not always with success. In 1526 he defeated the Hungarians in the Battle of Mohács and briefly took Buda. Three years later, he led another army into Hungary, occupied the entire country, and even besieged Vienna for three weeks. The Ottomans, however, found it difficult to hold what was conquered. The distance between Istanbul and these provinces, the custom of retreat after each campaign season, and the abilities of the Habsburgs to organize and mobilize opposing forces may have contributed to the Ottomans' shaky position. It was in fact not until the 1540s that the Ottomans felt secure enough to organize the regions around the towns of Buda and Temesvar into provinces. Furthermore, a relatively stable "march" area emerged between the Habsburg and Ottoman domains, which demarcated an unacknowledged but very real border between the two empires.

The Ottoman knack for creative organization is evident in these sixteenth-century conquests. For example, the state did not impose Ottoman methods of tax collection on the Hungarian lands as thoroughly as it had on previous European conquests. Even with such a fundamental tax as the *cizye* (head tax upon non-Muslims), which more than any other imposition denoted integration into the Abode of Islam, the government granted many exemptions. Other taxes often were gathered according to local customary rather than Islamic principles.[4]

Such flexibility was even more apparent in the frontier states of Transylvania, Wallachia, and Moldavia, which were conquered in sporadic fashion during the course of the fifteenth and sixteenth centuries. As

---

[4] Géza Dávid, "Administration in Ottoman Europe," in Kunt and Woodhead (eds.), *Süleyman the Magnificent*, pp. 85–88.

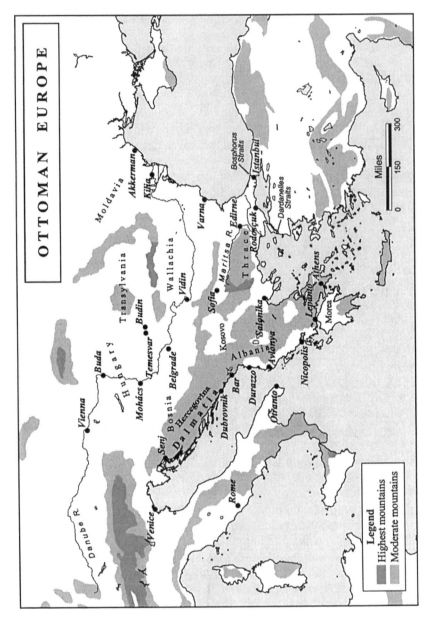

OTTOMAN EUROPE

Legend
Highest mountains
Moderate mountains

Miles
0   150   300

Map 5

early as the late fourteenth century, Bayezid had sent raiders against Wallachian territory, and it fell more directly under Ottoman influence when one of his sons, Musa, married the monarch's daughter in 1409 or 1410. It was not until after the second Battle of Kosovo (1444), in which Murad II routed the Hungarians and various crusading troops (including Wallachians) that the Ottomans firmly established the principality as a protectorate. His son Mehmed confirmed its status in 1460 when Vlad IV accepted Ottoman dominion. Moldavia finally fell under Ottoman sovereignty only two decades later, in 1484, when Ottoman and Crimean Tatar armies took the Black Sea port cities of Kilia and Akkerman. In 1503, both Hungary and Poland accepted these *faits accomplis*; but the Moldavian monarch did not do so until 1511, and it was not until 1538 that Süleyman, after the prince attempted to throw off Ottoman control, stationed Ottoman garrisons there.

Neither Wallachia nor Moldavia was ever fully assimilated into the Ottoman state and society. Ottoman garrisons occupied them and tributes were given, but no cadastral surveys of the provinces were administered; neither were *sipahis* granted *timars* or kadis appointed in these territories. Such methods of indirect rule were even more evident in Transylvania, which did not fall into the Ottoman orbit until later. As early as the 1440s, its ruler, John Hunyadi, had staged a series of successful campaigns against the Ottomans. Other than a few raids and a rather informal acknowledgment of sovereignty through a tribute, however, the Ottomans exhibited little interest in the principality before Transylvania became a prize in the struggle not only between the Habsburg and Ottoman Empires, but also between Catholics and Protestants.

In 1551, Süleyman sent an army under his grand vizier Sokullu Mehmed against Sigismund II, the prince of Transylvania, who had allied with the Habsburgs in part to help quash the mounting threat of Calvinism within his domain. Within a year, the Ottomans had recaptured most of Transylvania and returned it to vassalage. The war not only constituted a continuation of the long struggle between these two empires, but also again manifested the Ottoman ability to exploit rifts in Christendom: just as the Balkan lands had become Ottoman in part because their Greek and Serbian Orthodox inhabitants despised Catholic rule, so did much of eastern Hungary enter the Ottoman realm in part because its Protestant inhabitants feared the absolute Catholic intolerance toward their beliefs (newly manifested in the Inquisition). In the case of Transylvania, however, the Ottoman hand was particularly light. Unlike the Wallachian and Moldavian principalities, it saw no Ottoman garrisons, its diet elected its own princes, its princes sent no hostages to Istanbul, and its taxes remained unusually low.

Map 5   Here is depicted a highly stylized and fearsome troop of Ottoman soldiers from the mid sixteenth century.

The Ottomans managed the Danubian provinces as uniquely and creatively as they handled other regions of the empire. For example, the government modeled neither Selim's Arab land conquests nor Süleyman's Danubian ones on the example of its Anatolian and Balkan heartlands. In each case, if for very different reasons, it granted relative autonomy and left many customary laws in place. Even within each area the state proved flexible. The Ottomans understood historical and political peculiarities, and never brought either Transylvania or Egypt into as tight administrative control as even the rest of Hungary or Syria. The state could be bloodily harsh, to be sure; however, it also showed astonishing leniency as the situation demanded.

Süleyman as "king of kings"

This sultan did not extend his power and legitimacy only through martial exploits. Indeed, he treated travel to and from military campaigns almost as an elected official would; that is, as an opportunity for public display and enhancement of reputation. In 1534, for example, when an Ottoman army marched on Tabriz and won Baghdad from the Safavids, Süleyman left much of the hard campaigning to his grand vizier, İbrahim Pasha, while he dallied en route at Kütahya, Akşehir, Konya, Kayseri, Sivas, and Erzincan, and returned via Diyarbekir, Aleppo, Antakya, Adana, and Konya (again) to attend personally to the grievances of his subjects and visit holy and historic sites.[5] The sultan arrived at the military front just in time to lay claim to the conquest of the city of Baghdad. He thus opportunistically was able simultaneously to display to his subjects and to the world his concern for legal justice and his military prowess.

Süleyman's pursuit of the codification of the Ottoman legal code that his great grandfather Mehmed II had begun also displayed his interest in justice, an impression that he cultivated. One Ottoman choncler writing soon after the sultan's death describes how "the sweet perfume of his deeds was spread to the four corners of the earth ... talk of his justice was on everyone's tongue; thus was his concern for the care of the *reaya* made manifest."[6] Indeed, because of this focus, Turks today recall him not as Süleyman the Magnificent, but as Süleyman the Lawgiver (*kanuni*).

As striking as this sultan's concern for justice is the fact that he made sure that the entire world knew about it. Süleyman (or at least his advisors)

---

[5] Christine Woodhead, "Perspectives on Süleyman," in Kunt and Woodhead (eds.), *Süleyman the Magnificent*, p. 168.

[6] Petra Kappert, (ed.), *Geschichte Sultan Süleymān Kānūnīs von 1520 bis 1557, oder Tabakāt ül-memālik ve derecāt ül-mesālik von Celālzāde Mustafā* (Wiesbaden, 1981), fo. 28a; as quoted by Woodhead, "Perspectives on Süleyman," p. 165.

displayed an almost obsessive attentiveness to personal glory in his patronage of both architecture and literature, and in his personal habits. His great architect Sinan, a *devşirme* boy who began his career as a designer of military bridges, went on to construct some of the most important public buildings in the world, including the Selimiye mosque in Edirne and the soaring Süleymaniye mosque, that even today presides over Istanbul's skyline and reverberates with memories of this grand monarch and the empire over which he ruled.[7] He was equally attentive to his literary legacy. The sultan not only himself wrote verses under the pen name "Muhibbi" (affectionate companion), but also patronized such principal classical Ottoman poets as Bâkî and Hayali. These lyricists memorialized their ruler in such verses as Bâkî's

> in truth he was [the epitome of] elegance and beauty, of prosperity
>   and dignity
> the monarch with the crown of Alexander, the army of Darius
> the sphere bowed its head in the dust at his feet
> the earth before his gate served as prayer mat for the world.[8]

Süleyman also sponsored court historians, who unabashedly promoted their patron's character and exploits.

The historian Lokman, writing some twenty years after the sultan's death, remembered the ruler as "a mine of talent, a quarry of abundance and munificence; he had no equal in grace and charm; he was free from vanity and arrogance and wore no robe of pride."[9] It is striking how successfully Süleyman marketed himself. His reputation as military strategist, as just ruler, and as artist may have been deserved, but it certainly grew with time, until he was considered, both domestically and abroad, as a paragon among monarchs. He was so successful at promoting himself, in fact, that no succeeding sultan could measure up; the resultant harkening back toward a misplaced past probably contributed to a perception of subsequent disquietude and corruption, the condition into which the seventeenth- and eighteenth-century Ottoman empire is often said to have plunged.

The imagery of Bâkî's poem suggests how conscious Süleyman and his court were of the history of the domain over which he ruled as well as the regions he aspired to govern. The poet compares him favorably with Darius, the great king of the ancient Persian Empire, as well as Alexander, the Macedonian who conquered most of the known world and introduced

---

[7] Aptullah Kuran, *Sinan the Grand Old Master of Ottoman architecture* (Washington, D.C., and Istanbul, 1987).

[8] Quoted in Woodhead, "Perspectives on Süleyman," p. 180.

[9] Quoted in Woodhead, "Perspectives on Süleyman," p. 176.

Hellenistic civilization to it. The sultan not only measured himself against historical world conquerors, but also evaluated himself favorably against contemporary leaders. He sought consciously and deliberately to vie with the Holy Roman Emperor and the Pope as imperial successor to the Roman Empire as well as to link himself with the civilizations of Greece, Persia, and Arabia.

Süleyman inherited these ambitions from his predecessors, most notably from his great-grandfather Mehmed II, who with the conquest of Constantinople in 1453 had proclaimed himself heir to the Romans, had sought to secure that claim with the conquest of Italy, the Ottoman invasion of which aborted with his death in 1481, and symbolically had sought to prove the universality of his empire by inviting to Istanbul a bevy of European artists, most notably Gentile Bellini, who had come to Istanbul in 1479 at Mehmed's invitation and who painted several portraits of the sultan. Almost a century later, Süleyman's advisors charted a similar course. In the late 1520s and early 1530s, the grand vizier İbrahim Pasha and his expatriate Venetian comrade Alvise Gritti orchestrated a series of processions and celebratory displays during the sultan's campaigns deep into Hungary and Austria. At the city of Nish, for example, two Habsburg envoys observed "the Turkish emperor sitting in majesty and pomp on a golden throne . . . The columns or supports of the throne were completely covered with jewels and costly pearls."[10] Such a display clearly was meant not only to awe these Austrian emissaries, but also to project a perception of power westward.

Even in the imperial capital, Ottoman ceremonial began more to emulate the West. One manifestation of this change was that, beginning in about 1530, Süleyman no longer reclined crosslegged upon a divan in the manner of his predecessors when displaying himself to ambassadors and other dignitaries, but instead seated himself high above them upon a sumptuous and jewel-encrusted throne. Indeed, the sultan's very choice of attire and his ceremonials displayed what apparently was an objective to subvert the claims of his imperial adversaries. One manner in which he competed with European rulers, for example, was by adapting the crown and sceptre – regalia associated with Roman and Catholic imperial traditions but symbols of authority that resonated not at all in the Middle East or Central Asia.[11] Indeed, during the same military campaign into the Balkans in the early 1530s, Süleyman showed off a magnificent crown – designed and assembled by Venetian artisans – that markedly united motifs from the coronation crowns of the Holy Roman Emperor

---

[10] Quoted in Gülru Necipoğlu, "Süleyman the Magnificent and the representation of power in the context of Ottoman–Hapsburg–papal rivalry," *Art Bulletin* 71.3(1989): 409.
[11] On which, see the insightful and persuasive Necipoğlu, "Süleyman the Magnificent."

Map 5 Süleyman gives the impression of being the most magnificent
of the many sultans that illustrate this massive volume, published only
twelve years after that monarch's death. Uniquely among this work's
depictions, he alone boasts not only a turban, but also, balanced pre-
cariously upon it, the crown of an emperor. Lonicer, *Chronicorum Turcicorum*, vol. I (in one binding), p. 34.

Charles V and the Pope Clement VII. Woodcut images of Charles V's
coronation ceremony in 1529 were circulated throughout Europe, and
no Western observer could have missed the Ottoman sultan's challenge
to the emperor's universalist claims in this choice of headgear.

Whereas, in the fourteenth and fifteenth centuries, the Ottomans had borrowed some of the structures of the European state, under Süleyman they seem to have challenged the Catholic version of European history itself – to reimagine it as a vision that harkened back to the pre-Christian past and to fashion the Ottoman Empire rather than the papacy or the Holy Roman Empire as the rightful successor to Greek and Roman civilizations. Even though this attempt to refashion European history failed, the construct itself was not all that farfetched. Geographically it certainly made sense, and even historically what gave Germanic barbarians (whom Charles V represented) any more right to carry the banner of Rome than Turkic ones? Even ideologically, the Ottomans' case was strong: whereas Christianity claimed to have supplanted Judaism, followers of Islam insisted that it was the only pure monotheism, that it represented the Abrahamic faith, and that both Judaism and Christianity were merely badly corrupted versions of Islam. Under Süleyman, then, Ottoman authorities proposed to reinvent a Europe in the empire's own image, even as Protestantism was forcing western Europe to reinvent itself.

The Ottomans and the Christian schism of 1517

Few of us associate the Ottoman Empire with the Reformation. It represented a civil dispute within Christendom, and Christian states fought its wars and negotiated its peaces. Those of us who do consider the Ottomans tend to focus upon the realm of ideas. We embrace the image of the terrible Turk, the infidel whose intent was to destroy the Christian world and who did not bother to distinguish between Catholic, Calvinist, and Lutheran, a view that some contemporaries shared.

Nevertheless, most early modern Christians had a much subtler and more sophisticated view of the Ottoman Empire than many of us appreciate. Even Martin Luther himself, who is known for his scathing malevolence against just about everyone – peasants, the papacy, Jews, and others – wrote with relative moderation about the Ottomans in his "On War Against the Turk."[12] It is certainly true that he believed that "the Turk . . . is the servant of the devil, who not only devastates land and people with the sword . . . but lays waste the Christian faith and our dear Lord Jesus Christ." Nevertheless, he never actually labels the Ottoman sultan an anti-Christ, as he does the Pope, or Turks as devils incarnate, as he does Jews. Luther in fact acknowledges that there exist those who "actually

---

[12] Martin Luther, "On war against the Turk, 1529," in *Luther's works*, Vol. XLVI: *The Christian in society, III* (Philadelphia, 1967), pp. 155–205.

want the Turk to come and rule because they think our German people are wild and uncivilized – indeed that they are half-devil and half-man," and never bothers to rebuff this judgment on his countrymen. He further remarks that "although some praise the Turk's government because he allows every one to believe what he will so long as he remains temporal lord, yet this reputation is not true, for he does not allow Christians to come together in public,"[13] certainly a halfhearted condemnation at most.

This appraisal came in 1529, even as Süleyman besieged Vienna, whose fall seemed imminent. It was a moment in which one might have expected fear and loathing to grip Europe. Luther certainly expresses such emotions; but also perceptible in these passages and elsewhere in his text is a grudging esteem for a government that not only accorded to non-Catholic Christians the right to reside and worship but also was the arch-enemy of his own arch-enemies, the Pope and Holy Roman Emperor. Other religious reformers reiterated Martin Luther's uncertainties. The principal paradox for all of them, perhaps, was that even though the Ottomans posed a dire threat to Christendom, and especially to the Christian state, nevertheless, it was the Catholic world – and above all its Pope, represented by these same reformers as anti-Christ – that was most immediately threatened. The Ottoman Empire pounded away at the "soft underbelly" of Charles V's empire, and it was Charles and his Pope who had sworn to force Luther, John Calvin, and other Protestants to renounce their convictions. Many Protestants understood that only the Ottoman diversion stood between them and obliteration.

The actions of European states and representatives of various Christian denominations should further moderate and partially belie our expressions of universal venom against the "Turk." If the rise of the Italian city-state augured the political breakup of Christendom, Martin Luther's posting of his ninety-nine theses in 1517 signified its ideological fragmentation, and ushered in over a century of religious wars. Both the Holy Roman Emperor Charles V and the French king Francis were fully engaged in these wars, even as they contended with the Ottomans. The rulers were bitter rivals, however, and their methods of dealing with the "terrible Turk" were wholly opposed: Charles over and over again attacked Süleyman's realm in both the Mediterranean Sea and the Balkans even as Francis negotiated alliances with him, in 1535 going so far as to sign a short-lived commercial and military agreement with the sultan. It is certain that the Ottoman threat as much as dynastic claims and political ambitions in Italy distracted Charles V from his declared intent of crushing the Protestant revolt to his north.

---

[13] Luther, "On war against the Turk," pp. 174–75.

The Ottoman government was aware of and exploited this tear in the fabric of Christendom. Its experiences in Hungary and Transylvania were only the most direct of that state's involvement in the religious disputes. Süleyman wrote at least one letter urging the Protestant princes of Germany to hold firm and cooperate with the French against Charles V; the Ottoman government continued to support the Calvinists not only in Transylvania and Hungary, but also in France; and cooperation with France led to the wintering of an Ottoman fleet in French Toulon in 1543 and the attachment of a French artillery unit to the Ottoman army in Hungary. During those troubled decades, the empire also became a haven for the religiously oppressed. In the mid seventeenth century, for example, a cluster of Huguenots, forced into exile from France, resided in Istanbul, and several Anglican clergymen who had fled commonwealth England, Quakers, Anabaptists, and even Catholic Jesuits and Capuchins settled in and wandered through the empire.

Such an eclectic mixture of Christians suggests that North America was not the only refuge for western European religious dissenters in the early colonial period. Indeed, it was generally understood that spiritually oppressed Christians as well as Jews could find sanctuary in the Ottoman Empire. As early as 1529, Luther was aware of the relative moderation of Ottoman society, despite his grumblings that Christians could not worship openly there. By the 1580s, a thinker such as Jean Bodin could write in open admiration about this aspect of Ottoman society:

> The great emperour of the Turkes doth with as great devotion as any prince in the world honour and observe the religion by him received from his auncestours, and yet detesteth hee not the straunge religions of others; but to the contrarie permitteth every man to live according to his conscience: yea and that more is, neere unto his pallace at Pera, suffereth foure divers religions, *viz.* That of the Jews, that of the Christians, that of the Grecians, and that of the Mohametanes.[14]

Bodin held the empire up as a model of religious toleration, an assessment with which some even today would agree. The claim is sometimes made that minorities in the Islamic state constructed by the Ottomans lived more comfortably and with less fear than they did in rival European states, and even than they do in the modern secular state. Compared with other seventeenth-century states such as the Habsburgs, the French, the Venetian, or the Russian this argument certainly holds, and it probably

[14] Kenneth Douglas McRae (ed.), *The six bookes of a commonweale* (Cambridge, 1962), book 6, p. 537. On Bodin's and other early modern attitudes toward the Ottomans, see Hentsch, *Imagining the Middle East*, pp. 49–76. A persuasive article on western European attitudes more generally is Aslı Çırakman, "From tyranny to despotism: the Enlightenment's unenlightened image of the Turks," *International Journal of Middle East Studies* 33.1(2001): 49–68.

also is valid in comparison with those modern nation states that define citizenship exclusively in fabricated categories of ethnicity, race, or religion. Nevertheless, it would be a mistake to generalize Bodin's observation to include every polity. For example, it is difficult to imagine a Christian or a Jew willingly giving up the guarantees of constitutional equality that many modern democracies provide for the structurally guaranteed inequalities of an Ottoman *millet* or *taife*. It is no easier to visualize a Muslim willingly becoming a second-class citizen in a Christian or Jewish state.[15]

Crisis at the turn of the seventeenth century

The impression that Süleyman represented the zenith of Ottoman capacity, and that all that followed was decline, persists today. The stubbornness of this vision derives partly from an association of the Ottomans with the Habsburg Empire, which certainly divided (even if it did not utterly collapse) soon after Charles V's death, and partly from the rising power of France, England, and other European states that were to force the entire Mediterranean world into a secondary role. The insistence of several late sixteenth- and seventeenth-century Ottoman writers that their state indeed was becoming aged and feeble has lent documentary evidence to this argument. Mustafa Âli writing in the 1590s, Peçevi writing in the 1630s, and especially such critics as Koçu Bey, who "counseled" (*nasihat*) Murad IV about the inadequacies of their state, all warn of a rise in corruption, a decline in lawfulness, and a failure of leadership in the post-Süleymanic empire.

Many of these works hint that Süleyman himself ushered in this deterioration – with his jealousy-driven execution of his grand vizier İbrahim, his scandalous marriage to the concubine Hürrem, and his aberrant murder of his son Mustafa (although Süleyman's own father Selim may have established a precedent for this act by deposing *his* own father Bayezid and allegedly murdering Süleyman's brothers). Nevertheless, these authors believed that the imperial household became even more dysfunctional in the decades after this sultan's death. It abandoned the tradition of imperial fratricide in favor of debilitating confinement, it allowed power to seep away from the sultan and into the hands of members of his family and counselors, and it began appointing and dismissing officials on the basis

---

[15] The word *millet* is controversial. See Benjamin Braude, "Foundation myths of the *millet* system," in *Christians and Jews in the Ottoman Empire: the functioning of a plural society*, Vol. I: *The central lands*, ed. Benjamin Braude and Bernard Lewis (New York, 1982), pp. 69–88; "Millet," *EI*; and Daniel Goffman, "Ottoman *millets* in the early seventeenth century," *New Perspectives on Turkey* 11(1994): 135–58.

of favoritism rather than merit. The chronicler Peçevi implicitly censures leadership in the sixty years since Süleyman's death on just these grounds when he writes: "in his reign, no holder of a government post, no military or judicial appointee, was dismissed without good cause . . . Accordingly, all officials acted with justice and moderation for fear of losing all chance of further employment."[16] For Peçevi, Naimi, and many other Ottoman statesmen and scholars, it was principally a deterioration of leadership that diluted power, engendered corruption, bankrupted the treasury, dragged the empire into ruinous wars, devastatingly inflated the currency, diluted and undermined the janissary corps, and generally enfeebled the Ottoman state.

Modern-day historians did not quickly repudiate this tale of decline; rather, they turned it on its head. In other words, poor leadership often has been envisioned as a symptom rather than a cause of more structural difficulties such as inflation caused by the influx of silver from the New World, changes in military technology, and the creation of a new type of state in western Europe. According to much of the scholarship of the late twentieth century, many Ottoman institutions – the janissary corps, the provincial leadership, the sultanate itself – suffered in the state's efforts to react to such largely external and underlying transformations.

The Ottoman state began to manifest the strains of persistent and multi-fronted warfare in the 1570s and 1580s. The need to mobilize ever-larger numbers of ill-trained mariners and infantry troops was among the most apparent symptoms. The devastating loss of a whole generation of mariners and archers at Lepanto in 1571, for example, necessitated the hurried recruitment of ill-prepared replacement archers and less effective musketeers. Even more disruptively, long and bloody wars against the Habsburg and Safavid Empires broke the well-designed organization for the enrollment and training of janissary troops and forced the Ottoman government not only to hurry janissary instruction, increase the numbers entering the corps, and begin allowing even born Muslims to enroll, but also to supplement these troops with irregulars. Between the 1560s and the 1630s, for example, the number of janissaries in active service rose from about 16,000 to some 40,000. Supporting and gradually replacing them both in the navy and on military fronts were infantrymen hurriedly recruited and trained in the use of firearms, but oblivious to the complicated codes of conduct that historically had restrained and emboldened the Ottoman military establishment.

---

[16] İbrahim Peçevi, *Tarih-i Peçevi*; as quoted in Woodhead, "Perspectives on Süleyman," p. 165.

Map 5 This crude, almost cartoonish, drawing of a janissary seems more comic than chilling. Still, his weapons and bearing do suggest a capacity for violence. Helffrich, *Kurtzer und warhafftiger Bericht*.

One of the most dramatic of the many consequences of this military expansion was monetary.[17] Unlike the Ottoman cavalry, which lived off the land for much of the year, the government had to barrack and pay the infantry directly out of the imperial treasury. As the janissary corps and its auxiliaries grew, the treasury became more and more strained. One result was chronic inflation of the Ottoman silver coins (a consequence of an abundance of silver from the Americas as well as the government's policy of recalling coinage and paying its troops in debased money).[18] A second effect was growing pressure upon the authorities to generate increased revenue, which eventually led to the overthrow of the *timar* system and its replacement with a series of innovative direct taxes and tax farms. A third consequence was a proliferation of firearms and the increased availability of those trained to use them, because their drain upon the treasury compelled the Ottomans to discharge auxiliary troops as quickly as possible.

Renovation at the turn of the seventeenth century

All of these transformations tended toward a decentralization of Ottoman authority. Price rises stimulated the creation of a cash economy and helped encourage regional commerce (thereby encouraging the rise of provincial centers to rival Istanbul); increasing expenditures helped shift tax collection into private hands, especially through the farming out of taxes in order to raise cash quickly for campaigns. It was the last of these changes, however – the pervasive distribution of firearms – that most directly and profoundly affected Ottoman subjects, as the following imperial decree issued in 1587 illustrates: "The governor of Suğla and the kadi of Ayasoluğ collected one-thousand firearms from brigands and mariners in the area. They are now being stored in the castle of Ayasoluğ. My imperial armory urgently needs these firearms... You should send them immediately."[19] This command not only suggests how the release of thousands of young men into the Anatolian countryside quickly created a public-order crisis, but also how desperately the Ottoman army, locked in combat as it was in the 1580s with Habsburg and Safavid troops, needed this *matériel* of early modern warfare.

[17] On these and other consequences of the changes in warfare, see Halil İnalcık, "Military and fiscal transformation in the Ottoman Empire, 1600–1700," *Archivum Ottomanicum* 6(1980): 283–337. On Ottoman monetary history, we now have Şevket Pamuk's exhaustive *A monetary history of the Ottoman Empire* (Cambridge, 2000).

[18] But see also Şevket Pamuk, "The price revolution in the Ottoman Empire reconsidered," *International Journal of Middle East Studies* 33.1(2001): 68–89.

[19] Başbakanlık Osmanlı Arşivi (Prime Minister's Archives), Istanbul, Turkey, Mühimme Defterleri (Registers of important events) 64, p. 95.

Unfortunately for the government, however, it was not simply a matter of confiscating muskets from ruffians and transferring them to the army. There also were issues of civil and personal security. In 1593, for example, the inhabitants of Urla, a western-Anatolian coastal village, presented a petition to the imperial government:

> The people in Urla pleaded "we live on the frontier and the ships of the misbeliev-
> ers have come many times and plundered our province. It is likely that they will
> come again. We need firearms in order to protect our property." This situation
> is confirmed. It seems both useful and good that the inhabitants of Urla and its
> surrounding villages retain their firearms . . . As for the rest, you should take their
> firearms for the state. But repeat the warning to the inhabitants of Urla that they
> must not give their firearms to outlaws.[20]

Such petitions suggest a dilemma for the Ottoman government that should resonate especially in modern America: what rights should subjects have to bear arms? The Ottoman answer to this question was simple for non-Muslims; they already were denied that right according to Islamic law. Islam, however, not only allowed but also insisted upon that same right for believers, so that the Muslim could pursue his religious duty to battle the infidel, which is exactly what the inhabitants of Urla claimed to be doing. So, Istanbul had little choice but to allow Muslim subjects to bear arms in Urla and elsewhere in the empire, which of course encouraged the dissemination of firearms and an increase in brigandage and violent crimes.

It also was one of several factors that drained power away from the central government. Sometimes, warlords and provincial notables began drawing upon the flood of footloose young soldiers to create body-guards or even personal armies that at times grew large enough to challenge imperial armies, as happened in western Anatolia. At other times, it was traditional leaders who mounted challenges against the central authorities. One of the most serious such threats occurred at the turn of the seventeenth century when the Kurdish commander Hüseyin Canpulatoğlu first worked in and out of Ottoman administration as the governor of Aleppo before being executed, at which time his vengeful nephew Ali mounted an effective rebellion against the state. Ali managed to sustain his revolt for two years; he controlled much of northern Syria, negotiated with and guaranteed protection to foreign communities in Aleppo, and was finally defeated in 1607 when the Ottomans raised an entire army against him.[21]

---

[20] Başbakanlık Osmanlı Arşivi, Mühimme Defterleri 71, no. 653.
[21] Bruce Masters, "Aleppo: the Ottoman Empire's caravan city," in Eldem, Goffman, and Masters, *Ottoman city*, pp. 30–31.

Such rebellions occurred throughout the empire in the early seventeenth century. They are striking in part because their instigators almost never sought the establishment of new regimes. Rather than demanding independence, for example, Ali accepted the governorship of Aleppo from the same state that had had his uncle executed. Most of these strongmen simply coveted larger roles in administration and decisionmaking within the empire – sometimes on behalf of themselves and sometimes on behalf of their people (the question of identity, then, could become an important consideration in these disputes). They considered the crisis at the center an opportunity to wrest some authority away from Istanbul.

There were other types of rebellions that shook the early seventeenth-century Ottoman world. Young, idle students (*softas*) from religious schools (*medreses*) participated in anti-governmental activities in many cities during the early decades of the century, with Istanbul itself becoming a center for such unrest. Here, a theologian named Mehmed of Birgi and his student, Kadizade Mehmed, condemned various Ottoman "innovative" practices such as the attribution of healing and other powers to the tombs of the dead, the establishment of religious endowments, the drinking of wine and coffee and the smoking of tobacco, and especially the many Sufi orders that weaved through the fabric of Ottoman society. Mehmed of Birgi even criticized the *fetvas* of Süleyman's influential *şeyhülislam* Ebu's-Su'ud, and his disciple took on the entire religious establishment. As a Friday preacher and a powerful public speaker, Kadizade Mehmed rapidly rose through the most important postings, until in 1631 he achieved the *imamship* of Hagia Sofia, the sultan's own mosque. His sermons emphasized the evils of innovation, often quoting such Prophetic traditions as "every innovation is heresy, every heresy is error, and every error leads to hell." This fiery activist urged his followers to cast off the accretions of time and myriad civilizations, and restore the Prophet Muhammed's community of believers.[22]

The *kadizadelis* (followers of Kadizade) proved themselves as great an ideological influence as provincial rebellions were military and political ones. As mosque preachers they certainly felt threatened by the encroachments of Sufi *tekkes*, coffeehouses, and taverns upon the mosque as hubs of communal life and social and political activism. Both coffee and tobacco had established themselves in the empire relatively recently,[23] and in this arena the *kadizadelis* received support from the sultan Murad IV, who mounted several harsh if futile campaigns against them. The dispute

---

[22] See Madeline C. Zilfi, *The politics of piety: the Ottoman ulema in the postclassical age (1600–1800)* (Minneapolis, 1988), especially pp. 129–37.

[23] On coffee in particular, see Ralph S. Hattox, *Coffee and coffeehouses: the origins of a social beverage in the medieval Near East* (Seattle, 1985).

Map 5   Murad IV (1623–40) is the best known of seventeenth-century
sultans. He ruled during the most troubled years of Ottoman political
transformation. Happel, *Thesaurus exoticorum*, sec. 4, following p. 14.

even became a *cause célèbre*, and made bitter grist for such pundits as the *şeyhülislam* Zekeriyazade Yahya, who castigated the *kadizadelis* with the couplet: "In the mosque let hypocrites have their hypocrisy. / Come to the tavern where neither pretense nor pretender be."[24]

Despite such critiques, the *kadizadelis'* apprehensions were not merely self-serving. Many of them thought both the Ottoman military and high Ottoman society inept and morally bankrupt, and envisioned the recurring debacles on the battlefield as well as the persistent palace scandals as manifestations of a turn away from true Islam. In important ways, they constituted a forerunner to Islamic reformers in later centuries who, whether Ottoman, Egyptian, Wahhabi, or Iranian, consistently have argued that the West has defeated Islamic states only because their ostensibly Muslim leaders have forgotten their religious roots. Bring back the Muhammedan state, they all argue, and Islam will again take up its leading rank in the world order.

In the mid seventeenth century, though, spiritual disquietude extended beyond Islam. For example, the Ottoman Jewish world collapsed into ideological and social turmoil in the 1650s and 1660s when a charismatic and enigmatic person named Sabbatai Sevi proclaimed himself messiah.[25] Sevi had grown up in Izmir, at that time a town of unmatched demographic and economic vitality, and social and intellectual edginess. Not only was this individual intellectually gifted and probably a manic-depressive, but a gamut of blasphemous notions pounded him from several directions and helped him formulate his own peculiar theosophy. Most obviously, Jewish mysticism, especially a particularly accessible and popular form know as Lurianic kabbalah, was esteemed and almost universally studied in this period. Sevi became enamored with this system of belief. The young mystic also may have combined such ideas with notions from deviant Sufi orders, with which he probably had contact in that volatile world. Furthermore, Sevi's own father and brother were brokers for English factors stationed in Izmir, and it seems likely that he heard from them of an England absorbed in its own religious upheaval.

Sevi, his principal "prophet" Nathan of Gaza, and their followers combined these ideas to concoct an eschatological theosophy that resonated throughout the Jewish world. When in 1665 his message finally was accepted after fifteen years of futile and wandering preaching, the vast majority of Jews everywhere embraced him as the messiah. In communities as distant as Amsterdam and Hamburg, Jews began to sell their

---

[24] As quoted in Zilfi, *Politics of piety,* p. 177.
[25] On whom see Gershom Scholem, *Sabbatai Sevi: the mystical Messiah, 1626–1676,* trans. J. Zwi Werblowsky (Princeton, NJ, 1973). For the Ottoman context, see Avigdor Levy, *Sephardim,* pp. 84–89.

goods and prepare to depart for Jerusalem. As Glückel of Hameln, who lived in Hamburg at that time, reports:

Many sold their houses and lands and all their possessions, for any day they hoped to be redeemed. My good father-in-law left his home in Hameln, abandoned his house and lands and all his goodly furniture, and moved to Hildesheim. He sent on to us in Hamburg two enormous casks packed with linens and with peas, beans, dried meats, shredded prunes and like stuff, every manner of food that would keep. For the old man expected to sail any moment from Hamburg to the Holy Land.[26]

If Sevi had such an influence even at the northwest fringe of the Jewish world, at its Ottoman center the near universality of such zeal triggered a real social and ideological crisis. Ottoman Jewish zeal also paralyzed commerce and set off an economic crisis in the empire at large.

The Ottoman government responded to such unrest in the state's cities and rural districts in various ways. As we have seen, it often attempted to accommodate the demands of rebellious chieftains and provincial governors and absorb them into administration. Many high officials met the first large wave of *kadizadeli* protests – which occurred in the 1630s – sympathetically. Murad IV even worked with Kadizade Mehmed to suppress some of the most blatant displays of luxury and aberrant behavior. A second great wave of agitation against the Sufi orders occurred in the 1650s. The *kadizadelis* at first succeeded in persuading the *şeyhülislam* to issue decrees against various Sufi lodges; in 1656, however, the newly appointed grand vizier Köprülü Mehmed ordered their leaders rounded up and exiled to Cyprus. The organization never fully recovered from this blow. A decade later, Mehmed Pasha's son, Ahmed, contended with turmoil among the empire's Jews by first imprisoning Sabbatai Sevi, and then giving him a choice of conversion to Islam or death. The messianic figure chose to preserve his life, which quickly quenched his movement.

One of the more effective and ultimately far-reaching governmental responses to social and political unrest was to station garrisons of janissary troops in city fortresses and employ them against crime and civil disorder. As early as the 1590s, for example, the state ordered janissaries posted in the castle of Foça on the western Anatolian coast onto vessels carrying fruits and vegetables to Istanbul to ensure that the produce was not diverted elsewhere. It also ordered teams of janissaries to patrol gardens and villages and to confiscate hoarded foodstuff.[27] Although the

---

[26] *The memoirs of Glückel of Hameln*, trans. Marvin Lowenthal (New York, 1977), p. 46.
[27] Başbakanlık Osmanlı Arşivi, Mühimme Defteri 72, p. 202; and 71, p. 230.

government's intent was to guarantee adequate supplies of provisions for the palace and capital city, such policies produced unintended consequences. Some of these janissaries soon settled into the local economies and societies, as was the case with several corpsmen in the western Anatolian town of Seferihisar who in 1617 not only refused to join a military campaign, but also used their status to insert themselves into the local economy as "butchers, bakers, and market people."[28] They also married into their new communities and found ways to pass on their privileges to their heirs.

In the long run, such policies helped to convert an effective army into little more than an incompetent police force, the aspect of the adjustment that historians have tended to emphasize. The insertion of the janissary corps into the body politic, however, also diffused loyalties and produced a new and potent elite in many Ottoman cities. The janissaries were able to use their rights as members of the *askeri* not only to maintain their ties with the regime but also to control local associations of artisans and municipalities. They probably encouraged the development of a sophisticated civil society, often became effective mediators between local and central authorities, and helped ensure that decentralized authority did not spawn political fragmentation.

Indeed, it was under Süleyman that a process began that reversed the movement toward monarchical absolutism, gradually stripped the sultan of power (if not authority), and by the 1660s had turned the Ottoman state into a type of oligarchy in which the sultan ruled only titularly. This political makeover was set in motion at the highest levels with the routine of marrying imperial daughters to Ottoman statesmen. The convention of doing so had been in place since the late fifteenth century. Under Süleyman, however, began the habitual marriages between imperial women and the most powerful administrators in the empire. Süleyman had nine grand viziers: three of them married his sisters, one married his daughter, and two married his granddaughters (of the other three, one was aged, the second was a notorious profligate, and the third was a eunuch).[29] This peculiar domestic arrangement that literally wedded statesmen to royalty became policy in the seventeenth century. Although it certainly encouraged the factionalization and politicization of the imperial household, it also provided wider access to the palace and, through linkage with the sultan's family, helped ensure that even the most powerful vizierial households would remain loyal and that centrifugal tendencies might stretch, but could not break, the Ottoman polity.

---

[28] Başbakanlık Osmanlı Arşivi, Mühimme Defteri 81, no. 367.
[29] Peirce, *Imperial harem*, pp. 66–67. Her discussion of the specifics of these policies is fascinating and enlightening.

Map 5 In the center background looms the Imperial Gate, a line of carriages pouring through its portal and into the first courtyard of Topkapı Palace. On the left stands the great Byzantine church Hagia Sofia, with two of its Ottoman-built minarets prominently displayed. D'Ohsson, *Tableau général de l'Empire othoman*, vol. III, before p. 283.

If not decline, then what?

One tenet of the "decline paradigm," as applied to monarchies, is that the realm reflects the ruler; in other words, a weak central government by definition denotes a feeble society, and an incompetent monarch must pull his kingdom down with him. Consequently, the rise of the decentralized state – that is, the emergence of tax farmers, provincial elites, and cities that rivaled Istanbul – becomes merely a symptom of a state and society in crisis because the "great man" who heads it lacks ability. In part because of the emergence of social history and its concern with long-term causation, in the 1950s and 1960s Ottoman historians began to question this precept, and looked beyond the sultan for causes of decline.[30] Even more recently, and perhaps because of the widespread fear of big government and bureaucratization that marks modern society and its acceptance of devolution and privatization as viable options to centralization, historians have begun to question whether this early modern empire ever declined at all.[31]

If defeats on the battlefield, ostensibly insane sultans, scandals in the imperial household, threats from *kadizadelis* and other reactionaries, rebellions in the provinces, chronically mutinous janissaries, and widespread bribery were not symptoms of decay, then what were they? Some have argued that they manifested not decline at all, but rather a series of crises, many of which were resolved in ways that actually strengthened the empire. We know that the empire did collapse in the early twentieth century, this line of reasoning goes, and our search for the roots of that inevitable descent to extinction has led us to privilege the idea of Ottoman decline to the exclusion of other phenomena and opposing explanations.

It has been suggested, for example, that the chronic financial shortfalls that seemed to have crippled the empire from the late sixteenth century also obliged the government to find creative ways to raise money, such as an increasingly elaborate system of tax farming and new direct taxes, and to reassess and attempt to supplant an obsolete land-tenure system that supported a decreasingly effective but politically influential cavalry. Supporters of this conjecture further claim that tax farming not only reformed collection, but also opened up the ruling class (the *askeri*) to much-needed new blood and new ideas, for some merchants and

---

[30] A good summary is in Norman Itzkowitz, *Ottoman Empire and Islamic tradition* (Chicago, 1972).

[31] The most persuasive presentation of these ideas (even though focusing on the eighteenth rather than seventeenth century) is Ariel Salzmann, "An *ancien regime* revisited: 'privatization' and political economy in the eighteenth-century Ottoman Empire," *Politics and Society* 21(1993): 393–423.

provincial notables were able to use the access to the elite that tax farms and other innovations provided to move into it.[32] This view is very different from the familiar claim that tax farming's principal consequences were to weaken central authority and to exploit and demoralize Ottoman subjects (the *reaya*).

The canonical account of the imperial household during the early seventeenth century also has lately been amended.[33] This period has long been referred to as "the sultanate of the women," because of the apparently extraordinary power of the sultan's mother, his sisters, his daughters, and other female members of his household that resulted from the seclusion of princes in the harem and a diffusion of power. The phrase was meant pejoratively; it was not overlooked that these women presided over the palace just as decline was considered to have settled in. The implication is clear: the empire rotted at its core when it relinquished authority into the hands of women (and especially "foreign" women, as so many of the wives, favorites, and servants were).

Take for example the role of the sultan's mother (*valide sultan*), who has been roundly condemned for drawing power from the sultan. One Englishman observed that Safiye Sultan, mother of Mehmed III, "was ever in fauor and wholy ruled her sonne: notwithstanding the Mufti and souldiers had much compleyned of her to ther king for misleading and Ruling him."[34] Many voices, both Ottoman and foreign, echoed this condemnation of female meddling in politics; many commentators both contemporary and modern considered the trend ruinous. There is another way to consider the situation, however. The imperial prince's mother's principal task long had been the training and protection of her son. In the fifteenth and sixteenth centuries, her job was finished when her well-prepared and grown-up offspring defeated his brothers and gained the sultanate. In the seventeenth century, however, when her ill-prepared son often became sultan despite youth or the incompetence spawned by a life of seclusion, it can be argued that it was appropriate that the *valide sultan* remain as his guide.

Some Ottomans certainly realized this important role. Mustafa Âli for one wrote of this same Safiye Sultan:

Though the sultan does not condone oppression, his viziers... bring unworthy ones into service and destroy the order of the world by bribe-taking. They do not

[32] Suraiya Faroqhi, "Politics and socio-economic change in the Ottoman Empire of the later sixteenth century," in Kunt and Woodhead (eds.), *Süleyman the Magnificent*, pp. 105–6.
[33] Especially by Peirce, *Imperial harem*.
[34] Henry Lello, *The report of Lello/Lello'nun Muhtırası*, ed. O. Burian (Ankara, 1952), p. 2; as quoted in Peirce, *Imperial harem*, p. 242.

tell the sultan the truth, ... Do they imagine it will be easier for them if, fearing his anger, they tell the *valide sultan*? She would never allow such disruption of order or such affairs to besmirch the reputation of her dear son.[35]

Âli does not reject the hypothesis that the government was rotten; he does though deflect its origin away from the sultan's mother and household. For him, the fault lies with venal retainers and the corrupt Ottoman administration.

The sultan's mother may be seen as acting almost as a regent, simply continuing the service she had provided as trusted counselor while her son was a prince. Despite being condemned because it brought women to power, the system provided the state with stability and protected the throne far more effectively and reliably than did regents such as Mazarin and Richelieu during Louis XIV's minority or İbrahim Pasha under the young Süleyman. Not only would no one doubt a mother's loyalty to the monarch, but the scheme kept power within that most important of Ottoman social units – the family. Consequently, it has been argued, not only did the empire survive, but the state weathered such structural adjustments and grew more resilient because of them.

A similar case can be argued in regard to Istanbul's interaction with its provinces. Anatolia, the Arab lands, and the Balkans directly and dramatically felt the consequences of decentralization, as the power to tax and make decisions spun out of the hands of the central state and into the possession of its agents and local notables and merchants. Again, these consequences, it long has been argued, weakened the Ottoman state and made life more difficult for its subjects. This summation, perhaps because of our suspicion of big government today, also has been challenged. Was it such a bad thing that Istanbul lost some decisionmaking power? The rise of a more complex and localized political structure in cities such as Aleppo and Izmir granted provincial authorities, merchants, even foreigners and farmers, a role in the management of their cities and communities. Izmir, for example, could establish itself as an entrepôt only when Istanbul became unable to reserve the produce of its hinterland for itself and was forced to relinquish to local notables decisions about what was grown and for whom. The tremendous wealth that this city ultimately generated, not least for the imperial treasury, may not have materialized under a strongly centralized state. Izmir is only one of many examples of such innovations in the provinces during the period of "decline."

Even culturally, most scholars have imagined early modern Ottoman civilization as sterile and derivative rather than creative and productive. The standards against which the empire is judged in such evaluations of

---

[35] Peirce, *Imperial harem*, p. 239.

course are all western European: the intellectual revolution of the Italian renaissance, the military revolution that helped usher in the nation state, the scientific revolution, the American and French democratic revolutions, and the English industrial revolution. It is certainly true that the Ottomans came up with nothing comparable to the theory of gravity or the steam engine or constitutional democracy. Nevertheless, there are other measures for creativity and achievement than the western European ones.

Those who embrace diversity and multiculturalism in the early twenty-first century, for example, must admire the enduring Ottoman aptitude for cobbling together myriad ways of life into something dynamic and original, even as western Europe invented the exclusive identities that helped propel it toward modern nationalism and imperialism, and then spawned modern racism, economic exploitation, and genocide. This tendency toward eclecticism, which was so noticeable in the emirate's first decades, persisted into the empire's mature years. In social life, it is seen in the continuing vigor of non-Muslim subject communities; in scholarship, it is evidenced in the conscious borrowings of Mustafa Âli and others from Arabic, Persian, and central Asian traditions;[36] in architecture, the public constructions of Sinan, who designed and supervised the raising of over 100 mosques, and his followers exploited and triumphantly transcended Byzantine and Seljuk traditions; and in poetry, Bâkî in the sixteenth century and Nâ'ilî in the seventeenth both vividly adapted Persian forms and imageries to their own times and cultures. Nâ'ilî produced such evocative and fatalistic *gazels* as:

> The simple-minded, who hope for
>   kindness from the sphere,
> Hope also for intoxication from an
>   overturned wine cup.
> Let the one who seeks benefit from the
>   decrees of the sphere,
> Be the one who hopes for tasty food
>   from a handful of straw.[37]

Nâ'ilî here and elsewhere proves himself as skilled a poet as his more illustrious predecessor Bâkî, using established forms to evoke razor-sharp and original associations and sensations. Despite his vividness, he unjustly has shared obscurity with many of his contemporaries simply because he wrote during a time of assumed Ottoman decay, obscurantism, and imitation.

---

[36] Fleischer, *Bureaucrat and intellectual*, pp. 273–92.
[37] Walter Feldman, "The Celestial Sphere, the Wheel of Fortune, and fate in the gazels of Nâ'ilî and Bâkî," *International Journal of Middle East Studies* 28(1996): 207–8.

The fact remains that the empire did in the end collapse, and that perhaps at first a malaise and then a decline must at some point have settled in before the final dissolution. Nevertheless, we can at least try to contextualize this hard reality by recollecting that the historian always has the advantage of hindsight. We need to remember that until after the First World War, the Ottoman Empire still existed. For someone living in 1669, for example, it surely seemed more likely that Italy rather than the Ottoman Empire would disintegrate; for someone living in 1789 it seemed more likely that France would cease to exist than that the Ottomans would do so; and even for someone living in 1919 it still must have seemed probable that some truncated Ottoman entity would endure. It makes good sense, I think, to conceive the early modern Ottoman world broadly as a multi-faceted entity rather than narrowly as a state embarking on a long death march, to insist that rot in some of its components did not mean consuming decay, and may even have reflected brilliance onto other features of the state and society. In other words, we need to understand that the decline model is not so much wrong as entirely insufficient; it conceals behind its visage simply too much that was creative, enduring, and resolute.

Part 2

The Ottoman Empire in the Mediterranean and European worlds

Kubad in Venice

The Venetians have no king, but their form of rule is a commune. This means that they agree on a man whom they appoint to rule over them by their unanimous consent. The Venetians (*Banādiqa*) are called Finisin. Their emblem is a human figure with a face which they believed to be that of Mark, one of the Apostles. The man who rules over them comes from one of the noted families among them.[1]

No one outside of the imperial council knew of Kubad Çavuş's secret instructions, and so he officially traveled to Venice as the representative not so much of his monarch or even his grand vizier, but of Joseph di Segura, an affluent and influential Jewish merchant of Istanbul.[2] Kubad much resented having to travel in the company of di Segura's son to the capital of the mysterious Venetian Empire, particularly since the long-standing treaty between the two powers had not yet been renewed after Süleyman's death while on military campaign in Hungary. The envoy now knew that the Ottoman government might not extend the agreement but instead was considering an invasion of the Venetian colony of Cyprus. Should that occur the bailo certainly would spend the war in an Ottoman prison; was there any doubt that the Venetians would take advantage of Kubad's presence to retaliate?

After an uneventful three-week sea passage – including a brief layover on the island of Chios which only the previous year had embraced the Abode of Islam and where the envoy delivered an imperial firman directing the new commander of Chios town's stronghold to stop beleaguering the island's inhabitants with demands for money and services – Kubad disembarked at Venice in late October 1567.[3] There he spurned both the palatial quarters provided

---

[1] Shihāb al-Dīn al-'Umarī, *al-Ta'rīf bil-muṣṭalaḥt al-sharīf* (Cairo, 1312 A.H.), p. 80; as quoted in Bernard Lewis, *The Muslim discovery of Europe* (New York, 1982), p. 211.

[2] On the envoy's journeys to Venice, see Arbel, *Trading nations*, pp. 135–40.

[3] On the question of "distance" in the early modern Mediterranean world, and the advantages and disadvantages of sea over land travel, see Kurt W. Treptow, "Distance and communications in southeastern Europe, 1593–1612," *East European Quarterly* 24.4(1991): 475–82. The author concludes that most couriers preferred the more reliable and secure if longer (perhaps forty or so days) overland route from Istanbul to Edirne, up the Maritsa River (by boat), Philippopolis, Pristina, Hercegovina, Cattaro, and (by boat) Venice, to

to honored guests by the Venetian government and the cramped and secluded housing offered by his compatriot Muslims, and instead took lavish shelter in a mansion rented by some of the Seguras' relatives on the serpentine island of Giudecca (Long Spine in the local patois).[4] The envoy almost immediately attained an audience with the Signory, the small body of powerful Venetians led by the doge.[5] The çavuş recognized that such an interview was comparable to an audience in the Imperial Divan. He also realized that although the Venetian heads of state had had years to study and learn the manners of his master the grand vizier Sokollu Mehmed Pasha, they were still trying to fathom Selim II's character.[6] The Venetians had no idea how he, Sultan Süleyman's successor, would react to a loss of merchandise and feared that the new padishah in retribution might lash out at Venetian shipping and ports in the Levant.

Kubad cannily concealed the awful truth that such a plan already was afoot and that a powerful faction was opposing the cautious grand vizier himself by counseling an all-out assault upon Cyprus, one of the last two major Venetian outposts in the eastern Mediterranean. Instead he exploited Venetian uncertainty to carry out his grand vizier's orders. The Ottoman envoy did not again have to visit the Signory; the Venetian government instead came to him at his residency on Giudecca island in the person of Alvise Grimani, a member of a powerful Venetian family.[7] Kubad found the choice curious, for Grimani's most famous forebear, by hesitating before guiding a Venetian armada against a much weaker Ottoman fleet, had forfeited to the Ottoman sultan Mehmed II the Venetian colony on Negroponte. Following this disaster, he had been banished from his city in disgrace, and then somehow had recovered decades later to become an octogenarian doge.

Over a period of two weeks, Grimani, Saruq, and di Segura spent several intense sessions with Kubad at his lodgings hammering out a compromise between

the sea voyage through the pirate-infested Aegean and Adriatic seas. A çavuş, perhaps even Kubad, did deliver such a *firman* to the commander of the castle on Chios (it is preserved as Başbakanlık Osmanlı Arşivi, Mühimme Defteri 7, p. 489). The Ottomans of course followed the lunar Islamic calendar, the dates from which I have chosen to convert for the sake of simplicity.

[4] We know where and how long Kubad stayed in Venice, but not why he remained or what he did there other than negotiate.

[5] On the Venetian state and its institutions, see Frederic C. Lane, *Venice: a maritime republic* (Baltimore, 1973), especially pp. 251–73.

[6] The Venetians expended great efforts and money in ascertaining Ottoman attitudes and policy. The bailo's later summary of Selim II's character, that he had "a very cruel face, and cruel he is indeed," while certainly unflattering may have been colored by the sultan's triumphant strike against Venetian Cyprus. The quotation is from Valensi, *Birth of the despot*, p. 39.

[7] Other than the existence of Grimani as his partner (see Arbel, *Trading nations*, pp. 134–36), the description of Kubad's negotiations with the Venetians and of his stay in Venice are all conjecture.

the two Jewish merchants. The Signory, anxious to calm Ottoman outrage, finally agreed to give Kubad over 10,000 ducats to carry back to the sultan to cover di Segura's imperial debts. In addition, the Venetian state transferred into the envoy's possession various other goods, including a supply of alum. The Ottoman official brought these goods with him back to Istanbul, where he employed them to build his own lucrative business.[8]

Kubad still had in his possession a copy of the hüccet *that fastened the Venetian bailo and thus the Venetian state to Ottoman justice. He informed Grimani that he might be willing not only to destroy the document but also to arrange that it be expunged from the record at the kadi's court in Galata. After some deliberation the Venetian Council of Ten consented to pay the envoy 2,000 ducats to do so: 1,000 for the certificate that he carried on his person and a second 1,000 upon fulfilling his task in Galata.*

By the end of November 1567 Kubad had sufficiently concluded his business in Venice. He decided not to set sail at once for home, however, for he was becoming intoxicated both with the authority he commanded in this foreign realm and with the delights of the place. In Istanbul, Galata had a reputation as an outpost for Christian European peoples and cultures. Venice, with its pageantry and riches, its markets and vendors, its inns, taverns, and brothels, made Galata seem pale and tawdry.[9]

The city's wines were a special treat. Kubad had often availed himself of Galata's offerings. Because of Islamic law,[10] *they were with few exceptions fermented in the cellars of diplomats only after a special dispensation (periodically withdrawn) from the imperial government. The envoy had not appreciated how foul these home-brews often were and he now understood how marvelous wine could be! The Venetians imported it from all over the Mediterranean world, and even though he quite enjoyed Majorcan* vin blanc *the envoy developed a particular fondness for, and more and more understood his* padishah's *mania for, the robust reds imported from Venetian Cyprus.*

In other ways though Kubad longed for the luxuries of his own city. The hard Venetian wooden chairs and tables were a poor substitute for the plush silk-upholstered divans to which he was accustomed. How could one enjoy one's leisure in a bolt-upright position? Congenial and languorous banter was nearly impossible! One might as well join the throngs wandering the canals or the nobs promenading along the Liste d'Oro. Even worse was the lack of coffee. Kubad had become a coffeehouse habitué soon after these marvelous haunts had appeared in Istanbul, where they were now a craze. The Venetians knew

---

[8] On this agreement and Kubad's expunging of the record of the bailo's promise to abide by Ottoman justice, see Arbel, *Trading nations,* pp. 138–39.

[9] On Galata, see Eldem, "Istanbul." On Venice see Jan Morris, *The world of Venice* (Orlando, FLA, 1993).

[10] On which, see Hattox, *Coffee and coffeehouses,* pp. 46–60.

nothing of such amusements, and how the envoy suffered without his relaxing habit.[11]

For almost three months after his negotiations had ended, the çavuş dallied. He maintained his residency on Giudecca even as he strolled through the squares and back alleys of the great city, explored its canals, scrutinized its Arsenals – both old and new – from afar, and as an esteemed guest attended meetings of its Senate. In the process, he learned much about the attitudes, procedures, and strengths and weaknesses of the Venetian polity as well as about the position of Ottoman merchants in the city's economy.

He absorbed even more during the long hours he whiled away in the shops, inns, and taverns of the Rialto deep in conversation with his shrewd if unlettered fellow countrymen. Despite an intense rivalry between them, their shared existence as expatriates had drawn together these Ottoman subjects – Armenian Christian, Greek Orthodox Christian, Jewish, and Muslim.[12] *Kubad quickly realized that, despite their sense of camaraderie, the trade of Ottoman subjects was delineated along ethno-religious lines. Ottoman Armenians dominated the exchange of Persian silks, Greeks of goods indigenous to the Ottoman realm, and Jews of precious stones, spices, and wines.*

The Muslim merchants' range was less certain.[13] *They were trying to carve out a monopoly as dispensers of mohair textiles, but were having a hard time of it. In one memorable conversation with several Turko-Muslims from central Anatolia (one of whom, of Circassian descent, was Kubad's own distant relative) they had complained bitterly about the difficulty of marketing Angora mohair in a Venice that could depend upon an inferior but serviceable enough mohair woven on Cyprus. The envoy conceded their contention that an Ottoman Cyprus would much enhance their business and intimated coyly that their ambitions might soon be realized.*

Although impressed and much enamored with the Serenissima, a deep resentment grew within Kubad's breast. In his beloved city of Istanbul, the large and thriving communities of Christians and Jews fraternized with Muslims

[11] According to the Ottoman chronicler İbrahim Peçevi, two Syrian brothers brought the first coffee shops to the city in 1555 (*Tarih'i Peçevi*, 2 vols. [Istanbul, 1864–67], vol. I: 363). D'Ohsson reports, perhaps with some exaggeration, that twenty years later there were over 600 of them in the city (cited in Hattox, *Coffee and coffeehouses*, p. 81). The drink did not arrive in Venice until 1580 (Jan Morris, *The Venetian Empire: a sea voyage* [London, 1990], p. 184).

[12] On Ottoman merchants in the international economy, see Halil İnalcık, "The Ottoman state: economy and society, 1300–1600," in İnalcık, *Economic and social history*, pp. 188–216. We have almost no information on relations between Ottoman merchants overseas. What follows is an informed guess.

[13] What follows relies in part on Cemal Kafadar, "A death in Venice (1575): Anatolian Muslim merchants trading in the Serenissima," *Journal of Turkish Studies* 10(1986): 191–218. We know little about Muslim Ottomans in Christian Europe during the early modern period.

on the streets and in the work places of the city. They worshiped openly in their churches and synagogues. One could even wander the quarter of Hasköy on a Saturday afternoon and watch believers pouring out of their synagogues, and the next morning observe the Christians attending church in Kumkapı. He himself had sat through both Christian and Jewish services, and welcomed misbelieving friends into his own house of God.

What a contrast Venice was, and what a gaudy hubris the Venetians exhibited, with their mangy flying lions and piteous Stato da Mar in which even churches, if Greek Orthodox (a mosque was unthinkable!), were often razed! The entire eastern-Mediterranean world loathed the officious Venetian colonizers.[14] *It is true that in Venice itself the state had permitted the Greeks, both exilic and Ottoman subjects, to establish their own community nearly 100 years before, and even to raise an almost-completed church, San Giorgio dei Greci, just next to the Arsenals. Nevertheless, the authorities had taken this measure reluctantly, and no Jews at all had been allowed to live in the city until some 50 years before. Now a small German Jewish community eked out a living as moneylenders, and survived in a cramped and overcrowded quarter, the Ghetto Novo. This community attended religious services not in temples built in honor of God, but in gloomy, moldering, and often-flooded private residences. It remained segregated in both its domestic and professional lives and existed under constant threat of expulsion.*

It had been a shock to learn that his Jewish associates, of Spanish rather than German origin and thus banned from residency in Venice, coveted similar refuge and considered such an abysmal shelter as Venice offered one of the choicest sites in Christendom! Such treatment was inconceivable in the Well-Protected Domains. After observing such squalor and impermanence how easy it was for Kubad to understand why Venice and other European cities served only as outposts in the Jewish commercial network, while Ottoman port cities had become its core.

Even more disheartening was the Venetian attitude toward his own co-religionists. The sixty or so Muslim merchants (not all Ottoman) laboring in Venice boasted no ghetto. They did not even have their own fondaco *in which to live, work, and worship.*[15] *Instead they lived scattered among the many neighborhoods adjoining the Rialto, the city's central marketplace. Here they were easy prey to the explosions of anti-Ottoman sentiments that occasionally visited the Catholic city. Even more disturbing was the resultant lack of community. There was no prospect that a mosque could be raised in that most Catholic state. The authorities were not willing even to provide running water in order to*

---

[14] Morris's *Venetian Empire* is a delightful and stylish if baldly orientalist journey through the ever-changing Venetian domain.

[15] They would gain such a factory, the *fondaco dei turchi*, sometime between 1592 (İnalcık, "Ottoman state," p. 189) and 1621 (Kafadar, "Death in Venice," p. 203).

accommodate the ordained ablutions that preceded a Muslim's five-times-daily prayer. Without such concessions Kubad could not imagine the organization of a substantive Ottoman commercial presence in Venice, or anywhere else in Christian Europe. He found it appalling to think that western Europeans considered this paranoid city-state a paragon of spiritual pluralism (or more usually censured its perceived permissiveness). If this was the ideal, how fanatical and stifling must the rest of Catholic Europe be![16]

[16] The social formations of western and Ottoman Europe are contrasted in Goffman, *Britons*, ch. 2.

5   The Ottoman–Venetian association

In an aesthetic sense at least, [Venice] still holds the east in fee, as the place where orient and occident seem most naturally to meet: where the tower of Gothic meets the dome of Byzantine, the pointed arch confronts the rounded, where hints and traces of Islam ornament Christian structures, where basilisks and camels stalk the statuary, and all the scented suggestion of the east is mated with the colder diligence of the north. Augsburg met Alexandria in these streets long ago, and nobody fits the Venetian *mis-en-scène* better than the burnoused sheikhs so often to be seen these days feeding the pigeons in the Piazza, leading their veiled wives stately through the Merceria, or training their Japanese cameras upon St Theodore like that contorted sightseer in the old picture.[1]

After the Ottomans conquered Constantinople in 1453 a few key cities more and more constituted that empire's nexus with the rest of Europe. Some, such as Venice or Vienna, existed outside of the empire; most, such as Istanbul, Izmir, and Aleppo, were Ottoman. The principal cause for this skewed situation can be found in the tenets of Christianity and Islam as displayed in the two halves of the early modern Mediterranean world. Whereas, in the Catholic northwest, Iberian and Italian states strictly restricted access to their cities, in the Muslim southeast the Ottoman state allowed diverse settlement.

There were some partial exceptions to this rule. The most famous certainly was Venice which as a port city drew its principal economic strength from seaborne commerce with the eastern-Mediterranean world. This contrast between the attitudes of the two civilizations produced a chronic and fascinating tension in Venice between a religious ideology that conceived a perpetual Crusade against the Islamic world and a situation that demanded bonds with Islamic states that controlled the international commercial routes to the east. From the point of view of the Catholic world, the Venetian reliance upon such trade led to a series of understandings with its Muslim adversaries that were deemed shameful.

---

[1] Morris, *Venetian Empire*, pp. 178–79.

The most infamous such case occurred in 1204, when Venetian ships diverted a crusading army intent upon undertaking holy war against the Seljuk Turks in Anatolia. Instead the vessels carried the army to Constantinople, resulting in an almost sixty-year occupation of the capital city of the Christian Byzantine Empire. The quick accommodation between Venice and the Ottoman Empire after 1453 is another notorious example of Islamic–Venetian accommodation. As soon as it heard of the fall of the capital of the Eastern Roman Empire, the Venetian Senate rushed an emissary with plenipotentiary authority to the new Ottoman capital to placate and negotiate terms with its conqueror, Sultan Mehmed II. Such accommodation, so often interpreted as sycophancy, not only produced Venetian commercial settlements in the principal cities of the expanding Ottoman realm but also engendered colonies of Ottoman subjects in Venice itself.

Uneasy harmony

Between the two most powerful states in the early modern eastern Mediterranean, the Ottoman and Venetian Empires, relations were always tangled. In retrospect, the two states seem to have been forever either on the brink of war or actually fighting. The truth is more complicated and more engrossing; the long war (1463–79) that dominated the last years of Mehmed II's reign was an anomaly. Between his death in 1481 and 1645 the two states fought only three relatively brief times, each about three years in duration. At other times the two empires coexisted, sometimes uncommonly well.

One can ascribe the relative calm to several factors. First of all, the fact that in the early sixteenth century each side had implacable enemies close to home complicated the Ottoman–Venetian relationship and tempted the two states to settle their quarrels amicably. For the Venetians, both mainland Italian rivals, spasmodically stirred up by the French and Spanish, and later the Holy Roman Emperor Charles V stretched the city-state's diplomatic skills, exhausted its treasury, and sapped its military strength.[2] For the Ottomans, land-based enemies to the east, south, and north confounded a government determined to push westward across the Mediterranean. Such distractions would block any future Ottoman monarch from menacing Italy as directly as had Mehmed II in 1480 when his troops landed at Otranto in readiness for an advance upon Rome, from which the Pope prepared to flee. Only the sultan's death in the following year aborted this bold lunge for the "red apple" of the West.

[2] On which, see Garrett Mattingly, *Renaissance diplomacy* (Boston, 1955) pp. 72–86.

Geographic considerations also loomed large in Ottoman–Venetian dealings. The Mediterranean Sea over which both states claimed pre-eminence bound its African, Asian, and European littorals not only culturally; it also politically divided its surrounding lands into eastern and western zones, the sea boundary being the slender passage between Sicily and Tunis. No state since the Roman one had constructed a system that unified the entire Mediterranean basin under a single sovereignty, and even Rome had been unable to hold both peripheries forever, but had in the fourth century broken apart into eastern and western realms.

In the fifteenth century political fragmentation on both sides of that line had left a vacuum into which a single city-state – Venice – had been able to step. In the second decade of the sixteenth century, however, the sultan Selim I conquered Syria and Egypt (1516–17) and brought the entire eastern Mediterranean under Ottoman control. At virtually the same moment a series of fortuitous inheritances united the western Mediterranean under the Spanish king Charles I (who was coronated as Holy Roman Emperor Charles V in 1519). Thus was launched the Habsburg hegemony over Catholic Europe. With the emergence of these two colossi, the Venetian Republic became transformed into a type of frontier principality. Just as an individual residing on a march or a borderland tends to adopt the attributes of its neighbors, indeed just as the Ottomans themselves in their formative years had mimicked many Persian and Byzantine forms, so more and more did Venice imitate its neighbors. The city-state simply could not compete with its two great rivals materially and militarily, and its survival depended increasingly upon diplomacy, accommodation, and emulation.

The acculturations of individuals at times became remarkable, and bore a striking resemblance to the plasticity found a century earlier on the Byzantine–Ottoman frontier. Andrea Gritti, a Venetian nobleman long stationed in Istanbul, for example, had five sons: one by his Venetian wife and four by his Ottoman concubine, with whom he lived during his long residency in Istanbul. This sojourn in an enemy's capital proved no liability for advancement: Gritti was elected doge in 1523 despite his love for Ottoman culture and the burden of his sons who were fully assimilated into the Ottoman world (and one of whom, Alvise, was the grand vizier's bosom friend and led an Ottoman army against the Hungarians at Buda).[3] Gritti and his progeny were among the most distinguished of a flood of ambitious Venetians who, captivated by the opportunities, vigor, and refinement of the Ottoman polity, stepped across and blurred

---

[3] On Gritti and his sons see Valensi, *Birth of the despot*, pp. 17–19; on his son Alvise, and especially on the latter's role in the transmission of culture between Venice and the Ottoman court, see Necipoğlu, "Süleyman the Magnificent," pp. 403–7.

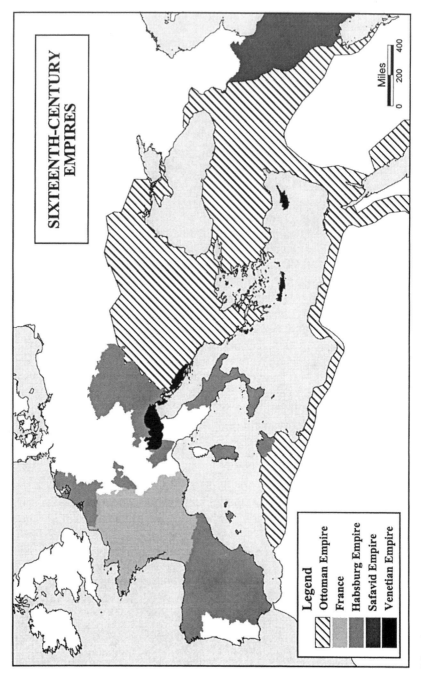

SIXTEENTH-CENTURY EMPIRES

Legend

- Ottoman Empire
- France
- Habsburg Empire
- Safavid Empire
- Venetian Empire

Miles
0 200 400

Map 6

the boundaries between the Christian and Islamic civilizations and became cultural chameleons, or even, in the vernacular of that age, "turned
Turk."[4]

Rounding out the western flank

Venetians were not the only "renegadoes" from Christian Europe. Far
better known and notorious were the thousands of Europeans who provided expertise to Muslim pirates and swelled corsair ranks in the Barbary
states. Nevertheless, because of the city-state's historical position as a
conduit for the distribution throughout Europe of spices and other im-
ports from the east and because of its many possessions in Greece and
the Aegean Sea, Venice (and thus Venetians) felt particular pressure to
indulge the Ottoman Empire. The results of the first of three Ottoman–
Venetian wars in the sixteenth century manifested this need. The engagement began in 1499 with the appearance of an Ottoman fleet in the
Ionian Sea.

The Ottoman campaign at the turn of the century in many ways was
unfinished business, a mopping-up operation from the long Ottoman–
Venetian War (1463–79) that had seen the Ottoman acquisition of the
Aegean islands of Negroponte and Lemnos and Venice's agreement to
pay a tribute in return for the right to trade in the Black Sea (which
the Ottomans, in possession of the Dardanelles and Bosphorus straits,
now absolutely controlled). The Ottomans had in that war captured all
of Greece except for the port towns of Lepanto, Modon, Coron, and
Navarino and their immediate hinterlands – which Venice retained as
colonies.

One reason for the new operation was an Ottoman determination to
seize control of these remaining Venetian strongholds. Equally critical
was Ottoman anger that the Venetians had refused refuge in a Cypriot
port to an Ottoman fleet, battered and made vulnerable by a tempest that
had struck it while en route to Egypt to engage the Mamluks. Particularly
maddening for Ottoman statesmen was that Venice had gained Cyprus –
indirectly to be sure and at the expense of a French despot rather than
the Ottomans – as an incidental result of the earlier contest between the
Venetian and Ottoman empires. Finally, the sedentary Sultan Bayezid II,
his younger brother Cem having finally passed away (however suspi-
ciously) in Naples in 1495, may have felt suddenly free to go to war
against those Christians who had held Cem hostage and thereby arrested
Ottoman expansion westward.

---

[4] To turn Turk had no national, ethnic, linguistic, or even cultural connotation. It simply
signified conversion to Islam.

This turn-of-the-century war also signified a further Ottoman incorporation into the European political infrastructure. Several of the lesser
Latin states – as well as France – had goaded the Ottomans to attack,
presumably in order to distract the Venetians from the Italian mainland,
which concurrently was tormented with chronic civil conflict and swarm-
ing with French and Spanish armies.[5] By accepting the Ottomans as a
player in this complicated war these states helped marginalize ideology in
the Mediterranean world.

In June 1499, Küçük Davud Pasha lifted anchor at Gallipoli and maneuvered a fleet, the size of which startled and terrified Venetian observers, out from the Dardanelles southwestward. At the same time the
Sultan Bayezid II marched a large army overland from Istanbul to Edirne
and down toward the Greek peninsula. The plan, not particularly innovative in itself (Xerxes had tried much the same thing some two millennia
before), was to crush Lepanto between the Ottoman army and navy. More
novel was the ability of the Ottoman state to float an armada large and
competent enough to challenge the Venetians in open battle. Mehmed II
had employed a fleet during the siege of Constantinople, but in an auxiliary capacity. He also had used one during the conquest of Negroponte,
but merely to assist the movement of troops from the mainland. Even
with land troops to back him, in neither 1453 nor 1470 would he have
dared risk conflict with a whole Venetian fleet. Thirty years later the great
sultan's son was prepared to use his flotilla more aggressively.

Even though the Ottomans did not take the Venetians unawares, their
naval operation proved decisive in the conquest of Lepanto. Antonio
Grimani, the Venetian commander, had his own fleet waiting at Modon,
from which he advanced to guard the passageway into the Gulf of Corinth.
Despite winds that favored the Venetian force, two Venetian and one
Ottoman vessel went down in flames after a brief engagement and the
outmanned Venetian commander panicked and withdrew to the island
of Corfu where he awaited reinforcements. This retreat enabled Küçük
Davud Pasha to rush up the straits into the Gulf of Corinth, where the
combined might of the Ottoman army and navy forced Zoan Mori, the
commander of the fortress, into a quick surrender.

The loss of the town of Lepanto doomed the Venetian cause, for control
of the entire Corinthian shoreline gave the Ottoman galleys, able both to
re-provision easily and to use the shore to its advantage, an insurmountable strategic edge in any coastal engagement. Even though Grimani
later was stripped of his honors and exiled from Venice because of his
ignoble retreat, neither he nor any other Venetian commander had ever

---

[5] On which see Francesco Guicciardini, *The history of Florence*, trans. Mario Domandi
(New York, 1970), pp. 79–117.

confronted such an armada, and it is doubtful that a more experienced commander would have been any less baffled.

Venice had long since accepted the near invincibility of Ottoman ground troops. Nevertheless, the Republic's naval superiority throughout the fifteenth century had helped preserve its seaborne trade and protect its islands and ports even in the littoral heartland of the Ottoman world. Despite the arrival of an Ottoman army before Lepanto's walls in 1499, the Venetian garrison at first gave little thought to submission. After all, the defenders must have reasoned, the sea-lanes remained open and their potent navy was cruising the Adriatic and could quickly reach Lepanto with provisions and reinforcements. When the fleet that arrived in early August flew not Venice's lion of St. Mark but the Ottoman star and crescent, the startled defenders succumbed at once to what seemed the inevitable.

The heat of the Greek summer already had driven Bayezid II from the lowlands surrounding Lepanto. So it was not he but Mustafa Pasha, the military commander (*beylerbeyi*) of Rumeli, who accepted the figurative key to the city. After this victory the Ottomans set out to secure the Gulf of Corinth from seaborne attack by raising fortresses at its entrance, sent home the fleet (which had accomplished its amphibious operation), and soon thereafter ended the campaigning season. Even though the Ottomans still may have deemed their navy ancillary, it had comported itself well, for the first time having challenged and repulsed a Venetian armada.

During the winter of 1499–1500 the Venetians sent an envoy to Istanbul, Lui Maventi, who in audience with Bayezid demanded freedom for Venetian merchants and the restoration of Lepanto. The sultan allegedly replied: "If you want peace, you will surrender Modon, Coron, and Navarino and pay an annual tribute."[6] This response displays an assurance that must have thoroughly unnerved the Venetian envoy and Senate. It also produced an impasse, and Maventi departed.

The Ottoman campaign against Venice's Morean strongholds resumed the following summer. Bayezid again used his new-model navy at Modon, just as he had the year before, to fend off a Venetian relief fleet as his army enveloped and overwhelmed the city in mid-August 1500. The Ottomans next took Navarino and Coron without a fight and by 16 August the entire Peloponnesian Peninsula had yielded to Ottoman arms, an accomplishment that stripped the Venetians of their last mainland territories in the eastern Mediterranean and rounded out Ottoman dominion along its western frontier.

---

[6] İsmail Hakkı Uzunçarşılı, *Osmanlı Tarihi*, Vol. II: *İstanbul'un fethinden kanuni Sultan Süleyman'ın Ölümüne kadar* (Ankara, 1943), p. 218.

Not that the Venetian campaign was a complete disaster. In the following year the Republic's navy again commanded the seas because of that state's success finally in convincing the Pope, the Knights of St. John, and the Hungarians to ally with it (although Venice never again would "do it alone" against its Muslim rival). This "holy alliance" first attacked the island of Mytilene, just off the coast of Ottoman Anatolia. When this campaign failed Benedetto Pesaro, Grimani's successor as Venetian admiral, convinced his allies to backtrack into the Ionian Sea and strike against the island of Levkas, which they captured. Pesaro was able to secure also for Venice the important Ionian islands of Corfu, Cephalonia, and Zante. This cluster of Ionian islands was strategically crucial for they (and especially Corfu) guarded access to the Adriatic Sea, which Venice chose to regard as its own.

The war ended with this reassertion of Venetian sea power, for by the end of 1502 both sides had had enough. Bayezid might have been tempted to push his advantage, particularly since the Ottomans must have been feeling vengeful against Venice's Hungarian ally who had that summer pillaged villages along the frontier – particularly in the Danubian valley near Vidin – and brazenly brandished spiked rows of severed Ottoman heads before the palace of Ladislas II in Budin. Nevertheless, rumors from the east that the Safavid Shah Ismael of Persia might soon strike against Ottoman territory made it seem urgent to calm the empire's western frontier. Consequently, on 14 December 1502 the Ottomans and Venetians agreed to a treaty that not only conceded to the Ottomans their Greek gains and to the Venetians their Ionian ones but also committed the Venetians to an annual tribute of 10,000 ducats. In short, this treaty granted just what Bayezid II had demanded two years earlier.

From the military standpoint, the 1499–1502 war seems a decisive moment in the construction of a hardening line between the Christian and Islamic Mediterranean worlds. As a result of this conflict the frontier between the Ottomans and the Venetians became almost entirely coastal, and thus clearly delineated. This hard geographic and ideological division is illusive, however, for in the military sphere a shift in power continued through the century, and in other spheres borders between the empires in fact were becoming more permeable and in some instances fading away entirely.

The dissolving of barriers was particularly pronounced in economic and diplomatic arenas. In the former case the Venetians concentrated with renewed vigor upon preserving and expanding commercial corridors into the Ottoman Balkans, Black Sea, Anatolia, and (after 1516–17) Syria and Egypt. This strategy secured commercial agreements with the Ottoman government, settled large trading communities in Istanbul

and other Ottoman cities, and taught the Republic much about the per-
plexing world of Ottoman politics and society. The foundation of this
emerging bond was a flood of expatriate businessmen and a skilled corps
of consuls, bailos, and envoys – in other words a sophisticated diplomatic service – who could serve as the interface between the Ottoman
and Venetian states. The resulting societal overlap inescapably produced
myriad Venetian cultural chameleons.

A seaborne ascendancy

The war of 1499–1502 demonstrated a novel Ottoman competence at sea.
This new ability matured as the century progressed, due as much to native
know-how as, in the more accepted explanations, to the service in the Ottoman fleets of skilled Greek mariners or the celebrated coalition with the
deys of the Barbary Coast, the most celebrated of whom was Hayreddin
Barbarossa Pasha. By 1537–39 when the second Ottoman–Venetian War
of the century occurred, a fully developed Ottoman navy with Barbarossa
at its helm was able not only to confound and vanquish the combined
forces of the entire Catholic Mediterranean world, but also to take the
war to Venetian citadels in the Aegean Sea and even into the Adriatic.

The immediate cause of this war was the Habsburg Charles V's ongoing
tussle with the Ottoman Süleyman for supremacy over the Mediterranean
seas. Charles two years earlier had enjoyed a victory (which would prove
ephemeral) with his conquest of Tunis.[7] The Pope's ability to pull together an alliance between the papacy, Venice, and the Habsburg Empire
established favorable conditions for a direct strike against the Ottomans.
Venice proved the Pope's most reluctant ally in this strong coalition. The
city-state had spent the previous thirty-five years cultivating Ottoman
friendship. In the process many of its most influential notables had spent
time in Istanbul. Some, such as Andrea Gritti through his long residency
in that great city, his founding of a household there, and the presence of
several of his sons in the Ottoman administration, had put down deep
roots in Ottoman society. In 1537 the Venetian Senate declared war only
after long debate and despite the impassioned opposition of Gritti and
others of like mind. Almost as if it were a civil war rather than one between
states, the intersection between the two societies was such that many a
Venetian father found himself fighting his son and a Venetian brother
killing his brother.

In this war, the Ottomans repeated their earlier strategy, so successful in the Morea, of blending their army and navy into an amphibious

7 See especially Hess, *Forgotten frontier*, pp. 71–99.

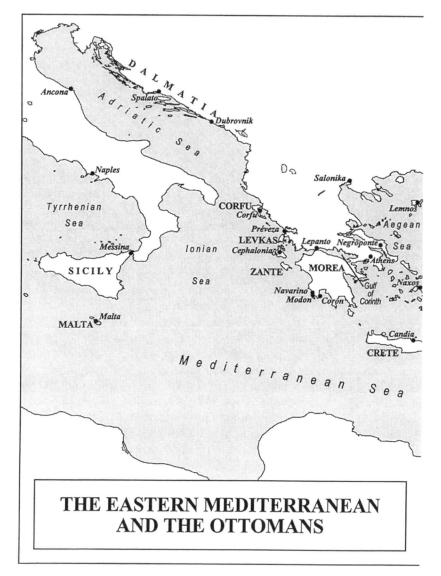

THE EASTERN MEDITERRANEAN
AND THE OTTOMANS

Map 7

machine that conducted pincer movements against Venetian and other
strongholds as the navy used the cover of castles, armies, even beaches
to repulse relief fleets. A vital novelty was that the navy no longer was
auxiliary to the army; now it was ground troops that attended mariners.

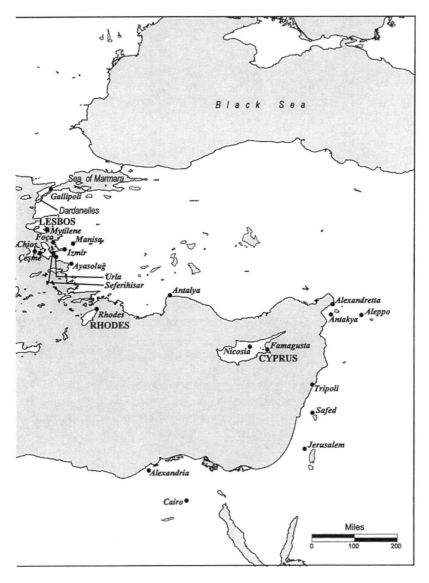

In short, Ottoman command of the entire eastern-Mediterranean littoral now allayed its fleet's logistical obstacles. Whereas the huge crews of the galleys of Catholic states risked fatigue whenever they pushed into eastern seas, Ottoman vessels had to pass all the way into the Tyrrhenian

Sea before they were further than a day or two from fresh water, victuals, munitions, and manpower.[8] This strategic gain is evident in the very first engagements of the war, when Barbarossa aggressively sailed up the Adriatic into the heart of the so-called "Venetian sea" even as two of the sultan's sons, Mehmed and Selim, led an army to Avlonya on the coast of Ottoman Albania. The army's mission was not only to put down a local revolt that Venetian agents had helped inspire, but more importantly to furnish the fleet, so far from its home base, with men, provisions, and arms.

When Andrea Doria, the Genoese commander of the combined Catholic fleet, retreated to the Sicilian port of Messina after a brief skirmish, Sultan Süleyman ordered an attack on the Venetian island of Corfu, which lies opposite Otranto at the mouth of the Adriatic Sea. This operation was completely seaborne and thus exposed Barbarossa's flank; he could not depend upon direct strategic support from Ottoman Albania. In addition, he encountered an innovative defense – squat and broad walls engineered expressly to absorb the force of Ottoman artillery. The invasion failed. Then in the following summer Barbarossa turned to the Aegean archipelago with much better results. Here he took the island cluster of Naxos and several other Venetian isles and pillaged towns along the coastlines of Venetian Crete.

The major battle of this war was fought at sea in 1538, off the coast of Préveza. Andrea Doria's fleet perhaps was larger than the Muslim one, but was disadvantaged because it had to perform in Ottoman coastal waters. With his galleys' backs defended and his crews replenished and kept fresh by the Ottoman units along the Albanian shores, Barbarossa could play a waiting game. The personnel of the enemy fleet, exposed on the open seas, gradually weakened. Reluctantly, Doria had to order a retreat, at which point the numerically inferior Ottoman fleet, with fresh oarsmen driven steadily forward by its pugnacious admiral, darted out and overtook the now bedraggled allied flotilla between Préveza and the island of Levkas on 28 September 1539.

In the ensuing engagement Doria found himself with neither the space to prevent the Ottomans from ramming his ships nor the winds to maneuver behind them. The consequence was a rout of the Catholic forces. Whereas thirty-six Alliance ships were captured, about 3,000 mariners enslaved, and Doria forced to flee ignobly to the haven of Corfu Town, Barbarossa lost not a single ship (ironically a storm two days later threw his fleet against the Dalmatian coast and wrecked sixty or seventy galleys).

---

[8] On this war and the ones of 1565 and 1570–73, see John Guilmartin, *Gunpowder and galleys: changing technology and Mediterranean warfare at sea in the sixteenth century* (London, 1974).

In the treaty that followed, Venice, the most reluctant ally, was the big loser. The Sultan Süleyman compelled the Serenissima not only to sign over to the Ottomans its fortresses along the Dalmatian coast but also to relinquish formally the Aegean islands that the Ottoman fleet had taken the previous summer.

The Pope and his allies had coerced an unwilling Venetian Senate into the war of 1537–39, from which Venice lost more than any other state. The ability of the Ottoman navy simultaneously to restrain a combined Catholic array and to overpower several Venetian fortresses and islands proved that the city-state no longer could mobilize a convincing military presence in the eastern Mediterranean. Its appearance in those seas would thereafter hinge upon the indulgence of the rival Ottoman state. In these circumstances, Venice was likely to drift into an accommodation with Ottoman ambitions and even to launch a metamorphosis toward the Ottoman "way." The only alternative would have been for the "mistress of the seas" to forsake its maritime empire. Venetian awareness of its martial frailty probably was the principal impetus for the city-state's construction of a sophisticated diplomatic grid, in which Istanbul was to become the most vital posting in the late sixteenth century.

Even more devastating than the loss of a scattering of Aegean islands was that the Ottomans now were able to incorporate into their empire much of the southeastern Adriatic coast. The Venetians long had considered the coastlines of this sea as their own and had succeeded in staking their claim against the city-state of Dubrovnik (Ragusa), the papal port of Ancona, and other regional pretenders. To do so against the behemoth that now governed much of Dalmatia (from where Venice long had drawn most of its precious mariners and oarsmen) and that possessed almost invincible armies and navies lay far beyond the Republic's means. The loss of the Dalmatian coast and the potential dismantling of the vital commercial termini that bound the Balkans to the rest of Europe warned against confrontation and more than ever counseled accommodation and adaptation.

Setback in the west

It probably was for these reasons that the Venetians missed the siege of Malta in 1565, the first major Ottoman naval reverse of the sixteenth century. The Islamic state sought the island of Malta in part because it had become the sanctuary of the crusading Knights of St. John after the Sultan Süleyman threw them out of Rhodes in 1522. More vital, however, was the island's location at the juncture between the eastern and western Mediterranean seas. The reach of galleys, the principal weapon of early modern Mediterranean naval warfare, was limited. Not only did they have to touch friendly shores every two weeks or so because of their large crews of oarsmen and soldiers who consumed vast quantities of food and water, but also they could not safely sail winter seas. Consequently, for fleets as for armies, provisioning demands and campaign seasons severely limited ranges of operations.

Just as Vienna may have represented a logistical limit for an Ottoman army whose commander and many of whose troops set out from Edirne or even Istanbul each year, so might Malta have signified a boundary for a fleet that had to embark at the Dardanelles and could move only as quickly as its slowest vessels (perhaps two nautical miles per hour). Furthermore, since neither any Balkan nor Barbary city had the resources to support the vast numbers involved in an Ottoman mobilization (although the state exploited each region as far as it could), all major campaigns had to draw upon Istanbul's vast resources.[9] Similarly, just as the conquest of Vienna, which did have the means to become a new logistical center, might have opened central Europe to the Ottomans, so the conquest of Malta, where a substantial host could have wintered, might have exposed Italy and even Iberia to their armies.

The siege of Malta miscarried, if only just, for the same reasons that each siege of Vienna faltered. It was certainly not because of incompetence; Guilmartin has proved the great skill with which both the Ottomans under Piyâle Pasha and the Spaniards under Don Garcia de Toledo maneuvered, even calling this engagement "the apex of sixteenth-century amphibious warfare."[10] Nevertheless the commander of Ottoman forces had much longer and more brittle lines of communication than did his Spanish foe, and he failed to take the fort of St. Elmo, which protected the entrance into the Grand Harbor at Malta, quickly enough to seize the stronghold at Malta Town before his men and the weather collapsed. Because he was so far from home Piyâle Pasha could afford to make no errors at all; the few he did make were enough to deprive him of essential time and resources.

Another critical factor in this Islamic state's setbacks at Malta as well as Vienna involved methods that had yielded earlier conquests. In their thrusts into the Christian Balkans and Muslim Arab lands the Ottomans had relied upon the abuses of alien administrations to gain support from indigenous subjects. Just as in the fourteenth and fifteenth centuries the Ottomans became adept at stirring up Greek Orthodox passions against

[9] The "natural limits of expansion" thesis has been challenged though. See, for example, Caroline Finkel, *The administration of warfare: the Ottoman military campaigns in Hungary, 1593–1606* (Vienna, 1987).

[10] *Gunpowder and galleys*, p. 178.

Catholic lords in the Balkans, so in the early sixteenth century did they exploit an inept Mamluk administration, taking advantage of its structural inability to blend indigenes into political and administrative life, and its impotence against Portuguese incursions into the Indian Ocean to garner the assistance of Syrian and Egyptian Arabs against alien rulers.

Unlike these earlier situations the religions, languages, and even ethnicities of the Austrian and Maltese inhabitants matched those of their rulers. Furthermore, centuries of conflict and indoctrination had thoroughly institutionalized in these societies a demonization of the "Turk," whom the inhabitants had never resided with and therefore could not imagine as human beings. Consequently, not only could the invaders not implement the effective dividing-and-conquering feature of the Ottoman method of conquest,[11] but they confronted natives who carried a communal horror of Islam and the Ottoman state and zealously resisted the invaders. Süleyman's army in 1529 and Piyâle Pasha's navy in 1565 were not only the victims of insurmountable logistics; each was left isolated in a remote territory populated by a malevolent people. The odds simply proved too long and the Ottoman state never figured out how to shorten them.

Occupying an Aegean island

Such was not the case in the eastern Mediterranean, where on several islands a Catholic nobility still ruled over Greek Orthodox commoners. Even though the Ottomans seemed invincible in this region, in the 1560s even the Aegean itself was not yet entirely theirs. Chios, a strategically and economically vital island nestled against the central Anatolian coast, lingered through Süleyman's entire reign in the hands of the Giustiniani, a prominent Genoese family. A scattering of small islands, along with Crete, which stretches across the southern approach to the Aegean Sea, remained Venetian.

The long-lived character of these Latin satellite communities reflects more a lack of Ottoman concern about them than effective resistance. Certainly after the battle of Préveza Venetian and Genoese colonials accepted, with however much loathing, Ottoman dominion over the Aegean basin. Most of them relinquished genuine liberty – usually yielding a tribute, guaranteeing Ottoman commercial access, and tolerating intermittent pillaging by Muslim corsairs – in return for nominal authority. The Sublime Porte in return invested these petty potentates with the illusion of sovereignty.

---

[11] On which see İnalcık, "Ottoman methods of conquest," pp. 104–29.

Chios, ruled since the fifteenth century by a Council of Twelve over which the Giustiniani family presided, is a case in point.[12] In return for continuing autonomy after Mehmed II's conquest of Negroponte in 1470, the island's elders agreed to pay an annual tribute which Selim I in 1512 had raised to 10,000 ducats as part of a renewed treaty (really an *ahdname* or imperial decree declaring specific privileges and responsibilities) that granted the Chians notable commercial rights.

Probably more important than this tribute, produced through customs revenue and the export of silks and resin from the rare mastic tree, was the island's situation as a "middle port" between the Ottoman Empire and the western Mediterranean Sea and Europe. Throughout the early sixteenth century, bullion and textiles from western Europe and cottons and dried fruits from western Anatolia were funneled through Chios Town via its sister mainland port of Çeşme. In this regard its situation differed little from Dubrovnik's, which concurrently served as an Adriatic entrepôt for the Ottoman Balkans in return for some autonomy.[13] Both also manifested that fecund pluralism associated with crossroads between civilizations.

An economic recession in the 1560s put the Chian tribute seriously into arrears. This monetary crisis, combined with Ottoman frustration at the botched invasion of Malta in 1565 and suspicions that the Genoese of Chios had given intelligence to the Knights of St. John that had helped frustrate that assault, sufficed to alter Chios's fortunes. One of Sultan Süleyman's last angry acts in the spring of 1566 as he prepared for his "death march" into Hungary against the Habsburgs was to order his grand admiral (*kapudanpaşa*), Piyâle Pasha, to confiscate the island.

The ease with which the naval commander implemented this command confirms that the island's long semi-independence had been an Ottoman artifice. Rather than moving directly against it, Piyâle Pasha anchored his seventy or so vessels at Çeşme. To this mainland port, only hours away from Chios, he summoned many of the island's aristocracy, and then detained them. Only then did he ferry his troops across the thin channel, occupy the Genoese fortress in Chios Town, and appoint as its commander Muzaffer bey, the *sancakbeyi* of Kırşehir, who at once began restocking its munitions and repairing its fortifications.

Having accomplished his task virtually without bloodshed, Piyâle Pasha loaded Chios's principal Genoese families aboard his galleys and sailed off for the Black Sea port of Kefe. The admiral probably had meant to sell these former overlords in the slave markets that marked the northern

[12] Philip P. Argenti, *Chius Vincta or the occupation of Chios by the Turks (1566) and their administration of the island (1566–1912)* (Cambridge, 1941).
[13] On which see chapter 6 below.

fringe of the Empire. The Genoese somehow avoided this fate, however. The Ottoman government later resettled most of them in the old Genoese colony of Galata, just across the Golden Horn from Istanbul. A few of the boys were taken to the palace of İbrahim Pasha in Istanbul itself, where they were converted to Islam and became servants of the sultan.

Ottoman handling of the Greek majority on Chios was even milder. In fact, the populace probably knew that its island's incorporation into the Ottoman polity would be virtually painless, perhaps even an improvement over the notoriously brutal Latin dominion. Recognizing the Greek loathing of the Latin goes far toward explaining the ease not only of this occupation but also of other Ottoman progressions into the Aegean and Balkan worlds. The foundation of Ottoman successes was moral rather than military; former regimes had been simply loathsome. Even though Ottoman conquests liberated no one (if liberation was even conceivable in an early modern context), they did produce both the cessation of Catholic contempt for the heresy of Greek Orthodoxy (often manifested in a fiercely proselytizing clergy and the razing of churches) and some relief from the onerous taxes and levies that Latin imperialists so infamously exacted from their Greek vassals.

Such amelioration certainly was the immediate result of the Ottoman occupation of Chios in 1566. Without delay the government undertook to survey the peoples and products of the island, in part to determine Chios's assets and exploit them fully and consistently and in part – since most inhabitants had joined the Abode of Islam (*dar al-islam*) without resistance – to establish the inhabitants' customary laws and minimize any spiritual or legal disruptions that inescapably would accompany the island's integration into the Ottoman world.

The outcome was an extraordinary tax break for the island's Greek Orthodox, Armenian, and Jewish inhabitants, an increase in immigration from other parts of the empire, and an immediate upswing in Chian commerce. The new regime reduced to perhaps 8 percent the tithe upon the Greek peasantry, which under the Genoese may have reached 50 percent of agricultural production. At the same time it scrupulously regulated the island's thriving silk industry, monopolized its lucrative trade in mastic, and strove to sustain its position as a middle port between civilizations. Ultimately of course the Ottomans expected the resources and peoples of Chios (as with any occupied territory) not only to sustain its own garrison, but also to contribute troops to the government's military and treasure to its coffers.

The palace and populace in Istanbul long had benefited just as much as did the Genoese from the proximity of this entrepôt to the fertile Anatolian seaboard. The Sublime Porte considered that territory, so rich in cottons and grapes, olives, figs, and other fruits, a chief provisioning zone for the capital city. As such, the government discouraged any diversions from this fundamental purpose. Consequently, it energetically stifled the development of mainland towns that might have evolved into commercial or demographic competitors with Istanbul, and in 1566 Foça, Çeşme, Izmir, and other western Anatolian port towns remained little more than transit stations for products en route to Istanbul and western Europe via Chios.

The legal code (*kanunname*) that prefaces the Chian cadastral survey (*tapu-tahrir*) of 1567 reflects the Ottoman intent to sustain the island as the region's paramount commercial interchange. In it, Selim II sheltered the island's Greek Orthodox, Jewish, and even Latin communities from potential exploitation by Muslims and by each other. He also agreed to exempt Chian children from the *devşirme*, to confirm all prior legal decisions, and to permit (with the kadi's consent) the repair of demolished, damaged, and abandoned Greek Orthodox churches, and also retained and strove to broaden the established Genoese commercial system. Istanbul allowed Chians to transfer luxury and other goods, especially silks, wheat, and barley, duty-free, imposed no new charges upon other goods imported from the mainland, exempted from duty vessels in transit from the Black Sea unless their merchandise was marketed on the island itself, and endorsed Çeşme's special commercial relationship with the island.

Venetian Cyprus subdued

The ease with which the Ottomans had occupied Genoese Chios probably encouraged the government's militancy. Indeed, it may be said to have constituted the opening act in the War over Cyprus, the most celebrated Ottoman–Venetian drama of the sixteenth century.[14] Cyprus's location within sight of the southern Anatolian coastline and close to the caravan terminals of Syria made it strategically and economically vital. Under the French Lusignans it had constituted the last of those peculiar Catholic feudalities that had sprouted up along the Syrian coast after the first Crusades. Also as a result of its location it has always been subject to invasion and consequently has long boasted a mélange of peoples; until divided into "Greek" and "Turkish" zones in the twentieth century the island had been wildly multi-religious, ethnically diverse, and polyglot.

The Signory, desperate for an eastern Mediterranean island to replace Negroponte, lost to the Ottomans in 1470, spent the next two decades

---

[14] On Cyprus, see Sir George Hill, *A history of Cyprus*, Vol. III: *The Frankish Period, 1432–1571* (Cambridge, 1948).

maneuvering for Cyprus (even becoming its figurative paterfamilias in order to gain it). In 1489 the Republic finally attained control of it as the result of a clever dynastic marriage and naked force.

Over the next eighty years the Venetians bent the island's people and topography to their particular requirements. In its most grim hour of imperiousness, the Republic demolished ancient and often exquisite edifices, constructed in their places ugly barricades and fortresses specifically designed to frustrate the huge artillery pieces that the Ottomans had employed so effectively against Constantinople, and fashioned a cruel colonial administration that pitilessly taxed (at least one-third of production) and corvéed (for as many as three days each week) Cyprus's Greek Orthodox serfs. The catalysts for this brutality were not only an imperious psychology but also contempt for the religion of the Greeks and terror of the Ottomans, whose territories after 1516 were within 35 miles to the north and 60 to the east of the island and whose galleys incessantly prowled the Cypriot coasts. In the name of security and for the sake of empire, then, the city-state fashioned a frenzied bitterness. When the Ottomans did finally land in 1570, most Cypriots exulted in each Venetian reverse.

Cyprus remained Venetian until 1571 for the same reason Chios had remained Genoese until 1566. Between 1489 and 1570 the Venetians labored hard to placate and accommodate first the Mamluks in Cairo and, after 1517, the Ottomans in Istanbul. The Serenissima even honored the substantial tribute that the Mamluks had earlier obliged the Lusignan despots to pay. The Ottomans could have snatched the island – at a bloody price to be sure – at almost any time after their absorption of Mamluk territories. Principally because of economic and political expediencies, however, the Sublime Porte for decades was willing to accept Venetian appeasement.

Unfortunately for this Ottoman–Venetian rapport, Cyprus lies astride the sea roads that join the Syrian coasts, Egypt, and southern Anatolia to Istanbul. After the Ottoman conquests of Syria and Egypt, that empire encompassed all of these territories, and pirates soon took to haunting the seas near the island, and pouncing upon and plundering Istanbul-bound Ottoman vessels heavily laden with rice and grain from Egypt and luxury items from Syria, before sprinting back into Cyprus's many protective harbors, coves, and inlets. Venetian garrisons in the myriad fortresses scattered along the island's coasts found themselves in an awkward dilemma. They believed it honorable to shield these semi-sanctioned vessels whose crews insisted that the holy war excused such raids, a stance that of course provoked Ottoman reprisals against Cypriot coastal towns. Such retaliatory forays became frequent, even chronic. Although the bailo over and over again attended the Imperial Divan to disavow Venetian responsibility for compatriot marauders, Christian privateering and Ottoman retaliation produced a festering sore in relations between the two empires.

Süleyman's death in 1566 probably sealed Cyprus's fate. The legacy of expansion almost required that each Ottoman succession begin with a legitimizing conquest. Mehmed II had subdued Constantinople, Selim I Syria and Egypt, and Süleyman Belgrade and Rhodes. The only exception during the previous century had been Mehmed II's son Bayezid II, whose father's draining militancy and whose own prolonged struggle for the succession with his younger brother Cem had curbed his pugnacity until late in his reign. This one deviation ended badly: displeasure with Bayezid's passivity had convinced discouraged counselors to help his son Selim I depose him in 1512 and (so hearsay had it) have him poisoned soon thereafter. In 1566 several of his key advisors (although not his grand vizier) maintained that Selim II also required such a maneuver, and that Cyprus could provide it. A dispatch from Dubrovnik in early 1570 notifying the Imperial Divan that Venice had just joined an anti-Ottoman alliance with Spain and the papacy merely designated the moment for an enterprise that already had been conceived, debated, and probably decided upon.

The Ottoman attack proceeded swiftly. In late June 1570 a large armada of some 300 vessels passed down the Dardanelles and into Aegean waters. Soon thereafter lâlâ Mustafa Pasha, Selim's childhood mentor, fiery leader of the "war party" in the Imperial Divan, and Sokollu Mehmed Pasha's implacable opponent, landed an army – composed mostly of *sipahi* troops mobilized in southern Anatolia – on the southern coast of Cyprus. Just as had happened on Chios four years before, an elated Greek Cypriot people greeted Mustafa Pasha as a liberator from its Latin oppressors. This local ardor helped the Pasha realize a quick march to the interior Venetian capital city of Nicosia, which succumbed after a short if brutal siege.

With most of the indigenous inhabitants backing the invaders, the war soon became a rout and by the end of July lâlâ Mustafa Pasha held the entire island except for the stoutly fortified port town of Famagusta. Under the inspired if reckless command of the Venetian Captain of Cyprus, Marco Antonio Bragadino (who was for his labors in the end flayed alive, stuffed, and publicly displayed in Istanbul), and thanks to the bold dash of a small fleet of Venetian galleys through the Ottoman sea blockade, the town held out for a full ten months. Nevertheless, without sustained seaborne assistance, which a desperately preoccupied allied fleet could not provide, the defense proved useless and the town finally was taken on 1 August 1571.

Even though Cyprus was "conquered," and thus passed as property to the sultan, Selim II's administration chose to regard the seizure of the island also as a deliverance. This attitude was not entirely fantasy, for the essentially Greek Orthodox island had been under first Lusignan and then Venetian rule since Richard I of England had seized it during the Third Crusade, and most of its inhabitants had learned to hate and fear their Catholic overlords. The fiction also was convenient, for it permitted the state to deny its *gazi* warriors their rights of plunder and to organize a smooth transition to Ottoman rule.[15]

Just as Venetians and other Fourth Crusaders in 1204 had disfigured and plundered Constantinople more thoroughly than did the Ottomans in 1453, so was it Venetians rather than Ottomans who pilfered most of Cyprus's treasures (some of which are proudly exhibited in Venetian museums to this day) and demolished most of its monuments. This is not to declare a particular Ottoman compassion in either case (the janissaries and other Ottoman troops plundered what they could); but neither were they more vicious, more savage, or more avaricious than their Christian rivals.

Immediately after Famagusta fell, the Ottoman state undertook a census to assess the wealth, population, and laws of the island. The Sublime Porte considered Latins, many of whom fled to Venice and elsewhere, as vanquished enemies; it treated Greeks as a subject people. A close reading of the census of 1572, for example, divulges not only a dramatic drop in direct taxes from the Venetian to the Ottoman era but also the termination of the reviled corvée and the excise on salt.

On Cyprus the Ottomans departed in one noteworthy way from the procedures they had executed on Chios. This deviation concerned the coerced migration of peoples (*sürgün*), one of the Ottomans' most debated and condemned policies in modern Cyprus, Greece, Serbia, and other Balkan states (and probably the empire's most visible legacy in these territories). Since the late fourteenth century the government had used *sürgün* for two often complementary purposes: the removal of recalcitrant communities from their sustaining habitats and the replenishing of under-populated regions and cities. One example was the successful (and notorious) forced migration of nomadic Turkomans from eastern Anatolia into the Balkans, where they served effectively on the Hungarian and Habsburg marches as latter-day *gazi* warriors (*akıncıs*); a second was Mehmed II's resettlement of Armenian Christians, Orthodox Greeks,

---

[15] İnalcık, "Ottoman policy," is the classic discussion of this transition to Ottoman rule. See also, though, Ronald Jennings, "The population, taxation, and wealth in the cities and villages of Cyprus, according to the detailed population survey (*Defter-i Mufassal*) of 1572," *Journal of Turkish Studies* 10(1986): 175–89.

and Jews in Istanbul (soon after 1453 Anatolia and the Ottoman Balkans were essentially divested of their Jewish communities), where they helped energize an almost abandoned city. At first many resented this uprooting by which

> the *padishah* having conquered the city sent troops to all the provinces, proclaiming "those who desire should come to Istanbul. We shall give you houses, fields and gardens, and properties." Whoever came was given these things. They settled in this city and made it flourish. The *padishah* also decreed that both rich and poor be driven from their homes. He sent men to the police and magistrates in every province and ordered them to do everything they could to drive inhabitants out, promising houses for a fixed period also to people who came in this manner.[16]

Many eventually learned to relish the fantastic possibilities of the booming metropolis, and Istanbul soon came to act as its own magnet.

The *sürgün* to Cyprus was a different matter, for it was Muslim nomads and agriculturalists from Anatolia whom the Ottomans transported to this island in the years after 1571. From the perspective of the early twenty-first century, this resettlement seems a bid to inundate a Greek island with Turks. Such was not the intent, however. As far as we can tell, the Ottomans never implemented *sürgün* against particular ethnicities or religions, the usual motive for similar tactics on the part of nation states today. Nor is there much evidence that the Greek Orthodox inhabitants of Cyprus were particularly rebellious, even potentially so. The state's intent rather was to reinvigorate an economy that centuries of abuse and neglect had crippled. Indeed, the government did not bring only Anatolian Muslims to Cyprus. In the 1570s Istanbul also sent orders (some of which Joseph Nassi and other influential Ottoman Jews succeeded in having rescinded) that Jews from Safed, Jerusalem, and elsewhere in Syria should resettle and reinvigorate the wreckages of Famagusta and Nicosia.[17]

A grand reversal

The Ottoman–Venetian conflict that had begun with the Ottoman invasion of Cyprus in the summer of 1570 climaxed a year later in two almost simultaneous events: the Ottoman conquest of Famagusta and a sea battle off the coast of Lepanto. The capture of Famagusta happened first, after an investment that lasted almost a year and is said to have cost the lives of the entire Venetian garrison and over 50,000 Ottoman troops.

[16] *Aşıkpaşazade Tarihi* (Istanbul, 1333/1914–15), p. 142.
[17] Uriel Heyd, "Turkish documents concerning the Jews of Safed in the sixteenth century," in *Studies on Palestine during the Ottoman period*, ed. Moshe Mo'az (Jerusalem, 1975), pp. 111–18; and Bernard Lewis, *Notes and documents from the Turkish archives: a contribution to the history of the Jews in the Ottoman Empire* (Jerusalem, 1952).

The battle of Lepanto followed a month later, on 6–7 October. Its result seemed to reverse the outcome at Famagusta.

In this last great naval engagement in the early modern Mediterranean world a mighty armada of galleys and supporting vessels under the command of Don Juan of Austria smashed an equally huge Ottoman fleet under the command of Muezzinzade Ali Pasha, who the previous year had replaced Piyâle Pasha as *kapudanpaşa*. This battle is considered a classic of galley warfare, in which each commander positioned his ships perfectly, each fleet lined up and advanced against the other efficiently, and each unit carried out its task almost flawlessly. It may have been the innovative use of four Venetian galeasses, large merchant ships modified for military use by the installation of cannon on unusually high superstructures, that won the battle for the Catholic League. Don Juan's strategy of placing these monsters in front of his armada and directing them to fire point blank and repeatedly into the enemy line as it swept around them may have worked to blunt and perhaps break the Ottoman formation and expose Ottoman galleys to deadly broadside and flank assaults from a second and much more numerous line of Catholic-League vessels.

Whether the principal reason for the outcome was the novelty of these vessels or the Ottoman failure to flank the opposing fleet on its left wing and force a "mêlée"-style battle, for which Muslim galleys were well adapted, the consequence was catastrophic for the Ottoman cause. Not only were most of 200 or so vessels captured or destroyed, but some 30,000 Ottoman sailors and soldiers perished, Muezzinzade Ali Pasha among them. Catholic losses were negligible.

Western Europe and its historiographers long considered this sea battle pivotal even as they played down the events on Cyprus. With the triumph of a Catholic league at Lepanto in 1571 after almost two centuries of humiliation, the balance was considered to have swung away from the Ottoman "pestilence." The combat also was said to have launched the decline of the Ottoman Empire, which thus occupied itself over the next 350 years with slowly disintegrating.

This interpretation has been contested and largely rebuffed.[18] One argument against it is that the Ottomans so quickly rebuilt their fleet after the débâcle. They drew upon their enormous resources to recover from the destruction or capture of over 200 vessels; as anyone craning his neck from the Galata Tower could plainly see, the tempo of hard work at their principal arsenal on the Golden Horn became frenzied in the winter of

---

[18] Most cogently by Andrew C. Hess, "The Battle of Lepanto and its place in Mediterranean history," *Past and Present* 57(1972): 53–73.

Map 7 The iconography of this frontispiece from a 1631 history of the Turks suggests how alive a crusading mentality still was in western Europe even sixty years after the Battle of Lepanto. At the top stands Christ the king with awed but composed Christian soldiers to his right. To his left, though, cower defeated and terrified Muslim warriors. The triumphant crusader standing on defeated Muslims on the left side of the picture, and the enchained Turk with broken bow and arrow on the right side, reinforce this image. Baudier, *Inventaire de l'histoire Générale du serrail*.

1571–72; and in the following spring the state launched an armada that, symbolically perhaps, was said to have reproduced exactly the number and draft of ships lost. These are hardly the actions of an exhausted and disheartened foe. Nevertheless, it has been convincingly argued that in galley warfare men were more vital than ships, particularly when those lost were skilled archers and oarsmen.[19] Lepanto certainly saw a devastating destruction of Ottoman manpower as well as armaments, and it seems likely that the armada that appeared on the seas in 1572 was shoddily manned. It is less certain that rival powers, stunned into inaction by the rapidity of Ottoman recovery, at all comprehended such defects, that the obstacle persisted for very long, or that it permanently halted Ottoman strikes into the western Mediterranean seas.

The fact remains that in subsequent years the victors were not to press their advantage, and that this great achievement did not goad the alliance of Catholic states forward. Indeed, Lepanto terminated the making of holy leagues against the "Turk" (although not aspirations to do so), and in fact constituted the last great naval encounter between Christian and Muslim powers. It may be seen as proof that "control of the seas" was an impossibility (and perhaps not even a strategy) in the age of the galleys.

After 1571 the very nature of warfare on the Mediterranean changed, along with the composition of the participants. No longer did large and treasury-depleting armadas cruise open waters. Instead small, often self-interested fleets roamed the sea roads and coastlines, preying, usually indiscriminately, upon exposed communities and detached merchant vessels. This was the era of the corsair, the buccaneer, and the privateer, and it mattered little to the prey whether the flag flown by the hunter was Barbary, Dutch, English, French, Majorcan, Maltese, or Spanish.[20] Not only could one's own countryman slash one's throat as easily as a foreigner, but flags seldom meant anything to the thoroughly diverse seafarers aboard such vessels. Furthermore, any assault could readily be justified, for in that world of multiple diasporas every Venetian vessel carried the persons or goods of Jewish and Muslim heathens and every Ottoman vessel those of Christians. Ottoman and Venetian mariners and merchants learned to dread the sighting of any mast on the horizon. Ironically the imperial stalemate that, more than anything else, Lepanto represented probably increased borderland porousness, for the world of the marauder, the smuggler, and the renegade was an accommodating one. It was the dissimulator who best survived.

---

[19] Guilmartin, *Gunpowder and galleys*, pp. 250–52.
[20] See Fernand Braudel, *The Mediterranean and the Mediterranean world in the age of Philip II*, trans. Siân Reynolds (New York, 1972), pp. 865–91.

The Venetian drift eastward

However fleeting the military advantage was for the holy alliance, its achievements at Lepanto certainly represented a heart-stirring triumph for the Pope and the Spanish, just as it constituted a psychological catastrophe and an ill omen for the Ottomans. For the Venetians, despite their initial euphoria, the outcome was more ambiguous, and not only because of the simultaneous loss of Cyprus. By 1571 the Republic's sympathies and interests could no longer be unequivocally with western Europe. After all, it had been Christian kings and emperors who had ravaged the Veneto, Christian corsairs who had virtually destroyed the Venetian carrying trade, and Christian explorers who had undermined Venice's international commerce in spices and textiles. The Senators understood that both they and the Ottomans suffered from the plunder of Dutch and English privateers in the Mediterranean Sea and from the ventures of Portuguese sea peddlers in the Indian Ocean. Each Ottoman failure also damaged the Venetian capacity to trade; every Ottoman victory protected Venetian traffic in the eastern Mediterranean world.

Indeed, the commercial nature of the Venetian Empire determined a particular dread of long sea wars that disrupted seaborne communications and commerce. Francesco Guicciardini's observation about an earlier clash could just as well apply to this one:

Having supported the war against the Turks with the greatest difficulties and boundless expenses and without any hope of gaining any profit therefrom, and besides all this, fearing so much more that they might be attacked at the same time by other Christian princes, the Venetians were always very desirous of reaching an accord of peace with the Turks.[21]

From worry about commercial loss and fear of adversaries in Italy itself, the Senate routinely urged its allies to engage swiftly with the Ottoman fleet, hoping for a quick and clean end to the conflict. Financial and commercial expediencies also pressured the Venetians to bargain promptly with their foe and to send their merchants into Ottoman ports and hinterlands, often at the very moment their navies clashed. Even during the Cypriot war, which seemed so brutal on the ground and over which passions seemed so intense, Ottoman merchants continued to ply their trade in Venice and Venetians carried on in Istanbul, Aleppo, and Alexandria. Such "business-as-usual" practices not only help explain the briefness of Ottoman–Venetian wars in the sixteenth century, but also produced allegations of faintheartedness and betrayal from allies whom Venice's

---

[21] *The history of Italy*, trans. Sidney Alexander (London, 1969), p. 177.

acclaimed company of emissaries in Rome, Madrid, Vienna, and elsewhere worked so hard and cleverly to gain.

At the root of Venetian indecisiveness was the Senators' recognition that their own allies were a greater threat to the city-state's commerce, based as it was upon the shipment of spices, silks, and other goods from the East into western Europe, than were the Ottomans.[22] The Venetian banker Girolamo Priuli predicted as early as 1499 that the Portuguese discovery of an all-water route to Asia would ruin Venice's transcontinental commerce, and the Portuguese explorer Pedro Cabral returned from India, the holds of his thirteen ships loaded with Indian pepper and other spices, in the third year of the Ottoman–Venetian War of 1499–1502. By then both the Ottomans and the Venetians were well aware of the presence of Portuguese ships in the Indian Ocean, and both governments understood the Portuguese threat to overland commerce. Venice welcomed the Ottoman conquest of Syria and Egypt in the second decade of the sixteenth century as well as that Islamic state's launching of a fleet in the Red Sea as ventures aimed at quashing Portuguese incursions into the Indian Ocean. The Ottomans shared this enthusiasm; their conquests probably had more to do with Portuguese encroachments to the southeast than with vexation against the Mamluks or eagerness to oversee the sacred cities of Mecca and Medina.

It constitutes a striking foil to the notion of fixed boundaries that transcivilizational commerce persisted, even flourished, in the midst of the three Catholic–Ottoman conflicts of the sixteenth century. After (and even during) each war, more Ottoman and Venetian merchants resided in and freely wandered the other's territory. Venetian commercial colonies appeared not only in Galata. Venice also fashioned settlements in Edirne, Salonika, and (after 1517) Aleppo, Alexandria, and other Ottoman towns, a mutually beneficial movement that seems to have quickened as the century advanced. As the Venetian navy weakened, the commercial imperative overwhelmed the military and ideological constraints in that city-state's relations with the Ottomans.

There are many causes for this apparent contradiction, not least of which was that the Venetian Empire always had been commercial. Given a choice between land masses or islands and coastal regions, the Senate always chose the latter. Even as early as the Catholic division of Constantinople after its conquest during the Fourth Crusade (1204), when the ferocious if blind Enrico Dandolo could have picked whatever he wished from the Byzantine carcass, the determined doge had confined

---

[22] On which see Brummett, *Ottoman seapower and Levantine diplomacy.*

Venetian appropriations to strategically placed islands, choice harbors, and the right to trade freely within all of former Byzantium.[23]

In 1204 Venice had carved a seaborne empire out of the disintegrated Byzantine polity. Nevertheless, its physical loss three centuries later did not necessarily signify the absolute collapse of the Venetian Empire. One alternative, which the Venetians pursued, was to turn to the Italian mainland, the Venetian *terra firma*, where trading routes and the demand for secure granaries and woodlands already had directed their aggressions. Scholars recently have emphasized this option.[24]

Venice did not simply abandon the seas because of Ottoman mastery, however. There were countless diasporas that thrived in the *pax ottomanica* and beyond on commerce alone, and the loss of its possessions might have injured the Serenissima's pride more than its seaborne power. What was critical for commerce was access not dominion, which in actuality probably drained Venetian resources, through the demand of colonies for protection, more than it benefited the city-state. As the Ottomans hacked away at first Byzantine and later Hungarian, Mamluk, and Venetian lands, Venice more and more concentrated upon its trading diaspora by ensuring that its merchants could inhabit and trade freely in the port towns and hinterlands of the unfolding Ottoman seaboards.

---

[23] On Venice's role in the Fourth Crusade and Latin rule in Constantinople, see Donald M. Nicol, *Byzantium and Venice: a study in diplomatic and cultural relations* (Cambridge, 1988), ch. 8.

[24] S. J. Woolf, "Venice and the Terrafirma: problems of the change from commercial to landed activities," in *Crisis and change in the Venetian economy in the sixteenth and seventeenth centuries*, ed. Brian Pullan (Bungay, Suffolk, 1968), pp. 175–203.

Kubad between worlds

Anyone who saw the Venetians, a tiny nation living in such liberty that the worst rogue among them would not wish to be their king, ... anyone, I say, who saw those people and then went to the realm of the man we call the Grand Signor, and saw how people there reckon that the sole purpose of their existence is to serve this man ... would he reckon that these two nations shared a common nature, or would he not rather judge that he had left a city and entered a sheepfold?[1]

Kubad finally left Venice on 12 February 1568. Even though he would have preferred the speedy and convenient journey by sea across the Adriatic and Aegean seas, he chose instead the land route from Dubrovnik and via Sarajevo and Edirne because of escalating strikes by Uskok and Maltese pirates against Ottoman shipping.[2] Back in Istanbul he reported to his lords in the Imperial Divan and fulfilled his promise to the Venetian Senate by arranging for the obliteration of all references to Soranzo's contract with di Segura.[3] He even convinced the kadi of Galata to tear his copy of the vexing certificate out of his ledger and burn it.

Kubad's willingness to undertake this unlawful act derived partly from expectations for future rewards. Venetian relief at no longer being liable to Ottoman justice was enormous and a grateful bailo compensated the courier well. There was a darker cause, however. He could never have secured the kadi's consent

---

[1] Etienne de La Boétie, *Le discours de la servitude volontaire*, ed. P. Léonard (Paris, 1976), p. 135; translated as *Slaves by choice*, trans. Malcolm Smith (Egham Hill, Surrey, 1988), p. 54; quoted in Valensi, *Birth of the despot*, p. 66.

[2] Catherine Wendy Bracewell, *The Uskoks of Senj: piracy, banditry, and holy war in the sixteenth-century Adriatic* (Ithaca, NY, 1992), pp. 58–59, cites a Venetian emissary to Archduke Charles who wrote in 1568 about the escalation of Uskok raiding: "for not only subjects of the Turk who have escaped from their places and have gone to live there are given refuge under the name of uskoks, but also many who have been banished from Ancona, Urbino, and Apulia, and also exiles from all the islands and nearby towns of Your Serenity, and deserters from the galleys, who act as guides and leaders for these wicked men." See also Kafadar, "Death in Venice," p. 200.

[3] Although we have no account of Kubad's report to the Imperial Divan, as a *çavuş* it is likely that he appeared before it.

to destroy a page from his ledger (based as the pronouncements were upon the Shariah itself) without a direct order from the sultan. The seemingly treacherous exploit helped him gain the trust of Venetian officials, to carry on as a counselor to the bailo (from whom he collected a hefty fee), and to pass on intelligence to his grand vizier. In short, Kubad became a double agent.[4]

He was not so much informing on behalf of his sultan as of his grand vizier. Kubad knew that his government was riven with a factionalism in which the di Segura family was fully engaged through its co-religionist Don Joseph di Nassi. Nassi, the sultan's confidante and infamous provider of wine, had joined the chief Mufti Ebu's-Su'ud Efendi, Selim's boyhood guide Lâlâ Mustafa Pasha, and Selim's chief concubine Nurbanu Sultan (rumored ironically to be of Venetian parentage) in opposing Sokollu's policy, believed to be shamelessly pro-Venetian.[5]

Kubad of course had heard and dismissed the shocking gossip that Selim II had fallen under Nassi's influence and that he wanted Cyprus only because of its aromatic wines (exceptional though they were). The envoy was convinced that Selim's genuine motive for invasion was the same as his father's had been in 1522 when he took Rhodes: Cyprus had become an outpost for Christian pirates. Kubad sided with the war party and opposed his grand vizier in urging an immediate attack upon the Venetian Empire, whose intolerance vexed him and many of whose deficiencies he had fathomed during his five months in Venice. Indeed, his insistence that the conquest of Cyprus would assist the marketing of Anatolian mohair and especially intelligence gleaned from the bailo and his staff, whose trust he now possessed, proved influential in His Most Imperial Majesty's determination to move against the island.

By voicing these opinions, Kubad opposed his grand vizier who he knew feared that an attack upon Cyprus would inspire the formation of a grand Catholic alliance against the young and untested sultan. In support of his concerns, the envoy had witnessed that fearsome and august gentleman rise before

---

[4] Such agents seem to have been common in the Ottoman world. See, for two other possible examples, Virginia Aksan, "Is there a Turk in the *Turkish Spy*?," *Eighteenth-Century Fiction* 6.3(1994): 201–14; and Roderick Conway Morris's curious *Jem: memoirs of an ottoman secret agent* (New York, 1988), a historical novel set in the time of Bayezid II (late fifteenth century).

[5] Our best sources for such factionalisms are Ottoman chroniclers, who often were themselves members of them (or at least had patrons who were), and who wrote almost obsessively and most scathingly about them. For this period the most accessible such work probably is Selaniki Mustafa Efendi, *Tarih-i Selaniki*, ed. Mehmet İpşirli, 2 vols. (Istanbul, 1989). The most thoroughly examined such writer is Mustafa Âli, on whom see Fleischer, *Bureaucrat and intellectual.* The pedigrees of sultanic wives and concubines are notoriously difficult to ascertain. Nurbanu long was considered to have been born Cecelia Venier-Baffo, the illicit daughter of two Venetian aristocrats who was captured and presented to the sultan by Barbarossa Hayreddin Pasha in 1537 (see Peirce, *Imperial harem*, p. 92). Benjamin Arbel, "Nur Banu (c. 1530–1583): a Venetian sultana?," *Turcica* 24(1992): 241–59, casts considerable doubt upon this romantic tale.

the Imperial Divan and thunderously read out a letter recently received from the Ottoman dependency of Dubrovnik, whose rulers kept a useful eye on develop-ments in Italy.[6] *This intelligence advised the imperial council that, in response to rumors of an Ottoman offensive, King Philip had contributed and outfitted 100 vessels. They were even then en route to the Papal States to be used in defense of Venice or however else the pontiff chose.*

Despite such evidence of Christian readiness, the grand vizier's rivals con-vinced the sultan to mobilize his legions and besiege Cyprus. At Kubad's urging, though, the divan elected to play by the rules of international diplomacy and announce to the Venetian Senate its decision to attack the island, even though, given the Venetian possession's strategic and economic importance, there was no real hope that the Senate would peaceably relinquish it. In early 1570 Kubad convinced the divan to dispatch him, its expert on Venetian affairs, again to Venice to demand the secession of Cyprus. He arrived there on 28 March 1570, and immediately attained an audience with a doge frantic to delay the attack until he had concluded negotiations for aid from the Pope and other Catholic rulers.[7] Kubad gave him no opportunity to stall, but informed him instead that the Ottoman assault would begin immediately.

The envoy fully appreciated that he was the bearer of evil tidings, and that this ultimatum might effect a long confinement – or worse – in Venice. Such a response, Kubad reasoned, would simply be tit for tat, for the sultan routinely jailed the Venetian bailo during hostilities. Just as the envoy expected, his arrest was immediate. More surprisingly, his compatriots, both Muslim and non-Muslim, also were confined and their goods were confiscated, in reprisal, he later learned, for similar treatment of Venetian merchants in Istanbul.[8]

Threats from and negotiations with Istanbul and the urgencies of inter-national trade despite the intrusion of war soon led to the release of both Ottoman and Venetian expatriate communities. Kubad was not so lucky.[9] He remained in Venice throughout the three-year war that saw the Ottoman con-quest of Cyprus, the formation of a Catholic Holy Alliance against the Ottoman Empire and its success in a grand naval engagement off the shores of Lepanto, the implausible resurrection of the Ottoman navy, and the hard negotiations that followed.

[6] On Dubrovnik, see Francis W. Carter, *Dubrovnik (Ragusa): a classic city-state* (London, 1972). The letter from the city state is extant (Başbakanlık Osmanlı Arşivi, Mühimme Defteri 19, p. 118); there is no record that Mehmed Pasha recited it in the divan.
[7] On the doge's negotiations with other European states and the formation of a Christian Holy League, see Lane, *Venice*, p. 370. We do not know whether or not Kubad met with the doge; he had been active in negotiations in Istanbul (see Arbel, *Trading nations*, pp. 151–53).
[8] On treatment of the Ottoman nation in Venice during the Cypriot war see Kafadar, "Death in Venice," pp. 200–1; and Arbel, *Trading nations*, pp. 55–76.
[9] The only evidence for this statement is that Kubad's opposite number, the bailo, re-mained imprisoned throughout the war.

The envoy kept abreast of events through numerous visits from di Segura, Grimani, and his Circassian cousin. He also learned from his kinsman that the small band of Ottoman merchants bullheadedly had resumed their commercial ventures despite sporadic harassment from a frantic people as the Ottoman– Venetian war over Cyprus dragged on.

In late September 1571 an exultant di Segura burst into the envoy's cell to report that Venetian Famagusta had fallen after a frightful ten-month siege. The Muslim and Jew sat long into the night debating this milestone's meaning, and especially whether, as rumored, Selim II would present the island to Joseph Mendes, the Jewish refugee from Portugal and Venice and current Duke of Nassi.

Only a few days later Kubad heard a wild bustle on the canals outside his dungeon. In a few moments an elated Grimani called to announce that the galley Angelo Gabriele *had just entered port trailing a bright crimson Ottoman banner and myriad turbans, scalped from the severed heads of janissaries, and bearing the news that the Catholic League had routed a huge Ottoman armada in the Gulf of Corinth. Again the çavuş spent long hours discussing the ramifications of this catastrophe. The Ottoman envoy, reminding Grimani of his own ancestor's misadventure at Negroponte some seventy years earlier and of Andrea Doria's catastrophe at Préveza some forty years after that, scornfully brushed aside his Catholic comrade's sanguine certainty that Charles V's natural son Don Juan of Austria would now drive the Ottoman fleet against the very walls of the great city of Constantinople itself.*

In Venice, the Catholic triumph at Lepanto produced an exceptional imbroglio. Kubad had heard from his cell a jubilant and jeering mob threatening to slaughter his Muslim brethren, whose scattered and exposed condition in and around the Rialto only increased the danger. Luckily, the Venetian state had averted the threatened bloodbath by gathering the community together and guarding it with a phalanx of watchmen.[10]

As Kubad lay on his mat that chilly October night he could not sleep. Was it the icy bora *howling down from the northeast that chilled his bones? Or was it the galling revelry that had burst with unprecedented energy across the city, and that he knew even then was reverberating also across all of Christian Europe?*

[10] Such explosions hastened the Venetians to form an Ottoman *fondaco*.

6   Commerce and diasporas

My Exalted Self commands the kadi and *bey* of Jerusalem: the bailo of
Venice petitioned the Sublime Porte that those who visit Jerusalem
from the subjects of the nobles of Venice should not be injured. Nor
should any one of you interfere with the monks who live in the Church
of the Holy Sepulchre. When they repair and renovate according to
their old situation areas of that church which have fallen into ruin, they
seek a command that it is in accordance with Venice's capitulations
(*ahdname* and *nişan*). Such a decree is given to these Frankish
monks.[1]

In Pera they speak Turkish, Greek, Hebrew, Armenian, Arabic,
Persian, Russian, Slavonian, Wallachian, German, Dutch, French,
English, Italian, Hungarian; and, what is worse, there is ten of these
languages spoke in my own family. My grooms are Arabs, my footmen,
French, English and Germans, my Nurse an Armenian, my
housemaids Russians, half a dozen other servants Greeks; my steward
an Italian; my Janissaries Turks, that I live in the perpetual hearing of
this medley of sounds, which produces a very extraordinary effect
upon the people that are born here. They learn all these languages at
the same time and without knowing any of them well enough to write
or read in it.[2]

One must turn to Ottoman history rather than western European history
to explore how Venice and other western European states organized presences in the Levantine world, for the underlying design of Ottoman society did much to accommodate and make possible the development
of commercial and diplomatic settlements in the empire. During the
fourteenth and fifteenth centuries the Islamic state constructed a system, based upon a broad-minded interpretation of Islam's attitude toward
rival monotheists, that provided inclusion for the Christians and Jews who
populated the conquered lands of Anatolia and the Balkans.

[1] Başbakanlık Osmanlı Arşivi, Ecnebi Defteri 13/1, p. 14, doc 1 (imperial decree, 1604–5).
[2] Lady Mary Wortley Montagu, *The Turkish embassy letters*, intro. Anita Desai, ed. Malcolm
Jack (London, 1993), p. 122 (Lady Mary Montagu to Mady Mar, 16 March 1718).

The non-Muslim in the Ottoman world

Since the time of Muhammed (*c.* 570–632) Islam had confronted large communities of Jews and Christians almost everywhere it went. In response, the religion developed a doctrine not of impartiality but of indulgence, whereby those who followed the Torah or Christian Gospels (*zimmi* or "people of the Book") were allowed to live and worship according to their faiths in the Abode of Islam (*dar al-Islam*) as subject people in return for payment of a head tax (*cizye*) and certain other signs of subjugation. This precept enabled Christians and Jews to endure, and even to prosper, under the dominion of this rival faith.

In subsequent centuries and in various places Islamic rulers and states had sometimes interpreted such Qur'anic pronouncements broadly and with tolerance; at other times they had defined them narrowly and harshly.[3] The Ottomans, perhaps more from necessity than choice, embraced the former course. The swift conquests of the fourteenth, fifteenth, and sixteenth centuries established an empire that demographically at least was predominantly Christian, which made it imperative that the authorities indulge these non-Muslim subjects as much as doctrinally possible.

The circumstances of conquest helped the Ottomans do so. The vast riches delivered to the imperial treasury permitted the state to reduce the head tax that, according to the Shariah, signified the subjugation of non-Muslims in an Islamic state. In some cases Jewish and Christian communities even negotiated relatively negligible lump-sum payments (*maktu'*) in return for sweeping social and judicial autonomy.[4] The state often eased sumptuary restrictions, despite Qur'anic restrictions on non-Muslim wealth and display, and authorized the restoration of ruined churches and synagogues. Through such devices the Ottomans were able to obey the letter of the law even as they ameliorated its execution. At times the state went even further, for example by sanctioning the raising of new Christian or Jewish houses of worship in direct violation of Islamic law.

Mehmed II codified the previously tacit relationship with non-Muslim subject peoples when, with the conquest of Constantinople, the Ottomans inherited the spiritual as well as the political nucleus of Byzantium. The new monarch had not only to reform the political administration and economy of the ancient capital, but also to either reorganize or abolish the hierocracy of the Greek Orthodox church. Mehmed chose the

---

[3] A good treatment of this subject in regard to Jews and especially in comparison to the Christian world is Cohen, *Under crescent and cross.*

[4] On which see "Maktuᶜ," *EI*.

former course and appointed Gennadius Scholarius, who had welcomed Ottoman incorporation as the preferable alternative to orthodox union with Rome, as the first Greek Orthodox Patriarch under Ottoman dominion. On 5 January 1454 the sultan instated Gennadius as Patriarch and presented to him a "charter" (*ahdname*) – to be renewed or abrogated by each succeeding monarch – that delineated the organization, entitlements, and responsibilities of the Greek Orthodox community. With the full weight of Ottoman authority behind him, it also granted Gennadius far more intra-communal power than his predecessors had ever carried in imperial Byzantium.

Not only did the Patriarch, his subordinates, and his successors assume responsibility for the religion, laws, conduct, and tax payments of the Ottoman Greek Orthodox community, but Mehmed and his advisors also devised parallel organizations for the growing communities of Ottoman Armenians and Jews. This communal strategy, which never before the nineteenth century had any ethnic, geographic, or linguistic intent or justification, was not fully formed in the fifteenth century: not only was each organization rather ad hoc, but each reflected the particular requirements and qualities of its own religious community. The Armenian Gregorian Patriarch never attained the authority of his Greek Orthodox counterpart, largely because the Armenian community was so scattered and so much of it lived beyond the boundaries of the Ottoman Empire and thus beyond the Patriarch's control. The Grand Rabbi's authority was even more restricted, for the Ottoman Jewish community retained the largely decentralized political structure that had evolved during the oppressive Byzantine interval. Outside of Istanbul (and often even within that city's many synagogal quarters), leaders other than the Grand Rabbi retained much authority over their communities.

Over the next few centuries the societies and administrations of each of the three principal non-Muslim subject peoples were to evolve along distinct trajectories. Nevertheless, from their very inception these organizations (they only much later came to be called *millets*) did grant their members considerable autonomy. Especially in the spiritual, economic, and judicial spheres the state's policy of non-interference imparted to them the prospect of carving out productive niches in the Ottoman world.

Heterogeneity thus came to distinguish Ottoman society, especially along its seaboards and borderlands where the exigencies of war and the opportunities of commerce tended to diversify economies and throw together sundry peoples and ideas. Virtually every Ottoman city came to boast a rich ethnic and linguistic diversity colorfully woven through groups that defined themselves as Gregorian Armenian, Orthodox Greek,

Jewish, or Muslim. Despite some vocational specialization, these communities mixed freely in the markets and industrial districts that constituted their work places. Their residential neighborhoods leaned more toward segregation, clustering around churches, mosques, or synagogues; nevertheless even in this more personal environment there was some religious and ethnic mingling. In Ankara, Istanbul, Salonika, and other early modern Ottoman cities commercial districts were likely to become a mélange of peoples, and neighborhoods (*mahalles*) were apt to remain mainly (but not exclusively) Christian, Jewish, or Muslim. The Ottoman strategy of simultaneously welcoming non-Muslims into the polity and denying equality to them generated a municipal hodgepodge of faiths and peoples who, even as they lived and worked together, conserved ever-changing but often separate religious, legal, cultural, and at times even ethnic identities.

Dealing with aliens

Just as 1453 was a pivotal year in creating an Ottoman religious strategy, so was it decisive in the settlement of foreign subjects in the empire, for in that year the sultan inherited and had to manage not only Constantinople but also the Latin colony of Galata. Unlike the great city itself, the suburb of Galata had submitted to Mehmed's army without a fight. Consequently the sultan was not obliged to give it over to his troops to plunder. Instead he could construct his own relationship with the place. The outcome was a solemn pledge, presented as an imperial decree (named an *ahdname*, just as was Gennadius's proclamation), by which Mehmed contracted to leave intact the Genoese Council (the *Magnifica Communita di Pera*), grant the district legal and some political autonomy, and concede its alien inhabitants the freedom to trade in Ottoman domains. In return the Latins relinquished their weapons, quieted their church bells (which Mehmed and other Muslims seem to have found particularly galling), had their town walls pierced at strategic spots, and began paying a head tax.

From one perspective this *ahdname* exemplified a link between the Byzantine and the Ottoman periods. Latins (and since the Fourth Crusade particularly the Genoese) had replicated in Byzantine Galata an Italian city, complete with Gothic tower, Italianate churches, and piazzetta. Its character as an outpost for Italian culture continued under the Ottomans. Mehmed, looking for every advantage against his Venetian foes, even invited Florentine merchants to settle there and granted them indulgent liberties. Other Europeans soon followed, including first more Italians (Venetians among them) and later the French, the English, and the Dutch. Galata thrived under Ottoman rule. It became the commercial heart of the city, and, pushing slowly up the hill at its back into the vineyards and orchards of Pera, drew to its Italianate ambience ambassadors from Europe and their retinues and hangers-on.

In another sense Mehmed's bargain with the Genoese simply followed a legacy handed down from the Islamic world and more specifically from rival western Anatolian emirates. Venetian colonies long had existed in the cities of the Mamluk Empire, and as early as 1331 the emir of Menteşe, who controlled the caravan and sea roads at the southwestern corner of Anatolia, had concluded a commercial arrangement with Marino Morosini, the Venetian Duke of Cretan Candia. Six years later the same Duke concluded an accord with the emir of Aydın, who commanded a powerful navy based in the Anatolian port of Smyrna. Then in 1352 the Ottoman emir Orhan himself signed a similar contract with the Genoese, which yielded to its merchants access to Bursa and the caravan roads that radiated from that newly vanquished town. Looking for allies against the aggressive Venetian Empire in the Levant, Orhan probably signed this pact more as a political than a commercial tactic. Nevertheless, a similar agreement that Murad signed with his Venetian rivals themselves in the 1380s confirms also an Ottoman appreciation for trade.

Indeed, these pacts were principally commercial in layout and purpose, for they conceded to Latin merchants access to the vital caravan roads that ran through Turkoman-held towns such as Bursa and Smyrna in return for earnings from tariffs and other dues. They also facilitated political, ideological, and cultural objectives, however. The emirs gained Christian allies and acceptance into the eastern Mediterranean community of states, which helped to legitimize their governments, to achieve independence from their Seljuk overlords to the east, and to normalize their international relations. Orhan's 1327 striking of silver coins embossed with his name, only one year after the Ottoman conquest of Bursa, probably was as much a revenue- and visibility-producing scheme – generated through the circulation of Ottoman coinage along the caravan corridors – as a political maneuver, symbolizing as it did an assertion of independence. The Latins, meanwhile, not only gained allies and riches but also attained a better understanding of these important and potentially dangerous new states through access to their towns, subjects, and rulers.

Despite these precedents, Mehmed's *ahdname* of 1453 also was innovative; it constituted an ingenious twist on the emerging Ottoman approach toward its non-Muslim subjects. To the western outlanders the agreement may have seemed merely an arrangement that let them sustain and even expand their lucrative commerce under the *pax ottomanica*. The

25 This funeral procession is at Eyüb, the holiest soil in the vicinity of Istanbul and considered by the Ottomans as the fourth most important Islamic site after Mecca, Medina, and Jerusalem. It was here that Eyüb Ensari, companion to the Prophet Muhammed, had been buried after he was martyred during the first siege of Constantinople (674–78). It also was here that ascending Ottoman sultans girded their swords and assumed their offices in public ceremony. D'Ohsson, *Tableau général de l'Empire othoman*, vol. I, after p. 248.

Ottomans, however, perceived it also as a first step in the absorption of the foreigners into the "Abode of Islam," as according to Islamic law it was. Such agreements confirmed that the westerners were mere visitors (*müste'min*), and consequently able to retain allegiance to other, even non-Islamic, states and come and go at will. The length of residency theoretically was limited to one year only, however, and by consenting also to the imposition of a head tax (*cizye*) the European sojourners exposed themselves to eventual absorption through the category of *zimmi*. In theory at least the sojourner could become a subject simply by overstaying his welcome.

This is not to suggest that the sultan and his advisors necessarily intended this outcome (although there is some evidence that Mehmed had such a gradual incorporation in mind). Nevertheless, the kadi of Pera and his colleagues across the empire tended to envisage and to treat alien inhabitants as they did other non-Muslim Ottoman subjects. After all, these magistrates were *medrese*-trained members of the *ulema*. They had immersed themselves in Islamic law and managed their wards accordingly.

Extant Ottoman records from the early seventeenth century are packed with the protests of European diplomats against Ottoman officials who dared to try to manage them and their dependents as they did other Ottoman subjects. One, issued in 1605, records the Venetian bailo's insistence that Ottoman officials should not register the houses of his five dragomans and stewards in the tax rolls of subject non-Muslims. A second, promulgated just months later, resists the attempts of collectors to extract customs, janissary guards protection money, and candle-makers suet on livestock butchered for Venetian diplomats in Galata, Istanbul, and Üsküdar. A third, issued in the following year, states bluntly that Venetian merchants with shops in Galata and Istanbul "paid their customs and should not be put in the same category as non-Muslim Ottoman subjects in contradiction to the terms of their *ahdname*."[5]

Such complaints thread through relations between Ottoman officials and resident foreign communities. They are even more vividly displayed on the island of Chios, which as we have seen the Ottomans conquered in 1566 and aspired to transform into a *de facto* free port. Within decades local officials sought to impose *zimmi* status upon those Chian Latins who had remained after the conquest. In 1615 locals demanded extraordinary taxes (*avariz* and *kasabiye*) from a Venetian merchant who had "lived on Chios for a long time." Two years later and again in 1618 the Venetian bailo complained in the imperial divan that local collectors demanded the head tax from subjects of Venice who lived and traded on the island.[6] Such protests display tension over status that often is interpreted as Ottoman greed and corruption. While it is true that the Ottoman bureaucracy probably was no less venal than other bureaucracies, the circumstances nevertheless illustrate most strikingly different perceptions of the position the foreigner should assume in Ottoman society.

In short, although the *ahdname* that Mehmed presented to the Genoese in 1453 and those that followed certainly did ease commercial and social relations, they also signified one thing to the Ottoman mind and quite another to the alien European one. Furthermore, even within a specific context the impact of the tension between these culturally specific meanings changed over time. For example, because of drastically altered

---

[5] Başbakanlık Osmanlı Arşivi, Ecnebi Defteri 13/1, p. 28, no. 6; p. 29, no. 4; and p. 35, no. 5.
[6] Başbakanlık Osmanlı Arşivi, Ecnebi Defteri 13/1, p. 120, no. 1; p. 150, no. 1; p. 178, no. 2.

circumstances the terms that Mehmed II granted to the Genoese differed markedly from the more indulgent ones that the Sublime Porte was to grant to the French in 1569.

Venice's city-state rivals

The Ottomans had politics as much as commerce in mind when they negotiated and distributed capitulations. Just as a principal impetus for Orhan to grant the Genoese commercial agreements in the 1350s was mutual antipathy toward Venice, so was the long Ottoman–Venetian War (1463–79) a motivation for Mehmed II to favor Florentine traders in the late fifteenth century. Indeed, until almost 100 years later it was Mediterranean city-states rather than emerging Atlantic seaboard nation states such as France, England, and the Netherlands that the Venetians struggled to fend off in their contest for Ottoman commerce. Most of the time the Venetians prospered. During each Ottoman–Venetian war, however, Ancona, Florence, Genoa, Dubrovnik, or some combination of these cities were able to improve their commercial circumstances at Venetian expense.

Florence especially benefited from the long war between Venice and the Ottoman Empire that marked the second half of Mehmed II's reign.[7] Land-locked Florence, acclaimed for its fine woolen textiles, had had to funnel its precious commodity eastward by way of Venice and in the holds of Venetian ships until it secured the city of Pisa and its port of Livorno (Leghorn) in 1421. Thereafter its merchants attempted to break into the Ottoman market directly, an endeavor that their Italian rivals effectively blocked until the 1450s.

Mehmed II was sensitive to the paradox that his principal maritime rival Venice was also his chief trading partner in the Mediterranean world. After 1453 the sultan began to promote one of Venice's primary Italian rivals, Florence, in an attempt to break this dependence. Not only did Florence secure capitulations from Mehmed, but as early as 1454 Florentine ships laden with woolens began anchoring at Istanbul. In the midst of growing tensions between Venice and the Ottomans, the empire in 1462 expelled many Venetians from government houses in Galata and installed Florentines in their places. During the first years of the war, business between Ottomans and Florentines replaced the lost Veneto-Ottoman nexus, and flourished.

Florentine achievements proved ephemeral. Not only was the seaborne route from Livorno lengthy, but also that anchorage remained minor until

---

[7] İnalcık, "Ottoman state," pp. 230–34.

the Duke of Tuscany made it a free port in the 1590s. Furthermore, the Venetians simply were too entrenched in the eastern-Mediterranean world for another Italian state to dislodge them without sustained Ottoman assistance. Florentine prosperity depended upon a supportive Ottoman policy; when that patronage flagged (as it did after the peace of 1479) the new association languished.

In addition, Mehmed's abrupt promotion of the Florentines derived not from affection or even merely from political scheming; it was simply that the Ottomans had no alternatives to Latin merchants. For at least two centuries Italians had dominated Mediterranean commercial corridors. They settled their primacy in 1204 with the sack and occupation of the Byzantine capital, and until the late fifteenth century there was no assembly of Ottoman merchants who could challenge them. By 1500, however, several plausible rivals had arisen out of the Ottoman jumble of peoples. There were the Sephardic Jews, expelled from Iberia and resettled in Salonika, Istanbul, and other Ottoman cities as well as a scattering of port towns across the Mediterranean world and beyond; there were the Armenians who capitalized upon their management of the silk routes westward out of Persia to manufacture a far-flung trading diaspora;[8] and there were semi-autonomous dominions on the fringes of the Ottoman realm – entities such as Dubrovnik, Wallachia, and Chios – whose voluntary if sometimes wavering alignments with the Ottoman behemoth presented to them, it is true, the danger of absorption into that empire, but also offered the immense opportunities of a vast commercial hinterland in their Ottoman backyards. Such Ottoman subject peoples and dependencies matured into viable trading blocks, and as Venice became less of a military threat the Ottoman government lost interest in playing one Italian state off against another for military or commercial gain and began instead promoting its own merchants.

The case of Catholic, Italian-speaking Dubrovnik is particularly pertinent because it so resembled an Italian city-state and often competed directly with Venice.[9] Not only did this Dalmatian port town share with the Republic of St. Mark access to the Adriatic Sea, but also – despite some competition from Ottoman Adriatic ports such as Avlonya and after 1570 the Venetian Spalato – its location made it a western gateway into the Ottoman Balkans and their rich markets. Dubrovnikan merchants carried grains, salt, leathers, and wools into Italy and textiles and bullion into the Balkans.

The city-state's deliberate vassalage to the Ottoman Empire let it maximize its geographic position. Its peculiar station within the *dar al-ahd*

---

[8] On these and other such commercial networks see Curtin, *Cross-cultural trade.*
[9] İnalcık, "Ottoman state," pp. 256–69.

(Abode of the Covenant), a kind of theoretical middle ground between the Abode of Islam and the Abode of War, also accorded Dubrovnik a permanent sort of most-favored-nation status in trade within Ottoman domains, which it paid for with a hefty tribute. Colonies of Dubrovnikan merchants settled in major Ottoman cities throughout the empire. They also fanned out through the Balkans and came to dominate inter-regional trade in that province, where, as a conduit to the Adriatic Sea, Dubrovnik enjoyed the advantage of location.

The city-state honed this competitive edge through frequent and often effective petitions to the Sublime Porte against aggressive Ottoman pirates, harassing local officials, and its imperious Venetian competitors. Dubrovnik claimed and received Ottoman protection from the sea-*gazis* who darted out of such Ottoman Albanian ports as Avlonya, Durazzo, and Bar to raid Christian shores and prey upon Venetian and other Christian shipping. The Sublime Porte also shielded Dubrovnikan colonies in Rodosçuk, Edirne, and elsewhere from attempts to register them for various levies and taxes, and saved from Venetian encroachment the city-state's monopoly over salt brought to Bosnia and Hercegovina. The Ottoman government even condemned and threatened reprisals against the Venetians because of a naval blockade of Dubrovnik and raids against it in 1617.[10] Such privileges and protection helped frustrate Venice's many efforts to upset Dubrovnik's robust trade in its Balkan hinterlands.

Despite Dubrovnik's competitive edge domestically, in the international arena it ordinarily could not compete with Venice and other Italian states, and it thrived only when links between Venice and the Ottoman Empire collapsed utterly. Just as Florence had profited from the long fifteenth-century conflict, so during later Ottoman–Venetian wars did Dubrovnik's traffic burgeon. The principal cause in each case was Venetian distress, and Dubrovnik's ability to move aggressively into established Venetian markets increased enormously the Serenissima's need to maintain and make peace with the Ottoman Empire. For the most part, it succeeded. None of the three sixteenth-century wars lasted long enough for Dubrovnik to gain much advantage. The last great Ottoman–Venetian clash, the Cretan War (1645-69), was much longer than any previous conflict, however, and during it Dubrovnik's international commerce simply exploded. When the conflict began, Venice's challenger drew perhaps 20,000 ducats from the transit trade; by 1669 income had grown to about 500,000 (a 25-fold increase!); within a year after the Ottoman conquest of Venetian Crete it had plummeted again to about

<hr/>

[10] Başbakanlık Osmanlı Arşivi, Ecnebi Defteri 13/1, p. 4, no. 1; p. 3, no. 2; p. 84, no. 2; p. 145, no. 1.

60,000.[11] Venice must have suffered greatly – although it was still able to rebound quickly – from this extreme oscillation in commercial fortune; nonetheless, during the earlier sixteenth-century wars the Republic had endured relatively little financial distress.

Venice's Ottoman challengers

As these statistics suggest, in ordinary times Dubrovnik was no more able to compete with Venice's vast commercial experience and empire than were the Florentines. Each depended for prosperity not only upon Ottoman backing but also upon Ottoman repudiation of their Venetian competitor. Other Ottoman subject communities, however, could and did learn to challenge the Italian state's primacy. Principal among these in the sixteenth century were Jewish and Armenian subjects of the empire.

When the Ottomans came on the scene in the fourteenth century, a scattering of Jews already existed throughout the European and Mediterranean worlds. Centuries of coexistence with and accommodation to dominant societies – whether Mamluk, Byzantine, Italian, Germanic, or Spanish – had fractured these communities into a cacophony of lifestyles and beliefs. Even though they retained their Jewish identities, culturally Jews living in the Mamluk Empire much more closely resembled the Muslims with whom they shared Arab lands than they did their Germanic or Spanish brethren, who ate different foods, spoke different languages, embraced different attitudes toward marriage and family, and even practiced their religion in radically different ways.

Partly through conquest and partly through immigration, the Ottoman Empire drew together representatives from all of these types. Many settled in Istanbul, which by 1477 boasted over 1,500 Jewish households. Others lived elsewhere, in cities such as Safed, Jerusalem, Manisa, Alexandria, and Salonika. The last of these is perhaps both the most distinctive and most indicative of Jewish settlement in the empire. It seems that whereas no Jews lived in Salonika in 1478, by 1519 twenty-four Jewish congregations (*kehillot*) each with its own synagogue and rabbi comprised over half of the city's population.[12] It had become and long remained the only "Jewish" city in the world.

It also, and obviously, was a city of immigrants, to which Jews from throughout the European and Mediterranean worlds had flocked. Conveniently for tracing these migrations, congregations in the empire

---

[11] Carter, *Dubrovnik*, p. 397.
[12] Bernard Lewis, *The Jews of Islam* (Princeton, NJ, 1984), p. 126.

often identified themselves according to their places of origin. Those in Salonika were no exception. Their appellations – Apulia, Aragon, Calabria, Castilian, Catalan, Corfu, Evora of Portugal, German, Italy, Lisbon, Maghrib, Otranto, Provençal, Saragossa of Aragon, Sicily, and Spain – suggest diverse origins, congregational exclusivity, and Iberian dominance.[13]

These congregations at first fought bitterly over ritual, language, and what to do about the "marranos" (Jews who had been forced to renounce their religion in Catholic Spain and Portugal) who began trickling into the Ottoman Empire in the late fifteenth century and whose rejection of martyrdom Jews from northern Europe (Ashkenazim) particularly scorned. Despite their squabbling the overriding identity of this eclectic ingathering remained religious, and the congregations gradually resolved (or learned to live with) their differences. The amalgam they produced, while primarily Spanish (thus their heirs' appellation today as "Sephardim"), was infused also with elements from the Germanic, Arab, Byzantine, and other legacies.

The contributions of these subjects to the Ottoman body politic were considerable and varied. They brought with them from Iberia and Italy innovative methods of textile production and doctoring, helped develop and institutionalize Ottoman financial administration and tax gathering, and advanced Ottoman civilization in myriad other ways. They also, and more relevantly here, furthered the integration of the Ottoman Empire into the rest of Europe, particularly in the realms of commerce and finances.

The community's far-flung diaspora was instrumental in its commercial vigor. Not only did Spanish Jews resettle all along the Ottoman littoral, but they also established districts in Venice, Genoa, and other Italian states. As the sixteenth century progressed they even reintroduced themselves to Bordeaux, London, and other Atlantic seaboard cities from which their ancestors had been expelled centuries before, and established connections with their German co-religionists in Hamburg, Amsterdam, and elsewhere. Typically, the exiles from Spain and Portugal installed themselves in Christian European cities as converts rather than as Jews. Only later could they repudiate the faith that the Iberians had forced upon them. Even as "conversos," however, they often organized commercial links with Sephardic Jews in the Ottoman Empire and other cities in the rest of Europe, thereby advancing the new commercial net spreading out from the Levant as well as the process of binding together the two Europes.

[13] On Jewish settlement in the empire, see Levy, *Sephardim*, pp. 14–28.

Such was exactly the procedure that the best-known and wealthiest Ottoman-Jewish family of the sixteenth century undertook. The Portuguese Jews Beatrice da Luna and her nephew Joao Miguez (members of the influential Mendes family) converted in Lisbon under pressure from the monarchy and then fled the Inquisition along with thousands of other *conversos*. In their Catholic guises they migrated to Antwerp, and when the Spanish Inquisition established itself there escaped first to Lyon and then to Venice. At each stop the Mendes family established links with resident marranos and Jews, building a commercial network and their fortunes. By the 1540s the Mendes family had a substantial stake in the European spice trade, and in 1553 da Luna, at the invitation of the Ottoman government, resettled for a last time in Istanbul. Her nephew soon followed, bringing with him much of their money and forming through this relocation an Ottoman center to their vast commercial network.[14] Once safely in Ottoman lands they also peeled off their Catholic veneers.

Da Luna and Miguez were only the most eminent of the many marranos who entered the Ottoman domain during the sixteenth century. Joao in particular became known for his political dabblings. Although his power is often exaggerated, he probably was a confidante to several Ottoman viziers, encouraged the Ottoman boycott of the Pope's port of Ancona in 1554, supplied Selim II with fine wines from Cyprus, Crete, and elsewhere, nearly monopolized the export of Ottoman wines to Poland, and perhaps helped promote the Ottoman invasion of Cyprus in 1570. Nevertheless, there is little evidence that either he or other Ottoman Jews had real leverage over Ottoman policy, or even that he held a particular vendetta against Venice or Catholicism or that he tried to manipulate Ottoman authorities against them. Much to the contrary, perhaps aspiring to gain access into the city-state's lucrative market, Miguez, now the Duke of the island of Nassi, several times defended Venice against Ottoman censure.

Venice and the Ottoman-Jewish community nevertheless considered each other as dangerous commercial rivals. The Iberians' migration into the Ottoman Empire brought them also into the heart of the battered Venetian realm at the very moment when the Republic was most vulnerable, as it strained to transform itself from a political into a commercial empire. Sephardic settlements in Salonika, Istanbul, Aleppo, Alexandria, and other Levantine cities menaced Venetian pre-eminence in the eastern Mediterranean.

[14] Much of what has been written on the marranos and the Mendes family is hagiographic. Two brief and clear expositions on their power and commerce are Arbel, *Trading nations*, pp. 55–65; and Halil İnalcık, "Capital formation in the Ottoman Empire," *Journal of Economic History* 19(1969): 121–23.

Even more threatening to Venetian trade than the superb matrix of this commercial network were the abilities of the new immigrants to blend into and exploit both local and imperial Ottoman political and administrative organizations. The Ottoman state showed a willingness to rely on Sephardic Jews – who after all not only were Ottoman subjects but also could be trusted as comrade victims of Christian, and especially Habsburg, oppression – far more than on Florentines or even Dubrovnikans. Because of the government's confidence as well as the community's particular aptitudes, its members for a time came to dominate Ottoman tax farming, collection of customs, and financial advising to the Ottoman elite. The combination of their experience at the core of Ottoman administration and their diasporic existence made the Ottoman-Jewish community formidable competitors in the cut-throat world of Mediterranean and European commerce. The danger of losing to them lucrative trade, industry, and markets constituted yet another incentive for Italians and other Europeans to absorb and accommodate themselves to Ottoman behavior.

Nor were the Jews the only Ottoman subject people who rose to commercial prominence and threatened Italian arteries of commerce. Muslim traders dominated many Ottoman exchanges and a few international routes, particularly to the north and the east. More of a threat in the sixteenth and seventeenth centuries, however, was the Armenian community, a close-knit yet dispersed people who exploited communal characteristics as well as Ottoman flexibility to build a formidable trading diaspora. Even though the heyday of their trading network did not come until the seventeenth century, when Armenian dominance of the silk road from Persia across Ottoman Anatolia stimulated their economic activities also in the Mediterranean, European, and Indian worlds, Armenian settlements for centuries had existed in principal Middle Eastern and Mediterranean cities and served as the glue for various trading routes. Armenian communities inhabited Akkerman, Kaffa, Baghdad, Aleppo, Damascus, Bursa, and Istanbul; from these sites Armenian traders helped connect the Ottoman and Persian worlds to Poland, Russia, and India. Particularly in the Black Sea region, where even before the Ottoman conquest of Kaffa in 1475 Armenian merchants had begun patronizing trading centers, they constituted a notable rival to Italian and especially Genoese communities of traders.

Whereas Ottoman Jews became pivotal in linking the Islamic and Christian worlds, the Armenians, also a community marginalized in several rich civilizations, helped bridge the chasm not only between the Sunni world of the Ottoman Empire and the Shi'a world of Safavid Persia, but also between Christian, Islamic, and even Hindu civilizations.

Since neither the Ottoman nor Safavid states allowed the other's Muslim subjects to settle and trade in its domains, the Armenians eventually found themselves virtually monopolizing the movement of silks and other luxury goods between these two great empires and from them to the rest of the world.

The Ottomans in Renaissance diplomacy

However ambivalent the status of "alien" in Galata and elsewhere in the Ottoman realm was to become, Mehmed II's imperial decree issued to the Genoese of Galata in 1453 did allow foreigners to live in this remote world securely and according to their own laws and religious practices. The *ahdname* of Galata also became the prototype for a series of agreements between the Ottoman Empire and other governments that became known in western European parlance as "capitulations." The first of these immediately followed the conquest of Constantinople as Italian commercial powers – the Genoese, the Florentines, the Venetians – rushed to safeguard their stakes in the commerce of the eastern Mediterranean and Black Sea regions. France and the Ottoman Empire first negotiated – but probably never ratified – an agreement in 1536 during their anti-Habsburg rapprochement, finally sanctioning such capitulations only in 1569. England, the Netherlands, and other European powers followed suit in the late sixteenth and seventeenth centuries.

These documents came to symbolize not only the framework for links between the Ottoman government and the rest of Europe but also the relative positions of diplomatic and commercial representatives of other European states within the empire. For example, if Venice carried the choicest capitulatory terms at the beginning of Sultan Süleyman's reign, by the end of the century France and England had supplanted the Italian city-state. Such shifts reflect in part the rise of the western European state. They also exhibit Ottoman efforts to reward the enemies of its Habsburg rivals.

In the early modern period the Ottoman government did not conceive of such capitulations as treaties between equals. Rather, the Ottomans imagined the foreigners as members of a particular *taife*, or group, living within their polity.[15] Just as the state bestowed particular privileges upon religious, economic, and social clusters, so did it grant certain favors to subjects of foreign states; just as the state required from its subjects taxes and imposed upon them sumptuary conditions in return for these privileges, so did it demand from foreign merchants and envoys a surcharge upon goods traded and certain restrictions in residences and attire.

[15] On which see Goffman, "*Millets*," pp. 139–41.

26   Pera lies just above Galata, across the Golden Horn from Istanbul. In the sixteenth century, it became the quarter where diplomats lived, and drew a large number of non-Muslim Ottomans. This woman models the attire of a Greek inhabitant. Nicolay, *Le navigationi et viaggi nella Turchia.*

However mercantile the Ottoman purpose may have seemed in award-
ing capitulations to other kingdoms, the arrangement also served to im-
plant foreign diplomatic and cultural presences in the Ottoman realm.
Galata not only became the commercial heart of the empire, but also –
with its hauntingly western European architecture, churches, lingua
franca, and ambassadors – was perceived even before 1453 as a Latin
outpost in the Levantine world. Similar quarters soon were installed in
other Ottoman cities and by the end of the century an array of such sites
existed.[16] It was during the late fifteenth century that Italian city-states
began earnestly to heed the kingdom surging from their east. It also was
during this period that Italy is said to have invented the system of diplomatic representation that soon spread northward throughout Europe, and
whose basic pattern is employed to this day in relations between nation
states, fashioning this new diplomacy in the political microcosm that was
the fragmented world of Renaissance Italy. As an authoritative text on
this phenomenon puts it: "the immediate result of the absence of severe
outside pressures [during the late fifteenth century] was to set the states of
Italy free for their competitive struggle with one another, and so to inten-
sify their awareness of the structure and tensions of their own peninsular
system." These pressures, the author continues, "produced the new style
of diplomacy. Primarily it developed as one functional adaptation of the
new type of self-conscious, uninhibited, power-seeking competitive or-
ganism." In this cauldron, a more secularized and institutionalized diplomacy emerged, soon to be adopted by the great European states (Spain,
France, and England) to Italy's north and west. Furthermore, Venice was
a principal formulator of this new diplomacy and a key actor in this new
game, for "above the welfare of Italy or Christendom, above any considerations of religion or morality, the rulers of Venice preferred . . . the
self-preservation and aggrandizement of their own republic."[17]

The Ottoman empire materializes as little more than a shadowy back-
drop in this and most other studies of Renaissance diplomacy. Invariably, the key developments are considered to have occurred as a result
of the relations of Italian states with each other and with trans-Alpine
European kingdoms. Nevertheless, Venice certainly did experience "severe outside pressures" in exactly this period from the battering the Ottomans inflicted upon its empire and its navy. The Pope also experienced
enough disquietude for him to pack his bags when in 1480 an Ottoman
army disembarked at Otranto and prepared to march on Rome. Indeed,
there is little doubt that the Ottoman advance pressured Venice and other

[16] See Eldem, Goffman, and Masters, *Ottoman city*, pp. 207–13.
[17] Mattingly, *Renaissance Diplomacy*, pp. 61 and 95.

Italian states into a dramatic modification of their positions in the eastern Mediterranean world.

Contrary to Mattingly's claims, not only were Italian experiences in the Ottoman east critical in the construction of a new diplomacy, but resident envoys in Istanbul helped unmask (or at least temper) myths about the impenetrable Orient and the "terrible Turk," formed during centuries of enmity and warfare. In their place were assembled concrete and realistic details about Ottoman society. In short, despite the lack of interest of Ottoman officials in establishing their own diplomatic missions in other European capitals (none were organized before the eighteenth century, even though the terms of the capitulations gave them the reciprocal right to do so), the requirement that Italian states understand the Ottoman system together with the ability of that society to accommodate Christian settlements and missions determined that from the very beginning the empire would lie at the heart of the new diplomacy. Indeed, the formulating of some of the most essential elements of the modern world's diplomatic system – permanent missions, extraterritoriality, and reciprocity – drew upon the experiences of the directors of Florentine, Genoese, and Venetian settlements in the Ottoman domain.

From the very beginning the Italians felt it essential to protect their merchants in this most foreign place, especially from the monstrous calamities of enslavement and apostasy. They sought to do so in part by appointing permanent representatives (known variously as consuls, *eminis*, or baili) whose job was not only to shield the city-states' subjects from the perils of life in a foreign and perhaps hostile place, but also to fathom and describe in frequent letters and, upon their return to the Republic, in *relazioni* (recitations upon the empire that the representatives presented to the Venetian Senate) happenings in the pivotal and menacing Ottoman polity.

These envoys functioned similarly to and may have been models for the diplomats that Italians soon thereafter began posting in each other's capitals. The principal difference perhaps was that whereas the earliest resident ambassadors within the Italian peninsula simply confirmed and maintained alliances, the Ottoman appointees also endeavored to collect information about and predict the actions of a foreign and dangerous nemesis. The latter is a rather closer antecedent than is the Italian case, it seems clear, to Catholic Spaniard diplomats in Protestant England during the late sixteenth century, or to democratic American diplomats in the communist Soviet Union during the late twentieth century. In each case one of the emissary's principal tasks was to learn as much about the enemy as possible in order to predict, contain, and counter its policies and actions.

Just as reminiscent of modern diplomacy as the long-term residency of envoys in Ottoman lands was their acquisition of a form of communal governance that displayed many attributes of extraterritoriality. This stipulation, by which each expatriate people enjoyed the right to be judged according to its own codes, aimed to shield aliens from the supposedly cruel and certainly bewildering system of Ottoman-Islamic justice. It was an idea that was utterly foreign to most of Europe, locked as it was in the more and more fictitious concept of a universal Christian body politic. The Ottomans of course knew and used it as an extension of the system by which they administered their non-Muslim subjects.

The issue of freedom of worship lay at the core of extraterritoriality. In the century or so after the Protestant Reformation (1517) virtually all of western Europe adopted *cuius regio eius religio* – the idea that the ruler's religion should be the people's religion. In this climate, the display of heretical worship that most envoys demanded and most states proscribed paralyzed diplomatic relations between Catholic and Protestant states. Only in the seventeenth century did the concept of extraterritoriality resolve this dilemma. For the Ottomans, though, there never was such an issue. From the very beginning, each legate had a church or a chapel where he and his staff could worship freely and each ambassador and consul had legal jurisdiction over his "nation." No other European state employed such a sweeping extraterritoriality until long after the religious wars of the sixteenth century had helped shatter the idea of universal law. Thereafter the invention became and has remained an axiom of diplomacy in western Europe.

Even reciprocity – the idea that governments exchanged ambassadors – had some antecedents in the Ottoman world, even if not in the diplomatic sphere. The Ottomans insisted upon entering into each capitulation reciprocal rights for their merchants, with the result that European states had to allow settlements of Ottoman subject merchants (although perhaps because of cultural and societal impediments rarely Muslim ones) in Venice, Genoa, London, Amsterdam, and other principal European cities.

Such constructs yielded the implantation of western European organs into the Ottoman body politic and served as archetypes for the development of a new diplomacy in the rest of Europe. They derived from and undoubtedly were made possible by the Ottoman manner of structuring society. Having chosen to allow Christian and Jewish subjects to live according to their own laws and traditions, it was not a great step for the state to grant similar rights to foreign visitors. Indeed, the Ottomans gave the same name – *ahdname* – to the agreements that made each arrangement viable.

In the fifteenth and early sixteenth centuries Florence, Genoa, and Venice vied for control of Ottoman markets and goods. After about 1570 France, England, the Netherlands, and other northern Europeans joined

27   Each year, the sultan and all Ottoman grandees gathered in an
imperial mosque to rejoice in the birth of Muhammed. This print depicts
such a gathering at the Sultan Ahmed (Blue) mosque during Mahmud
II's sultanate (1808–39). D'Ohsson, *Tableau général de l'Empire othoman*,
vol. I, after p. 256.

and eventually displaced these Latin kingdoms. They shared the commercial terrain with Ottoman subject communities, who benefited as
much as did foreigners from the proto-laissez-faire approach that positive Ottoman attitudes toward both religious diversity and commerce
engendered. Venetians, Florentines, and others delivered to Italy some
of the arrangements that permitted such diverse communities to work
and live together and adapted them in their relations first with other Italian city-states and later also with the emerging nation states of western
Europe.

Kubad ransomed

> The greatest troubles I have had from [the Turks] have been caused by the men of Senj, who pass in their barks beneath Morlacchia toward Obrovac, come ashore, and do great damage to the Turks, who say that Your Serenity is responsible for guarding them from the sea, and demand that we give them recompense. And so I have chased the Senjani and the said uskoks as much as I have been able.[1]

It was not until almost two years after Lepanto that Kubad finally was homeward bound toward his beloved metropolis. The war between the Catholic holy league and the Ottoman Empire had sputtered along for over a year after the conquest of Cyprus and the battle off Lepanto. During that time, Kubad remained in Venice, first as prisoner and then as negotiator. The Ottoman captive received many visits from Grimani in the weeks after Lepanto. At first, it was clear, the venerable Venetian nobleman was dropping by merely to gloat. Gradually, however, the tone of his conversation changed, as he discussed with unease the contrast between a becalmed Venetian arsenal and one in Istanbul that reportedly hummed with unparalleled bustle. In early April, 1572, an edgy Grimani advised Kubad of the rumored launch at the arsenal in the Golden Horn of a fleet of some 200 refurbished and newly built galliots, galleys, and other vessels.

News from the wider world soon confirmed Grimani's fears that Lepanto would prove a sterile victory. Kubad noticed that the euphoric celebrations in Venice and elsewhere that followed Lepanto had slowly subsided, and heard from his Jewish compatriots that Latin optimism had gradually seeped away into despair as the grand alliance of Catholic powers grew distracted by the renewed threat from England, France, and a revolt in the Spanish Netherlands, and as the Ottoman navy, seemingly stronger than ever, re-formed itself and again prowled the Adriatic and even pushed into western Mediterranean seas.[2] He also

---

[1] Antonio da Mula, Rector of Zadar, Report to the Venetian Senate, *c.* 1543; as quoted in Bracewell, *Uskoks of Senj*, pp. 201–2.

[2] On Christian–Ottoman relations and especially warfare in this period, see Kenneth M. Setton, *Venice, Austria, and the Turks in the seventeenth century* (Philadelphia, 1991), pp. 1–39.

was made aware of the rising complaints of Venetian merchants and mariners against their state's and navy's increasingly futile efforts to safeguard their shipping from the predations of rival traders and pirates, Christian even more than Muslim.[3] It seemed clear to Kubad that the exertions of the war had not only utterly exhausted the Venetian fleet and driven the state toward financial catastrophe, but also provided an occasion for its European rivals to displace its trading empire. The commercial galleys of old rivals such as Ragusa and Genoa began anchoring in Ottoman ports; meanwhile new competitors such as France were making the most of modern and rugged sailing ships to push eastward out of Marseilles, and even from the Atlantic seaboard, to establish a diplomatic presence in Istanbul, and to negotiate such favorable commercial agreements with the sultan's government that the ships of other states – including even Venice itself – had begun to trade under the French flag. The Senate desperately wanted peace in order to focus on these perils that, as the Ottoman emissary mockingly reminded Grimani, came not from Islam but from fellow Christian states. The Venetians again turned to Kubad for advice about how to put an end to their debilitating conflict.

The envoy, who knew that the grand vizier Sokollu Mehmed and others had opposed the invasion of Cyprus precisely from fear of a unified Catholic world, urged the Venetians that their best course would be to break their alliance with the Habsburgs and the papacy. He argued that the Sublime Porte would welcome such a separate approach, and grant peace on reasonable terms. This advice merely confirmed what Venice's shortages of grain and other foods and reduced trade and industry already urged, and in early 1573 a delegation with plenipotentiary powers set out for Istanbul. Simultaneously, the doge also granted Kubad permission to leave.

In May 1573, Kubad, in a rush to get home, did not wait for a military fleet or set out on the long trek overland. Instead he boarded a Venetian merchant-galley "tramping" down the Adriatic – intending to stop over for trade at Spalato, Corfu, and Modon – en route for Istanbul. The ship never made it to its first port-of-call.[4] Just as it rounded Pola point, less than one day out from Venice, a swarm of some forty small boats suddenly darted in from the east and quickly infested the massive and clumsy galley. The courier knew that these were Uskoks, a community of destitute yet determined privateers – many of whom were fugitives from Ottoman Bosnia and Serbia – entrenched in the northern Dalmatian seaside town of Senj, sanctioned by the Habsburg state, and dedicated to struggle against Islam. Despite their sworn opposition to the Ottomans, it was Venetian shipping that most suffered from their attacks, which invariably occurred in the Adriatic "sea of Venice." Uskok zeal excused strikes

---

[3] On which see especially Alberto Tenenti, *Piracy and the decline of Venice, 1580–1615*, trans. Janet Pullan and Brian Pullan (Berkeley and Los Angeles, 1967).
[4] Bracewell, *Uskoks of Senj, passim.*

against Venetian vessels, which almost invariably carried Muslim and Jewish traders and their merchandise and thus, the corsairs' line of reasoning went, collaborated with the great Ottoman adversary.

Kubad appreciated that the danger was particularly his. Unlike the Venetian merchants and mariners, and Dalmatian oarsmen, who as Christians could plead for their lives, as a Muslim and an Ottoman official the Uskoks might summarily put him to death. With fervor did he thus aid his fellow sailors and passengers feverishly struggling to fend off a boarding of their ship: to no avail. Neither the self-indulgent merchants nor the malnourished seamen could match the sinewy and dogged mountain folk, whose myriad boats nimbly swirled around the lumbering Venetian vessel. With terrible speed, several craft had been attached to the great hull and dozens of Uskoks had swarmed the deck. The futile resistance ended, the galley was taken, and its passengers and crew stood huddled miserably in the bow.

Among these captives was Kubad, whose religion put him in particular danger, but whose rank also made him particularly valuable. He knew that these brutal pirates would do one of three things with him. They might unceremoniously execute him as a dangerous adversary. Although this option seemed logical, in fact it was unlikely as long as the pursuivant could conceal his mission to help negotiate a separate Ottoman–Venetian peace. The Uskoks were a desolate and destitute as well as a fanatic people who could ill afford to cut his throat and thereby lose the income of either selling him to the Genoese or the papal states as a galley slave or holding him for ransom. It also seemed unlikely that Kubad would be sold into bondage. The demand for galley slaves was much depressed in the relatively quiet aftermath of Lepanto, and the bandits could expect no more than ten or fifteen ducats for a middle-aged and rather flaccid statesman. As a high Ottoman official, however, he could fetch perhaps 300 ducats in ransom. Indeed, Kubad himself could guarantee such a payment out of his own pocket. Such was the upshot. Within a week, the pursuivant had arranged with the Ottoman military governor of the sancak *of Bihać for the immediate dispatch of a cavalry troop hauling 300 ducats to meet him near the town of Slunj on the Ottoman–Croatian frontier. Here the exchange took place, and Kubad again was on his way to Istanbul.*

Kubad had had to swallow his impatience to return to the imperial capital and travel home overland. His journey across Bosnia, down the Danube River, and then south from Plevna to Edirne did not get him to the Ottoman capital until late August. Much to his vexation at having been left out of the talks, the Venetians already had negotiated a separate accord; much to his relief, though, the great city of Istanbul remained haughtily and familiarly Ottoman. The sultan's servant settled once again into his routine.

7   A changing station in Europe

> For your Greek subjects of the island of Candia, and the other
> islands of the Levant, there is no doubt but there is some greater
> regard to be had of them, first, because that the Greek faith is never
> to be trusted; and perhaps they would not much stick at submitting
> to the Turk, having the example of all the rest of their nation before
> their eyes: these therefore must be watch'd with more attention,
> lest, like wild beasts, as they are, they should find an occasion to use
> their teeth and claws. The surest way is to keep good garrisons
> to awe them, and not use them to arms or musters, in hopes of
> being assisted by them in an extremity: for they will always shew
> ill inclinations proportionably to the strength they shall be
> masters of.[1]

Most historians have portrayed a post-Süleymanic Ottoman world in decline. Their evidence for such a downturn is principally military. It is often
argued that the Ottoman navy never fully recovered either its power or its
prestige after the débâcle of Lepanto (1571), and that the Ottoman army
never rediscovered its fortitude and fierceness after the long wars against
the Habsburg and Safavid empires that brought the sixteenth century to
a close and engendered the stalemating Peace of Zsitva-török (1606).
Consequently, the argument goes, concession, retreat, and retrench-
ment characterized Ottoman history during the seventeenth through the
nineteenth centuries. The reality, of course, was much more complicated than this representation suggests. Particularly in the seventeenth
century, many regions and sectors of the empire flourished economically;
innovation and bureaucratization engendered an unprecedented political stability; and even militarily, the Ottomans enjoyed some notable
successes.

---

[1] Robert Pashley, *Travels in Crete*, 2 vols., 1837 (reprint, Athens, 1989); as quoted in
Molly Greene, *A shared world: Christians and Muslims in the early modern Mediterranean*
(Princeton, 2000), p. 44.

International trade in the changing fabric of Ottoman society

A positive side of life in the seventeenth-century Ottoman Empire is seen most clearly in the commercial sector. While it is true that Ottoman merchants lost some ground to Dutch, English, French, and Venetian competitors in trade between the Ottoman and western European worlds as a result of a changing relationship between the Ottoman and other European states, many of these same merchants also profited from the consequent restructuring of commerce. The gradual loosening of Istanbul's control over foreign communities resident in the major cities of the empire, for example, increased opportunities for subject as well as foreign merchants to reorganize and streamline domestic trading networks, and for Ottoman agriculturists to diversify and market their produce.

A variance between the Ottoman and western European conceptions of the role of international trade yielded this changing relationship. As we have seen, after the Ottoman conquest of Istanbul, both Genoa and Venice had negotiated political and commercial agreements (*ahdnames* or capitulations) with the Ottoman state. These documents granted Italian merchants certain rights of domicile and commerce in Istanbul and later in other port cities of the Ottoman Mediterranean world in return for tariffs against commodities traded. As a result of Franco-Ottoman political agreements during their wars against the Habsburg Emperor Charles V, the governments of Francis I and Süleyman negotiated (but never signed) similar agreements. Then, in the last decades of the century, the Ottoman state granted the principal Atlantic seaboard nations – France (1569), England (1581), and the Netherlands (1600) – their own capitulatory treaties.

These documents differed little from the ones negotiated over a century earlier with the Genoese, Venetians, and Tuscans. Nevertheless, as the Italians themselves had discovered through repeated invasion, beginning with the French in 1494, these northern states were something new. Certainly they represented far larger societies than did either Genoa or Venice. Moreover, they were better organized, more purposeful, could draw upon more resources, and possessed considerable technological advantages over their Italian rivals. In other words, the relative power of these states was great, and the Ottomans did little in their treaties to acknowledge or compensate for this shift.

Furthermore, even within the Mediterranean world the balance of power had shifted. When the Genoese and Venetian states had negotiated their agreements in the mid fifteenth century, the Ottoman navy had been young and innovative. In subsequent years, it over and over again had defeated the combined forces of the Catholic-Mediterranean world, a success which helped the Ottoman government to define the terms of the Latin presence in its domains. The world after Lepanto (1571) was different. Ottoman naval power did not collapse. Indeed, on paper its navy became even stronger. Nevertheless, the terms of encounter had changed. There was never to be another sea battle of the magnitude of Lepanto, for neither the Ottomans nor any league of Catholic states again proved willing to gamble an armada upon a single engagement. Naval warfare in the late sixteenth century, rather, consisted of small sorties, feigning actions, and strategic occupations. With no dominant naval force, a type of vacuum emerged in the eastern Mediterranean seas.

The English, the Dutch, and the French used maritime technology developed in the heavy seas of the Atlantic and the organizational innovations of their centralizing states to step into this commercial void.[2] They introduced into the Mediterranean world a new type of vessel, the *bertone*, which, although smaller than the galleys used by the navies of this inland sea, was also quicker and more maneuverable in open waters, could sail in almost any weather, and demanded a relatively small crew. Although vulnerable in ports and close to shores, where winds, tides, and rocky coasts could give oar-propelled vessels an advantage, on the open seas the *bertoni* could be overpowering and provided their captains with choices. The speed and maneuverability of the *bertone* meant that, when confronted with a galley, the decision of whether to flee, chase, or fight was usually in its captain's hands. In a sea that in the aftermath of Lepanto swarmed with pirates and corsairs – many of them also sailing the new vessels – these same advantages pertained also to commerce and travel.

These new seafaring states also enjoyed administrative advantages. Peculiarly, perhaps, it was neither the English nor the Dutch states that signed capitulatory agreements with the Ottomans. Rather, enterprising individuals who had probed the opportunities of international trade established private companies – the English and the Dutch Levant Companies. These exclusive concerns secured monopolies over commerce between England or the Netherlands and the Levant by negotiating privileges first with their own governments and then with the Ottomans.

To take the English case: beginning in the 1520s, a trickle of enterprising young traders had proven the viability of Anglo-Ottoman commercial relations. This potential was fulfilled in the 1570s and 1580s because of the converging focus of several rich London merchants and Queen

---

[2] Tenenti, *Piracy and the decline of Venice, passim*.

Elizabeth's government. In 1575, the Ottoman government granted Edward Osborne and Richard Staper permission to trade in its domains, and three years later William Harborne settled in Istanbul as their envoy. In 1581, the Queen's government authorized Osborne, Staper, and ten other London merchants to establish the joint-stock Levant Company, the right to appoint representatives in Ottoman port cities, and a monopoly over English–Ottoman commerce.

This Company enjoyed several advantages over its Italian and Ottoman rivals. First, its charter shielded it from state interference. For example, whereas the Venetian government's principal consideration in its appointment of its bailo and consuls was political and Ottoman-subject merchants were under the vigilant tax-collecting eye of Ottoman authorities, the English Levant Company chose Harborne and subsequent envoys and consuls chiefly on the basis of commercial acumen; in other words, in the English case merchants rather than politicians or diplomats supervised commerce. Second, whereas French, Venetian, or Ottoman traders had to compete with innumerable compatriot as well as foreign merchants, English trade was restricted to factors of members of the Company. Finally, whereas other traders risked personal fortune with every venture, the shared-risk arrangement of the English Company diffused exposure to loss and allowed London merchants to hazard chancy but potentially lucrative enterprises at a fraction of the personal risk. With only slight differences (for example, the English consul was salaried whereas the Dutch one depended on surcharges on goods), the Dutch Levant Company resembled the English one.

The Ottomans were willing to agree to these potentially dangerous incursions in part because their attitudes toward commerce differed quite dramatically from western Europe's. In the late sixteenth and seventeenth centuries, the empire's statesmen considered their agreements with the rising western powers as more political than economic. On the one hand, merchants in Amsterdam or London sought the best possible commercial and communal terms. Consequently, they sought most-favored-nation status, demanded extraterritorial rights, tried to force "foreigner" merchants to trade under their flags, and worked to acquire the lowest possible tariffs, all in the name of increasing the Dutch or English share in international commerce. On the other hand, the Ottoman government thought more in terms of its treasury, its military needs, and its subjects' access to goods and services. Thus did it seek revenue from foreign merchants and strive to deny them access to commodities deemed strategically or communally vital. In other words, the Ottomans responded positively to English overtures because they wanted access to English silver, tin, gunpowder, and ships, and not because they wanted to sell commodities.

Furthermore, the Sublime Porte continued to justify and couch the *ahdnames* in Islamic terms. Thus, the *harbi*, foreign, non-Muslim "enemy," upon taking up residency in Ottoman domains, received an *aman*, or safe conduct, and became a *müste'min*, or foreign inhabitant. Theoretically at least, such residency lasted only so long – between one and ten years depending upon the school of Islamic law – before such visitors became *zimmis* and thus subject to the rights and impositions of the non-Muslim Ottoman subject. In other words, the Islamic worldview envisioned Dutch, English, and French traders, no less than Genoese and Venetian ones, as *taifes*,[3] and thus potential Ottoman subjects. It is clear, then, that a rupture could occur between the growing sense of extraterritoriality (which, as we have seen, ironically owed much to Latin–Ottoman relations) that accompanied the emergence of a more modern state in the West and an Ottoman Empire that remained ideologically wedded to a godly view of the state and its relationships with society and other principalities.

Commerce in the Ottoman borderlands

Whereas the seventeenth-century Ottoman government seemed not to pay much heed to this growing gap between the normative and the historically concrete, many of its officials took it seriously indeed. As the settlements of the Dutch, English, and French communities progressed into their second and third decades, differing interpretations of the rights and obligations of alien sojourners led to frequent clashes between officials and foreigners in Istanbul and elsewhere. The roots of the tension lay in the fact that these alien traders, of whom many spent decades in Ottoman port cities, established their own enclaves (often referred to as "nations" or "factories") and expected indefinitely to retain capitulatory advantage over their Ottoman rivals. Many Ottoman officials, operating within an Islamic worldview, saw things differently, and repeatedly sought to convert such habitués into Ottoman subjects.

They attempted to do so in several ways. The capitulatory agreements covered not only aliens themselves, but also their dependents – janissary guards, doormen, and translators. In the early seventeenth century, Ottoman administrators responsible for the community of foreigners at Galata persistently ventured to collect the head tax (*cizye*) from them as if they were unprotected Ottoman subjects. Also in Galata at about the same time, janissary watchmen, candle makers, and customs collectors tried to collect taxes on meat and suet bought and butchered for

---

[3] On which, see chapter 6 above.

the Venetian community as if it were a non-Muslim subject community. Finally, throughout at least the first half of the seventeenth century, these same officials repeatedly attempted to categorize as non-Muslim subjects (*zimmis*) Venetian and French merchants who leased shops in the bazaars of Istanbul.[4] Such behavior certainly threatened the self-rule of these communities of foreigners. Nevertheless, the Ottoman officials were behaving in neither venal nor deviant ways. They intended neither to extort, nor to exclude, nor to convert as their counterparts might have aimed to do in the rest of Europe. Rather, their methods were designed to integrate these long-term sojourners politically in accordance with Islamic law without subverting either religious or civil autonomy. Most foreigners, of course, insisted upon the legal and cultural security that their political autonomy afforded, and strove to preserve and even augment collective self-rule. They did so through a variety of means and with uneven results.

By the early seventeenth century, the principal trading nations of England, France, the Netherlands, and Venice had established rather intricate commercial and administrative networks that stretched across the Ottoman Empire and beyond. Although each of these webs had different strengths, weaknesses, and structures,[5] they also shared certain characteristics. At the head of each stood representatives (ambassadors, envoys, or baili) in Istanbul, whose responsibilities included not only representing their home governments and/or companies, but also their compatriots resident in the Ottoman Empire. Each government or company also appointed consuls who led and administered the nations or factories settled in particular Ottoman cities. Finally, each competed to ensure the best commercial terms for their communities and the most autonomy from the Ottoman government.

There also were important differences between these states' administrations of their communities in the Levantine world. Venice, for example, had long experience in the Levant and had developed a highly centralized administration. Its vast, if much eroded, colonial system in the Aegean Sea and its many wars with the Ottomans meant that it had to be as much concerned with diplomacy and politics as with trade. Consequently, the Venetian Senate made it state policy to appoint judicious and capable bailos, who could maneuver through and report astutely upon the Ottoman world, and to exercise strict control over both the bailo and his consuls by making them state officials and providing them with salaries and staffs.

---

[4] See Başbakanlık Osmanlı Arşivi, Ecnebi Defteri 13/1, p. 28, no. 6; p. 29, no. 4; and p. 35, no. 5; and Ecnebi Defteri 26, p. 144, no. 3, and p. 54, no. 3.
[5] On which see Neils Steensgaard, "Consuls and Nations in the Levant from 1570 to 1650," *Scandinavian Economic History Review* 15(1967): 13–55.

Western European states were much less organized. Paris, for example, applied almost no control over its representatives, who often bought their positions as tax farmers and whom the merchants of Marseilles loosely directed. In the early seventeenth century, the French ambassadors were notoriously venal, incompetent, and chronically in debt. The heads of the Dutch and English communities were only slightly more able to administer competently than were the French.

This relatively decentralized administration among Atlantic seaboard states helped produce a frontier-like spirit within many early seventeenth-century Levantine trading nations, which comprised mostly impoverished and adventurous young men seeking to make their fortunes, many of whom found the freedom and novelty of their new environments profoundly exhilarating. Robert Bargrave may serve as an example. In 1647 he sailed from England with Sir Thomas Bendysh, the newly appointed ambassador to Istanbul. His diary repeatedly suggests how thoroughly the Ottoman world mesmerized this young merchant, as evidenced by his description of an Ottoman estate near the shore of the Bosphorus Straits:

[It] was situat on the side of a litle Hill, over a pleasant narrow Dale, which was embrac'd by a Rivolett in two Branches, and fenc'd with woods almost round it: such as afforded a various and a pleasant chace of wild Boars, of wolves, of Jackalls, and of wild Deere: so that we seldome wanted Venison of sundry sorts, besides Phasant, Partridge, and wild=foule in cheap Plenty.[6]

The peoples and opportunities even more than the foods of that milieu inspired Bargrave and others like him. To a young Englishman that world must have seemed brilliantly colored and richly exciting. In his homeland, convention and expectations (probably frustrated) hemmed him in. He likely socialized and toiled within a restricted and rather uniform circle, he consumed a little-changing English fare day in and out, and his prospects for marriage were limited and perhaps early determined. Suddenly, he was the outsider, compelled to eat unfamiliar foods, called upon to fraternize with an unimaginably diverse people, and counted on to invent new ways to make money. In short, he was largely freed from the constraints of an unbending and oppressive society and economic order. Although some probably never escaped the loneliness and homesickness that typically accompany sojourns overseas, others must have found their positions liberating.

---

[6] Robert Bargrave, *A relation of sundry voyages and journeys made be mee*, fo. 11r. Preserved in the Bodleian Library as Rawlinson, MSS.799. Now published as Michael G. Brennan (ed.), *The travel diary of Robert Bargrave* (London, 1999).

The foreign residents' freedom was far from absolute, however. The London merchant who had appointed him factor, his consul, and his ambassador exercised some control over his activities. Even more than their own states, companies, officials, and employers, however, it was Ottoman authorities and Ottoman society that circumscribed the independence of these young men. Had they journeyed to the Americas, as did many of their compatriots, they would have been influenced by their new environment and the peoples who already inhabited it. Nevertheless, such Europeans exercised a good deal of control over this new world and by the end of the seventeenth century, the English, French, and Spanish were well on their way toward colonizing it, to creating the neo-Europe that much of the Americas was to become.[7] In Ottoman domains, however, the rules of engagement were different. In this land, it was the western Europeans who had to accommodate themselves to a strong and self-confident state and society. In the sixteenth century, they had done so (with mixed results to be sure) by negotiating rights of trade and settlement with the central authorities in Istanbul.

In the seventeenth century, the situation became more complicated. Although the Ottoman government remained confident, we have seen that it also had experienced a series of military, monetary, administrative, and social affronts. The accumulated pressures of defeats by the Habsburgs and the Safavids, unchecked inflation, the rising influence of provincial authorities, and chronic rebellions had subtly diminished the capacity of the central authorities to govern effectively. As a result, European sojourners sometimes found themselves in environments in which neither authority nor power were clearly defined. It often was not enough simply to rely upon the central Ottoman government to redress grievances. The reemergence of past elites in various parts of the empire, the emergence of new elites elsewhere, and the establishment of new cities along the Mediterranean coasts greatly increased the opportunities and the dangers of trade and settlement in the Ottoman Empire.

Ottoman cities, new and old

Western European states established presences in many seventeenth-century Ottoman cities, including, at various times, Edirne, Salonika, Bursa, Alexandretta, Syrian Tripoli, Ankara, Antalya, Chios, Cairo, and Alexandria. Throughout the century, however, the three most important

---

[7] On the process of mutual "engendering" between the new world and the old, see especially J. G. A. Pocock, "British history: a plea for a new subject," *Journal of Modern History* 4(1975): 601–24. On the English experience in the Americas and the Mediterranean compared, see Matar, *Turks, Moors, and Englishmen*, pp. 83–107.

28   Here is a sixteenth-century Italian portrayal of the noble Ottoman
relaxing at home. There are no chairs or other furnishings; instead the
artist represents the figure's wealth in his rich robes and the shadowy
servant entering with a tray of food. Vecellio, *Habiti antichi*, f. 381v.

Ottoman cities for Mediterranean commerce were Istanbul, Izmir, and
Aleppo, and it was at these sites that trading nations struggled to maintain
communal self-rule and vied for commercial predominance. These cities
had in common Dutch, English, French, and Venetian settlements, foreign districts, and foreign administrators. Nevertheless, the various lines
of authority and peculiar social structures frustrated attempts to develop
a template for conduct or adjustment.

One consequence of the several transformations that characterized the
early seventeenth-century Ottoman world was the emergence of semi-
independent notables (*ayan* or *derebeys*) in outlying regions of the empire.
In some cases, these powerful men were simply representatives of eminent
local elites, who used the opportunity of a destabilized and distracted
central government to reassert themselves and their families, clans, or
ethnic groups. In other cases, they were new elites, who took advantage
of political and economic changes to insert themselves into emerging
commercial networks or the tangled edifice of administration. Then there
were the rebels, who gathered around themselves disgruntled irregular
soldiers and carved out semi-autonomous fiefdoms in provincial towns
and countrysides.

Such new elites established themselves in various permutations and affected governance in a variety of ways. In the caravan city of Aleppo, for
example, the Canpulatoğlu, a Kurdish clan, in the early seventeenth century simultaneously disrupted the caravan trade and inserted themselves
into the top ranks of Ottoman administration (Hüseyin Canpulatoğlu in
1603 became the first local to obtain the governorship of the province of
Aleppo). In the neighborhood of the port town of Izmir, it was first out-
laws such as Cennetoğlu and later notable families such as the Araboğlus
and the Karaosmanoğlus who inserted themselves locally and muddied
the lines of Ottoman power and authority. Even in Istanbul itself, powerful officials occasionally directly challenged the government's authority.
In 1651, for example, it seems that a certain İpşir Pasha led an army to
the outskirts of the city before being bought off with the grand vizierate
in the following year.[8]

Foreign merchants and diplomats had to contend with such men, and
sometimes did so effectively. In 1625, for example, Nicolini Orlando,
the consul of the Netherlands in Izmir, sent tribute to Cennetoğlu, in
return for which the outlaw granted Dutch merchants protection as they
traded in those regions under his control.[9] In 1613, the Venetian consul
in Aleppo protested the inability of Ottoman authorities to rein in the

---

[8] Evliya Çelebi, *Intimate life of an Ottoman statesman*, pp. 64–66.
[9] Başbakanlık Osmanlı Arşivi, Maliyeden Müdevver 6004, p. 124.

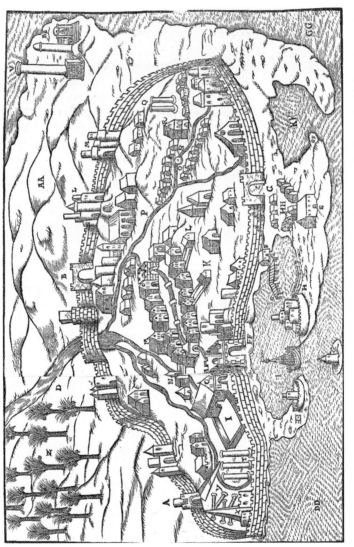

29   The walls, principal buildings, and sea defenses are clearly, if imprecisely, drawn in this late sixteenth-century map of Alexandria, one of the Ottoman Empire's principal commercial ports. Helffrich, *Kurtzer und warhafftiger Bericht.*

power of an Armenian, Bedik, who had assumed control of the collection of customs and felt confident enough to declare before the kadi: "I am the collector of customs. No one will imprison me."[10] Finally, in Istanbul in 1650, Henry Hyde agreed to pay an unnamed Ottoman pasha (perhaps Melek Ahmed himself), a "Rebell," a hefty sum in return for confirming his appointment as ambassador from England.[11]

Each of these men – Cennetoğlu, Bedik, and the unnamed pasha – operated in the gray areas at the borders of Ottoman law and society, if in very different ways. Even though in the long run none succeeded in challenging the Ottoman state, each did disrupt the terms of the capitulatory agreements negotiated between their government and the Dutch, English, and Venetians. Each also tempted foreign diplomats and traders, frustrated by the inability of the Ottoman government to protect them, to negotiate with such illegitimate authorities, thereby not only encouraging, but even contributing to their insubordination. The Dutch consul in Izmir, for example, approached Cennetoğlu only after issuing a number of futile protests to Istanbul that the brigand's army had disrupted Dutch trade in the woolens, leathers, and dried fruits of western Anatolia. Orlando's payments amounted to protection money, and thus an implied recognition of extra-governmental authority.[12] In much the same way, the Venetians, French, and other foreign nations in Aleppo resorted to direct negotiations with Bedik and other customs collectors after it became clear that the Ottoman state could not (or would not) protect them from what they perceived as abuses. Finally, in Istanbul, Hyde turned to an out-of-favor but potentially influential Ottoman statesman in his attempt to reverse the decision of a sitting grand vizier to confirm a rival's bid for the English ambassadorship.

As central control weakened, such confrontations and negotiations between local authorities and foreigners occurred repeatedly in all of the principal Ottoman commercial cities during much of the seventeenth century. The extra-governmental factions that surfaced were not the same everywhere, however, because of the dissimilar pasts and current particularities of the Ottoman cities and regions in which foreigners labored. In Aleppo, for example, newly settled Dutch, English, and French communities endeavored to plug themselves into a long-established and fixed commercial network, whose existence long predated the Ottoman conquest of 1516. Their Venetian and local rivals had long experience with this lattice, and, as the Ottoman government's ability to

---

[10] Başbakanlık Osmanlı Arşivi, Ecnebi Defteri 13/1, p. 83, no. 2.
[11] Bargrave, *Relation*, fo. 32v.
[12] On which, see Frederic C. Lane's classic study, "The economic consequences of organized violence," *Journal of Economic History* 18(1958): 401–17.

intervene effectively receded, the newer settlers were often outmaneu-
vered in competition for commodities, low prices, and various commercial accommodations.

As both the English and French factories in Aleppo became mired in
debt to local merchants, their frustrations grew. So much so that in 1642
the French consul and 55 merchants appealed to the kadi and Ottoman
military commander to allow them to refinance their debts to their
"notable" (*ayan*) creditors, which the Ottoman officials permitted.[13] In
this same decade, the English merchants in Aleppo went further, not only
petitioning the Ottoman government for succor against local leaders,
but also appealing to their compatriots in Istanbul and Izmir to lend
them money to pay for an imperial decree (*hatt-i şerif*) that they naively
believed would force the locals to abide by the terms of the capitulations.
A letter that Sir Thomas Bendysh, the English ambassador, wrote to
the directors of the English Levant Company some years later describes
how the Aleppan factory had been unwilling "to proceed unless some of
this Factory [in Istanbul] entered the lists [to obtain a *hatt-i şerif*] with
them." He then querulously declared that

wherin coining like friends, rather than politicians, crafty factors, or such as desired to draw the stream to their own mill, a Hautesheriff (the best assurance
granted in Turkey) was obtained by the hands of Mustapha Bassa for to take of
their chief aggrieances and Commands went from said visir to back the same,
as to exempt the said Factory from other inconveniences, which at first was supposed and accepted of as a piece of good service done them, when they not only
gave us hopes of great Intrades, but of latter times wrote us, they would be faithful
stewards, in levying and recovering those duties for us.[14]

According to Bendysh, not only had the factory of Aleppo not been
"faithful stewards," but they had ignored their debts to the factory in
Istanbul and kept profits for themselves. In short, the only consequence
of this effort to utilize one Ottoman authority to quash another was a
serious falling out between the English nations of Aleppo and Istanbul.

The frustrating experience of French and English traders in Aleppo,
much of which derived from having to compete with rivals who better
understood the city's commercial dynamics, was not necessarily repeated
in other Ottoman emporia. In seventeenth-century Izmir, for example,
the new trading companies from northwestern Europe thrived. Whereas
imperial weakness allowed established groups to reemerge in Aleppo,
in Izmir it was new groups who rose to prominence, among whom
were the foreign merchants themselves who settled in a small predominantly Turko-Muslim town of 2,000–3,000 in the first decades of the

[13] Başbakanlık Osmanlı Arşivi, Ecnebi Defteri 26, p. 29, no. 1.
[14] Public Record Office, State Papers 105/174, p. 398.

century and helped build it into one of the major trading centers in the
Levantine world, with large Armenian, Greek Orthodox, Jewish, and
foreign communities.[15] In other words, whereas in Aleppo, foreigners
constituted barely tolerated aliens, in Izmir they themselves merged into
and in many ways dominated the town's political and economic elite. The
consuls themselves here became almost Ottoman notables.

By mid-century, the French and English factories were even able to utilize local officials to overcome the combined authority of their own and
the Ottoman governments. In 1646, for example, the English ambassador, Sir Sackvile Crow, secured an imperial Ottoman decree ordering
the seizure of English goods and factors in Izmir. When his agents, accompanied by a çavuş, attempted to do so, they were met by a throng who

proclaimed in the Streets, that the Town would bee undone, the Trade lost and
go to wrack, if this was suffered; so that before the Consulls door were so many of
the scum of the Town, the Streets were packed thick of them. On the other side,
a more unruly enemy threatned worse things, [Nicolas Terrick] the Master of the
Golden Lyon . . . lands 40 men at Barnardistons [the English consul], and vowed
hee would have his money or goods, or swore hee would beat down the Town.[16]

The English ambassador's agents wrote this letter in order to report on
their inability to seize the goods of their compatriots, which explains its
contemptuous and condemnatory tone. Nevertheless, the letter's con-
tents make clear that the English consul and factory were able not only
to rally many of Izmir's most prominent citizens to oppose the imperial
seizure of their goods, but also to mobilize the manpower of English
ships riding in the town's harbor. Whereas in Aleppo foreigners appealed to central Ottoman authorities for relief from alleged misuse, in
Izmir they combined with locals to subvert imperial directives. Ironically, in each case a principal consequence of the quarrel was communal
factionalism.

It was the Ottoman world more than the western or southern European ones that gave rise to dissimilarities between foreign settlements in
various Ottoman cities, and which led to different individual experiences.
A European stranger residing in Aleppo usually restricted his social life
to the particular *khan* in which he and his compatriots lived and labored.
His social life might extend to neighboring *khans*, but his exposure to the
diverse peoples and languages of his milieu remained minimal. His compatriot in Istanbul also lived in a particular quarter within the city, Galata

[15] Goffman, *Izmir, passim.*
[16] *Subtilty and cruelty: or a true relation of Sr Sackvile Crow, his design of seizing and possessing himselfe of all the estate of the English in Turky. With the progresse he made, and the meanes he used in the execution thereof* (London, 1647), p. 61 (Hetherington and Zuma to Crow: 16 June 1646). The convoluted episode is more fully discussed in Goffman, *Britons,* pp. 73–85.

and Pera. Nevertheless, he could circulate more freely through the city, and the taverns and shops in Galata and the large numbers of Ottoman subjects who lived there meant contact with an assortment of peoples every time he stepped outside his home. Those who settled in Izmir could wander even more freely through Ottoman society. The "Street of the Franks" in which foreigners lived paralleled the quay and lay at the very heart of the town, and both geographically and politically these "Franks" grew to dominate the landscape of Izmir. In spite of such regional variation, however, one constant was that the social structure of the Ottoman realm in the seventeenth century continued to accommodate itself to the Christian sojourner, European or otherwise, even more than in the past. Ottoman society remained richly elastic and permeable, a point nowhere more tellingly seen than in its willingness to find room for the outsider, even for priests and clergymen traveling to and proselytizing in this ostensibly Islamic empire.

Proselytizing in the Ottoman world

For example, clusters of Catholics who had dotted the largely Greek Orthodox religious terrain of the Balkans since before the fifteenth century thrived after the Ottoman conquest. The elders of the Ottoman dependency Dubrovnik felt a spiritual obligation not only to protect their persons and property against Muslim and rival Christian proselytizers and expropriators, but also to counsel them in the Latin canon. Dubrovnik found it difficult to do so directly, however, in part because of several papal-inspired Catholic rebellions against Ottoman rule and in part because the "captive" Latin church was so small. So, much as the Aleppan English and French factories had appealed to Istanbul against local rivals, Dubrovnik also tried to employ the Ottoman state to protect the empire's Catholic subjects.

The city-state's policy precipitated a number of clashes with both Muslim and Orthodox Ottomans. For example, based upon an agreement signed with the Ottoman state in 1399 privatizing and giving Dubrovnik jurisdiction over certain Catholic establishments in the Balkans, the city claimed custody of various churches in Belgrade and its surroundings, and in the 1620s worked to renovate and settle priests in several of them. The region's Orthodox leadership, certainly opposed to such missionary ventures into its community, grew alarmed at these activities. In spite of a recent decree from the Ottoman government that confirmed Catholic ownership of these churches and condemning "Bosnians, and other *millets* of misbelievers" who interfered in their affairs in Belgrade, three "Latins of Dubrovnik" protested first in the law courts of Belgrade, and then directly to the Ottoman government in Istanbul in 1628 that people from these communities stood at church doors collecting alms, harassing Latin priests, and attempting to disrupt Catholic devotions.

A second incident in the 1620s concerned a monk who wandered the Balkans ministering to various colonies of Dubrovnikan merchants and other Catholics. Not only did "some people from the military order and others interfere with him for personal gain; in addition, monks, archbishops, and bishops who are in other *millets*... meddle with the fees that he has long taken from the Christian community." Yet a third incident involved the several Catholic monasteries dispersed across the province. The monks from these monasteries possessed commands (*ahdnames*) from the sultan allowing them to roam about, advise the "*reaya* who are in the Latin *millet*," and gather revenue from them. Despite these guarantees, some monks in 1640 petitioned against the harassments of "brigands and intriguers" as well as the persecution by "eastern monks, monks in other *millets*, priests, bishops, and archbishops."[17] Two years later, another petition described the actions of a Catholic priest, who gathered together a retinue of men, goods, baggage, and weapons, wandered through the administrative provinces of Budin and Temesvar, and read "the Gospels to Christians who are in the Latin *millet*." Certain Ottoman administrators and rulers, the petition asserts, disrupted his authorized movements and activities. Ottoman authorities in Istanbul insisted that the Catholic priest should be left to wander and preach in peace.

These incidents suggest a government more concerned with social and economic activities than with religious tenets, at least among its non-Muslim subjects, a laxness that gave seventeenth-century Ottoman society a particularly protean quality. It not only absorbed religious and other types of communities almost at will, but also was a massive and dynamic world that the foreign visitor had no choice but to engage on Ottoman terms. As we have seen, the Dutchmen, Englishmen, Frenchmen, and Venetians residing in Levantine communities did just that. The Ottoman state continued to conceive these alien communities just as they did their own subject ones – that is, according to a rather elastic rendering of Islamic law. Under such law, foreign infidels legally became *müste'min* – communities that were granted temporary rights of residence in the Ottoman domains. It followed that foreigners functioned as a component integral to, rather than an appendage disconnected from, Ottoman society.

Categorizing foreign merchants as *müste'min* put them on a virtually equal footing with those Dubrovnik priests and monks who wandered the

[17] Başbakanlık Osmanlı Arşivi, Ecnebi Defteri 14/2, p. 46, no. 1; 14/1, p. 62, no. 2; and 14/2, pp. 114–15.

Ottoman Balkans with such impunity. Even in the seventeenth century, however, it did not yet mean that their factories (or "nations") could function according to Western judicial traditions. Instead, a struggle ensued between foreign administrators, merchants, and divines who feared Ottoman jurisprudence and society and believed in the virtues of their own political, social, and religious structures, and Ottoman administrators determined to govern these interlopers just as they did other non-Muslims. Isaac Basire and Robert Frampton were two English clergymen who entered this world in the mid seventeenth century.

The 21-year-old Isaac Basire de Preaumont immigrated, perhaps from France, to Protestant England in 1628, married seven years later, and in 1636 received a Bachelors of Divinity at Cambridge. In 1641 Charles I made him a chaplain extraordinaire, and he attended upon the king during his hard days under siege at Oxford in 1645. In the next year, the parliamentarians seized this intensely royalist clergyman and imprisoned him briefly in Stockton Castle before driving him into exile.

Basire wandered to Paris, where in 1650 he met with Henrietta Maria, the recently executed Charles's Catholic wife, then to Italy, and finally arrived in the Levant in 1651, just at the close of the English civil wars and as the Commonwealth interregnum was beginning in England. He spent altogether fifteen years in exile, mostly in the Ottoman realm. In Basire's seemingly aimless driftings, which left him divided from his wife and five children for the entire period, he carried with him a strong sense of his spiritual and political purpose in the world.[18] He also served as a spy for the royalist camp.

Over the years, Basire wrote several long reports to the advisors of first Charles I and then Charles II. He described, from the comfort of an Aleppine *khan*, his sojourn and proselytizing in Venetian Zante, where he had produced "a vulgar Greek translation of our church's catechism."[19] This enterprise had led to his deportation to Ottoman Greece, where, undeterred, he preached and presented to the Greek Orthodox Metropolitan of Achaia a Greek-language copy of the Anglican catechism. After a brief return to Italy and travels through Sicily, Basire found his way to Aleppo, where he chatted with the Patriarch of Antioch and left him an Arabic version of the catechism, and then to Jerusalem, where he had long discussions with both Orthodox and Latin clerics and gained entrance into the Church of the Holy Sepulchre. He then passed into the Mesopotamian valley, where he discussed religion with Armenian bishops

[18] Basire's personal history can be culled from W. N. Darnell (ed.), *The correspondence of Isaac Basire, D. D., Archdeacon of Northumberland and Prebendary of Durham, in the reigns of Charles I. and Charles II. with a memoir of his life* (London, 1831).
[19] Bodleian Library, Clarendon MS 46, fo. 73v.

and arranged for the preparation of an Armenian translation of the catechism.

After wintering in Aleppo in 1652–53, Basire finally set out for Istanbul by land, traveling "without either servant, or Christian, or any man with me that could so much as speak the Frank language; yet, by the help of some Arabic I had picked up at Aleppo; I did perform this journey in the company of 20 Turks, who used me courteously."[20] Most arresting in this account is the image of a steadfast English divine wandering freely through the Ottoman Balkans and Arab lands, and even pushing across Syria and Anatolia in the company of twenty Muslim Turks. Traveling with this infidel throng, to whom, alone of all those encountered, he dared not preach, did not at all shake his faith in the inherent superiority of either his Anglican creed or his English society.

Basire's unshakable purpose was to convince the various churches of the East of the efficacy of Anglican worship. Even more remarkable than the man, however, was the realm in which he wandered. Unlike the Venetians, who banished Basire from the island of Zante for his proselytizing, the Ottomans placed few constraints upon him. Nor, as we have seen, was the government's turning of a blind eye toward Basire's ventures unusual. Ottoman sources describe a domain that must have seemed to bustle with Christian missionaries. Istanbul diligently defended foreign clerics from Greek and Serbian Orthodox slander and from abuse by local Ottoman officials. The Dubrovnikan and Venetian priests who ranged across the Ottoman Balkans, as well as the many Catholic monasteries situated there, found ready recourse in the Ottoman judicial system.[21] The Sublime Porte also protected Capuchin priests who wandered, proselytizing, across the empire, only ostensibly tending to French factories in Egypt, Aleppo, and elsewhere.[22] In a curious precedent to late twentieth-century disputes, the Ottoman government occasionally even tried to frustrate the export to western Europe of artifacts, as in 1656 when the Greek Patriarch accused "Frankish monks" of stealing statuary from the home of the Virgin Mary in Jerusalem and carrying it off to Europe.[23] The image that springs to mind from such Ottoman sources is one of Protestant clergymen such as Basire invading Ottoman lands not to convert Muslims or Jews, but to do battle with Catholic, Greek Orthodox, and other divines for the souls of Ottoman Christians. The role of the Ottoman authorities in these latter-day Crusades was to provide

---

[20] Bodleian Library, Clarendon MS 46, fo. 73v.
[21] In addition to those documents cited above, see also Başbakanlık Osmanlı Arşivi, Ecnebi Defteri 13/1, p. 114, no. 1; and Ecnebi Defteri 14/2, pp. 144–46, and 146.
[22] Başbakanlık Osmanlı Arşivi, Ecnebi Defteri 26, p. 38, no. 1; p. 59, no. 1.
[23] Başbakanlık Osmanlı Arşivi, Ecnebi Defteri 26, p. 88, no. 1.

ground rules, act as referees, and protect the Muslim faithful from such missionaries.

Isaac Basire was a restless evangelist who wandered the full breadth of the Ottoman Empire; other English clergy, however, were more settled. Basire's near contemporary Robert Frampton was in 1655 appointed chaplain to the English factory at Aleppo and remained in that city for twelve years. He also was an Anglican royalist, who fought for the king at the Battle of Hambledon Hill in 1645 and preached in London and elsewhere during the early Commonwealth years. Frampton was appointed chaplain in Aleppo during the heyday of Cromwell's regime with the charge "to keep that factory steady to the crown and church," which he seems to have accomplished.[24] During his period of service he helped convince Ottoman authorities in Alexandretta to allow the rebuilding of a crumbling Greek church; he persuaded the Greek Orthodox community to allow the burial of Mr. Hext, the English assistant consul in Alexandretta, in the hallowed grounds of that same church; he learned both Arabic and Italian (the Mediterranean's lingua franca) fluently enough to preach and converse freely in both tongues; and he journeyed to Istanbul to plead successfully on the English factory's behalf against a tyrannical (or so he claimed) Ottoman governor.[25]

As these events suggest, Frampton threw himself into the Ottoman world with alacrity, and developed a profound and useful understanding of it. He cultivated, for example, friendships with various religious officials, including the Orthodox Patriarch, with whom he regularly debated religious controversy, and the chief kadi in Aleppo, with whom he habitually exchanged wine-drinking visits.[26] Although his quick fluency in Arabic must have helped him infiltrate Ottoman society, it was the Ottomans who allowed the infidel, both subject and alien, to reside in their domains. It was also the Ottomans who granted them free access to each other, and felt confident enough in their own religion, their own civilization, and the legitimacy of their own government to allow social intercourse even between Muslims and non-Muslims – at least in the public, masculine, sphere.

There were limits to these activities. It was fine for the missionary to proselytize among fellow Christians and even Jews. The Ottomans could only push Islamic principles so far, however, and Muslims remained strictly out-of-bounds. Nevertheless, Frampton risked chipping away at this ideology wall. On several occasions, for example, the chaplain

[24] T. Simpson Evans (ed.), *The Life of Robert Frampton, Bishop of Gloucester, deprived as a non-juror, 1689* (London, 1876), p. 20.

[25] Evans (ed.), *Life of Robert Frampton*, pp. 38–42 and 65–73.

[26] Evans (ed.), *Life of Robert Frampton*, pp. 51–53.

harbored young Christian orphans and vagabonds whom he feared would become Muslim if left in the care of the state.[27] More perilously, he at least twice met converts who had come from Christendom and covertly persuaded them to renounce their new faith.

The first of these was a French renegade whom he met in Egypt, "many miles from Christian converse, especially of any Europeans" and in the "good round company of Turks and others." One evening, after everyone but Frampton, his servant, and one "Turk" had retired, the chaplain asked his servant, in Italian "as a language farthest from the stranger's capacity," why this young man tarried on. To Frampton's amazement, it was the young man himself who answered. When he queried further, it transpired that this was a French soldier who had fought with the Venetians at the siege of Candia during their long defense against the Ottomans (1645–69) and who, emaciated and near death, had thrown himself on the mercy of the besieging Ottoman army. He now lived, as a Muslim, in "a good plight," and had "good habit, freedom, and mony in my purse." Despite this renegade's insistence on "the justice and morallity of his new way," the devout Anglican minister considered this apostasy appalling. With fire and brimstone he exhorted repentance, to such effect that the renegade, trembling, proclaimed that he would the next morning go to the kadi and "renounce my error and by God's grace lay down my life to seal the truth of my repentance."[28] Frampton refused to allow this fatal step, and instead convinced the man to accompany him to Aleppo where he was released into the custody of the French consul and spirited off to Christendom.

Frampton later acted to rescue the soul of a second renegade, this time a Portuguese friar, "a man of some learning but more levity, who had scandalously deserted the faith," and led a contented life in Aleppo.[29] Contented, that is, until chaplain Frampton convinced him of the error of his ways and, again with the assistance of the French consul, had him also shipped off to Christendom. Frampton's work was less successful in this case. Perhaps it had been more haranguing than conviction that had brought the friar back into the fold, because several years later the mendicant, in Frampton's words, "return'd to his vomit again and liv'd in the same town."[30]

This English clergyman knew full well that he was testing the limits of Ottoman broadmindedness when he meddled with converts. In the first

---

[27] Evans (ed.), *Life of Robert Frampton*, p. 64.
[28] Evans (ed.), *Life of Robert Frampton*, pp. 56–60. All of this, of course, is according to Frampton!
[29] Evans (ed.), *Life of Robert Frampton*, p. 61.
[30] Evans (ed.), *Life of Robert Frampton*, p. 65.

case, he expressed fear that the young Frenchman intended to inform against him to Ottoman authorities. In the second case, the plot was indeed discovered. Frampton, fearing Ottoman reprisals, formulated, but for some reason never effected, a flight to England. Perhaps his friends in Aleppo shielded him. Or perhaps Frampton and other missionaries assumed wrongly that the Ottomans would abide exactly by the strictures of Islam in cases of apostates.[31] In any case, it was only several years later, in 1667, that he returned to England to marry Mary Canning, before returning with his bride to his chaplaincy in Aleppo for another three years.

These restrictions upon proselytizing remind us that the Ottomans were not tolerant and unprejudiced in any modern sense. Ottoman authorities were no less certain than were others of the exclusive truth of their faith; they punished the heretic and the apostate with no less fury. Nevertheless, Islam did provide a position in society for the infidel. Although Frampton and other Christians probably were right to fear reprisal for trying to win Muslims over to Christianity, neither he nor other English clergymen expressed much appreciation at being allowed to live and work in the Ottoman Empire. His Muslim, Jewish, or even Catholic counterparts would not have been allowed to settle, much less undertake professional religious work, in his own homeland, where religious difference, publicly at least, remained anathema.

Basire and Frampton probably were somewhat anomalous in their engagement with Ottoman society. English sojourners – whether diplomat, merchant, or divine – tended to exhibit much less interest in that world. In their writings, they stressed biblical and classical sites, the physical remains of which tell us little of their relations with Ottoman society. When their comments did drift into contemporary observations, they almost invariably discussed their own worlds of friends, family, community, and commerce. Only infrequently did English clergymen and others delve into the manifold Ottoman realm. When they did so, it almost always was to express either awe or contempt for this huge and elaborate world that, if they had stopped to consider, might have made their own isle seem almost bereft of human variety.

One result of this documentary void is that we have little direct knowledge of what the more established locals made of such exotic visitors. Shopkeepers, merchants, agriculturists, mariners, janissaries, religious officials, and administrators came into daily contact with these strange

---

[31] In the nineteenth century, at least, the Ottoman government was reluctant to take any action against apostates, on which see Selim Deringil, "'There is no compulsion in religion': on conversion and apostasy in the late Ottoman Empire: 1839–1856," *Comparative Studies in Society and History* 42(2000): 547–75.

characters who roamed across their landscapes, sketching the debris of dead civilizations and earnestly admonishing Christian Ottoman subjects to alter their spiritual practices. How much, though, does this superficial acquaintance differ from the modern tourist's, who travels to Jerusalem to visit Hebrew and Christian sites or Istanbul to see Roman and Byzantine ones? Are these modern sightseers any more aware of the people and society around them than were the Anglican clergymen who visited the Ottoman realm?

We must rely upon hints and reconstructions to contemplate the English clergyman's association with the Ottoman world. I am convinced that close relations existed and at times were strong. Otherwise Isaac Basire could not have journeyed the breadth of Anatolia with a band of Turks; Robert Frampton could not have whiled away the evenings sprawled across divans, sipping wine and deep in conversation with Ottoman pashas, kadis, and other dignitaries; and these and other clergymen could not have fraternized socially and intellectually with such a gamut of Ottoman society. It was the Ottoman world that made such encounters possible, and it is the Ottoman world with its manifold elasticity rather than the western European one with its excluding rigidity to which we must turn to explore how such encounters could have taken place.

A new-style conflict

Frampton's French renegade, who had defended Venetian Candia against Ottoman troops before "turning Turk," exemplifies both the persistent porosity of the military frontier between Christendom and Islam and the particular case of Crete, which experienced a surge of converts to Islam during and after the war.[32] He also articulates the lengthy and terrible Veneto-Ottoman struggle for the island of Crete that paralleled Dutch, English, and French movements into Ottoman commercial grounds previously occupied by the Venetians. It was typical of Ottoman relations with the rest of Europe that commerce and warfare persisted simultaneously. Whereas in the previous century, however, some Venetians had traded in Ottoman domains even as other Venetians fought the Ottoman government, now it was other Europeans who did so; and whereas in previous centuries, Mediterranean states were the most powerful ones in Europe, by the middle of the seventeenth century the states of the Atlantic seaboard had surpassed them.

Even though after the fall of Cyprus in the previous century Crete became the only significant Venetian colony in the eastern-Mediterranean

---

[32] On which see below, and Greene, *A shared world*, pp. 39–44.

seas, it was some seventy years before the Ottomans finally attacked it, and almost twenty-five more before they conquered it. Their hesitancy derived in part from consuming and exhausting wars elsewhere, first against the Habsburgs (the "long war" that punctuated the turn of the century) and then against a resurging Safavid Empire under the dynamic Shah Abbas. Only with the reconquest of Baghdad from the Safavids in 1638 were Ottoman borders again secure enough for the state finally to turn its attention to rounding out its eastern-Mediterranean frontiers.

Just as important as warfare in explaining Ottoman lethargy were transformations in Ottoman political life. Sultans eager to legitimize their new reigns had spearheaded earlier campaigns that led to the conquests of Constantinople, the Arab lands, Rhodes, Belgrade, and Cyprus. In the seventeenth century, however, not only did few sultans have the ability to lead armies, but also such public expressions of power were no longer necessary in the mature Ottoman state. Instead, it was factions, often led by grand viziers, imperial mothers, and favorite wives and concubines, that made high-policy decisions. Not only were such semi-legitimate committees often irresolute and short-lived, but also they had little to gain from aggressive military action. If such campaigns failed, they lost money, their positions, and perhaps their heads; if they succeeded, the glory was the sultan's and the state's rather than theirs.

A series of such coteries were in power in the years preceding and subsequent to 1645, when the Sublime Porte finally launched an invading fleet against Crete. The reign of the notoriously erratic İbrahim (1640–48) was particularly shaky. It began steadily enough, with a veteran and cautious, if uneasy, faction led by the sultan's authoritarian mother, Kösem, and his predecessor's grand vizier, Kemankeş Kara Mustafa Pasha, firmly in control. Relations between the sultan and his family soon deteriorated, however, as the Ottoman historian Naima explains:

> The sultan's mother would sometimes speak affectionately, giving counsel to the... *padişah*. But because he paid no attention to her, she became reluctant to talk with him, and for a long while resided in the gardens near Topkapı. During this time the sultan became angry as a result of some rumors and sent the grand vizier Ahmed Pasha to exile his mother to the garden of İskender Çelebi.[33]

In 1644, when the sultan finally had executed this vizier and had banished from the capital his own mother, Kösem sultan, Ottoman leadership became more volatile. Not only were the eighteen men who held the grand vizierate over the next twelve years generally incompetent, but

---

[33] Mustafa Naima, *Tarih*, 6 vols. (Istanbul, 1863–64), vol. IV, p. 290; as quoted in Peirce, *Imperial harem*, p. 246.

İbrahim also made a series of other unfortunate political and religious appointments (in the same period, İbrahim and his successor appointed twelve *şeyhülislams*, twenty-three chiefs of finance, and eighteen grand admirals).[34] With such rapid turnover in the most important posts, policy was bound to fluctuate. Sometimes missteps could be remedied; once war was declared, however, it was hard to reverse course.

In 1645, a war party led by Jinji Hoca, a spiritual advisor, and the grand admiral Yusuf Pasha, convinced the sultan to attack Venetian Crete, over the objections of a peace party led by the grand vizier Semin Mehmed Pasha. In late April, a fleet under the command of Yusuf Pasha set sail from Istanbul, and within two years the Ottomans had conquered most of the island other than the north-central port city of Candia. That the progress was so rapid was due only in part to Ottoman arms; many of Crete's Greek Orthodox majority were fed up with Catholic Venetian rule and welcomed the invasion. At the walls of Candia, however, the operation stalled. It took another quarter-century of grinding hostilities and destructive barrages against Candia before the Ottoman military finally completed the conquest.

During this quarter-century, the Ottoman military controlled all of Crete but Candia, and during this period thousands of Cretans converted to Islam and joined the Ottoman army. This phenomenon was unique among Greek Orthodox peoples under Ottoman rule, and requires some explanation. Some probably converted at sword point, as had Frampton's French renegade. Most, however, must have done so voluntarily. A widespread and festering resentment against Catholic Venice only in part explains the unusually high rate of Islamization; otherwise, Greek Orthodox antipathy on other Venetian-held islands would have led to similar rates of conversion. Several other factors also help illuminate its occurrence. For one thing, hundreds of years of repressive Latin control had left the peasantry of the island with hardly even a memory of an Orthodox ecclesiastical hierarchy. The consequent lack of guidance in orthodoxy and steadfastness disconnected Cretans from their religious roots and left them exposed to deviation and spiritual drift. In other words, many parts of the island existed as those isolated in-between worlds that are so characteristically Mediterranean and have been described eloquently as "a separate religious geography" that "constantly had to be taken, conquered and reconquered" by organized religions and settled states.[35] Thus, large sections of Crete and other out-of-the-way Mediterranean places shared with the more infamous Ottoman Albania reputations for

[34] See Robert Mantran, "L'état ottoman au XVIIᵉ siècle: stabilisation ou déclin?" in *Histoire de l'empire ottoman*, ed. Robert Mantran (Paris, 1989), p. 237.
[35] Braudel, *Mediterranean and the Mediterranean world*, p. 33.

religious fickleness. It was in such pockets that Islam tended to make the quickest progress.

Nevertheless, perhaps it is changes in the Ottoman state and military between the great conquests of the sixteenth century (the Arab lands, Hungary, Cyprus) and the capture of Crete a century later that best explain the inclination of Cretans to convert.[36] First of all, the seventeenth-century dispersion of power meant that viziers, pashas, other influential Ottoman statesmen, and especially the important Köprülü family, rather than the sultan and his household controlled the lands of conquered Crete. The desires of these notables to exploit the subject territories in different ways than would the monarch gave native converts new economic and social opportunities. Secondly, that same erosion in the value of the Ottoman cavalry and the simultaneous growth of the janissary and other infantry corps that had compelled the state to loosen recruitment in the Balkans, Anatolia, and elsewhere also provided Cretans the opportunity to move directly into the military (and thus the ruling order) through the simple act of conversion. It seems, in fact, that the long war, during all but the first year of which the Ottomans controlled most of the island, encouraged displaced agriculturists, viticulturists, and other workers opportunistically to convert in order to enter themselves into Ottoman military rolls. In the end, not only did the Muslim proportion of the island's population become greater than in the rest of the Greek Orthodox Ottoman world, but the makeover occurred without the disruptive transplantations of population that had followed Ottoman conquests in the Balkans and on Cyprus. In short, it was a principally home-grown and consequently relatively smooth transition from Venetian to Ottoman rule on Crete.

Ironically, it was the inability of Venice to call Christendom to its aid that was most critical in prolonging the war and motivating so many to "turn Turk." In previous conflicts, the crusading ideal had promoted at least tacit support from Mediterranean states. At times, as in the Battle of Lepanto and the defense of Malta, Venice had been able to effect holy leagues. The Serenissima did try to cobble together such a league in this war, reaching out even to distant England. As late as 1655, for example, the Senate drafted an appeal to Oliver Cromwell as a fellow Christian in which it complained of "these most barbarous Infidells, whoe have noe other end but the oppression of Christendome," and who "doe multiplie their forces utterly to subiugate the Kingdome of Candie, beinge the bullwarke of Italy, and an entrance, wherby the most insidious nation of the Turks may thrust themselves forwards to the oppression of the better

---

[36] On which see Greene, *A shared world*, pp. 41–42.

part of Europe." The Venetians may have couched their letter in the language of holy war, but they understood that, with Cromwell, they also needed a practical tone, and added: "never will there be seene a more propitious conjuncture to suppresse the Ottoman Empire, being nowe tired under the burthen of eleven yeares warre, directed by the counsell of women, exhausted of souldiers and money and can hardly resist the [Venetian] comonwealth alone."[37]

This bleak assessment of Ottoman fortunes seemed accurate in 1655. The war was stalemated; İbrahim had been assassinated in 1648; his successor, Mehmed IV, was a minor firmly under his mother Turhan's control; Mehmed's grandmother, Kösem, had herself been assassinated (rumor had it poisoned at Turhan's behest) in 1651; a desperate treasury was grasping money wherever it could find it (for example the grand vizier Melek Ahmed Pasha in that very year imposed extraordinary taxes on all *timars*; and between May 1655 and October 1656 the sultan appointed and removed seven grand viziers, six şeyhülislams, and five grand admirals). Cromwell nevertheless ignored Venice's plea, instead sending his navy to wage war against the Spaniards in the Caribbean and continuing the longstanding English policy of leaving the Mediterranean theater to the directors of the English Levant Company.

In the war over Crete, not only did Venice have to stand alone, but also England joined other northern European powers in playing off one side against the other. They were able to do so largely because the increasing naval dominance of Atlantic seaboard states in the Mediterranean world after the Battle of Lepanto not only insulated their shipping from the Cretan war, but also reduced the two contestants into supplicants for military aid. By the 1640s, Dutch, English, and French vessels were faster, more maneuverable, and better armed than were Ottoman and Venetian ships. Indeed, the Ottomans had surrendered the open seas to their rivals. In other words, whereas in the sixteenth century, Ottoman power had projected itself across the Mediterranean as far as Malta, by the 1640s it extended no further than the shorelines of the Aegean Sea. This reduced power meant that when the Ottoman surge that had begun the war faltered at the walls of Candia, the authorities had great trouble provisioning the army that they had landed on Crete, and the conflict deteriorated into one of attrition.

During this war a principal Ottoman weakness lay with its navy, a fact no more tellingly proven than in its sporadic inability to defeat the Venetian strategy of blockading the Dardanelles. By the 1640s, Istanbul was probably the largest city in Europe, with a population that had swollen

---

[37] Bodleian Library, Rawlinson MS A.31, pp. 13–15.

to perhaps 300,000. Food and clothing for these people came from throughout the empire. Thousands of sheep raised in the Balkan provinces were driven to the outskirts of the city and slaughtered each year, and countless tons of grain, fruits, and vegetables were transported by ship from the port towns of the Black and Aegean seas. It was a matter of urgency that the sea lanes be kept open. The Venetians, then, countered the Candian siege not by attacking the Ottoman army directly, but by harassing its supply lines and by attempting to cut off Istanbul's access to the entire Aegean by blockading the Dardanelles Straits.

A century earlier, when the Mediterranean lay at the economic, political, and ideological heart of Europe, this tactic probably would have been effective. In the seventeenth century, however, not only was the Ottoman–Venetian conflict regional, but also western European powers supported the Ottomans, whom they might previously have spurned as an Islamic state, as well as the Catholic Venetians, whom they might previously have backed as a Christian state. Although such aid was not unprecedented (witness the Franco-Ottoman understanding against Charles V during Süleyman's reign), it was new in the sense that Venice constituted even less of a threat to the other states of Europe than did the Ottomans. In short, the cause for Dutch, English, and French interference in this war was neither ideological nor military; it was commercial.

The vacillating participation of English ships in the war makes unmistakable this mercantile foundation. Granted, English vessels often took part informally. Renegade ships' captains made enormous profits from the desperate plight of both sides, by sometimes breaching the Ottoman cordon at Candia and at other times running the Venetian blockade of the Dardanelles or provisioning Ottoman troops on Crete. Nevertheless, English officials also involved themselves more formally. In 1649, for example, the English ambassador authorized thirteen English ships, laden with Ottoman soldiers and provisions, not only to sail from Izmir and land them near Candia, but also to join a large Ottoman fleet (together with a few French and Flemish vessels) whose purpose was to break the Venetian blockade of the Dardanelles.[38]

The willingness of northern European governments to allow their ships to join an Ottoman naval fleet suggests that neither avarice nor ideology was the only factor in foreign participation in the Cretan war. Indeed, this particular flotilla had created quite a stir in Istanbul. As one of the English ambassador's clerks observed, its launching in the spring of 1647 had been

---

[38] *Calendar of state papers, Venice*, vol. XXVIII, p. 98, no. 268; and p. 99, no. 272 (Alberti and Vianuol to Doge and Senate: 15 May 1649). See Goffman, *Britons*, pp. 150–54, for a more thorough treatment of this incident.

One of the most glorious sights the City yeelds: It consisted then of about :60: Gallies, and Gally-grosses, and :30: Shipps, all which were richly guilded, painted, and furbish'd, new out of theyr Arsenall, full laden with Men, Gunns and Provisions, and clad from Stemm to Sterne with most glorious Bandiers: (theyr gunns all thundred together, wth such an Eccho as the World has scarse the Like.[39]

Even though some contemporary observers may have shared historians' belief that this fleet of some ninety ships was far more shoddily constructed and technologically backward than the fleets that the Ottomans had floated a century earlier, nevertheless it must have been an inspiring and fearsome sight to look down from the hills of Pera into the Golden Horn and see such a forest of vessels materialize below.

Not only did such displays influence the approach of western Europeans toward the war, but so did Ottoman ability to disrupt commerce. That state's capacity to control the high seas may have been much reduced. Nonetheless, foreign mariners and traders still had to mingle with Ottoman peoples in port cities, and all merchant ships still had to anchor in Ottoman harbors. Inhabitants understandably incensed at both food shortages and the Venetian enemy could easily become mobs and make even an evening stroll risky. As one English observer, demonstrating all of the prejudices of his time, notes: "the dayly hazards of being stabb'd by the drunken sottish Turkes: who supposing all to be Venetians that wore our westerne habit, (as if the world were divided between Venetians and Turkes) and they having lost in the war perhaps some neer relations, were allways apt to mischief us."[40] Most such harassments of course occurred in Ottoman rather than Venetian cities simply because many more merchants lived and traded in Ottoman than in Venetian territory.

Foreign merchants and diplomats perceived the Ottoman and Venetian governments themselves as even more of a threat to international trade than the subject peoples of the two empires. This peril derived from the ability of such authorities to harass traders, imprison representatives, and, most ominously, deny vessels the right to enter or quit anchorages in Ottoman ports. One result of the Venetian blockade of the Dardanelles, for example, was that all Dutch, English, and French merchant vessels sailing to Istanbul became subject to searches and confiscations. The English ambassador in 1648 had to obtain special permission from the Venetians before his ships could pass through the Dardanelles. In the same year English ship captain Edward Maplesden protested that he had twice attempted to traverse the Venetian blockade of the straits and had twice been turned back. Not only had he lost much time and money

[39] Bargrave, *Relation*, fo. 21v.
[40] Bargrave, *Relation*, fo. 22v.

from these failed sailings, but he feared that if he tried again to pass through to the capital city, the Ottomans might conclude that he "went up only to victual and furnish their enemies with provisions (which they do already mutter and begin to report) so by that means may not only bring an Avania upon himself and ship, but also upon the whole nation."[41] The Venetians of course suspected that foreign ships were doing exactly the same thing for the Ottomans. Two years earlier, the English ambassador had ordered English ships to steer clear of the port of Izmir, ostensibly in order to avoid the threat that the Ottoman government would seize such vessels for service in the Cretan war.[42] No such threat in fact really existed, for until the Ottomans built a fortress at the mouth of the Gulf of Izmir in the late 1650s, vessels could sail into and out of the harbor with impunity and it was more a case of the foreigners harassing the populace of Izmir than the other way around.[43]

One should not conclude from these examples that individual diplomats and merchants always acted on behalf of their states and compatriots. In the early months of the war, and just as the Ottoman campaign had begun to falter at the walls of Candia, the English ambassador Sackvile Crow several times visited the grand vizier Salih Pasha to accuse the English factory in Izmir of persistently supplying the Venetians with grains, weapons, soldiers, and oarsmen.[44] He twice secured orders from the Ottoman government forbidding English ships from lading in that town. Crow's motives were both personal (he bore a grudge against the English consul in Izmir) and political (his king, Charles I, had ordered him to seize the merchants' goods on behalf of the monarchy's doomed campaign against the parliamentarians). Nevertheless, such actions must have considerably raised fears of meddlings in the Cretan War.

The risk that Dutch, English, and French vessels would become more actively involved in the war created dilemmas for both the Venetians and the Ottomans. For example, should the Venetians refuse foreign ships ingress into the Dardanelles, the captains of these same vessels might be tempted to help the Ottomans break their blockade; should they let such vessels through, however, then not only was the very purpose of the

---

[41] Public Record Office, State Papers 105/174, pp. 149–50. On the term "avania," see Merlijn Olnon, "Towards classifying *avanias*: a study of two cases involving the English and Dutch nations in seventeenth-century Izmir," in *Friends and rivals in the East: studies in Anglo-Dutch relations in the Levant from the seventeenth to the early nineteenth century*, ed. Alistair Hamilton, Alexander H. de Groot, Haurits H. van den Boogert (Leiden, 2000), pp. 159–86.

[42] The real cause may have been dissension within the English nation, on which see Goffman, *Britons*, pp. 148–53.

[43] Eldem, Goffman, and Masters (eds.), *Ottoman city*, pp. 106–9.

[44] Başbakanlık Osmanlı Arşivi, Mühimme Defteri 90, p. 43, no. 130; and p. 44, no. 139.

blockade defeated, but they were helping their commercial rivals to fabulous earnings in the desperate markets of Istanbul. Such quandaries occurred only because the Mediterranean governments were losing control of their own seas to rivals for whom ideological issues were less important than economic and political ones. This willingness to negotiate with and support an infidel power even against a Christian one not only reflected an emerging attention to commerce (mercantilism), it also was a consequence of exposure to myriad peoples in the Americas, Africa, and Asia. Furthermore, the societies of western Europe were themselves becoming more open-minded about religion. At this very time, both non-Calvinists and Jews were migrating to the Netherlands, a spirited discussion about the resettlement of Jews had become part of a larger debate about toleration in England, and Huguenots had (temporarily to be sure) become part of the overwhelmingly Catholic body politic in France.

In an environment in which exclusive religion was being questioned even at home, it should be no surprise that political expediency began to replace religious ideology also in the eastern Mediterranean. Factors and other representatives of Atlantic seaboard companies urged abandonment of their Venetian coreligionists simply because it made political and economic sense to do so; their suggestions more and more became company and state policy. Consequently, Venice not only had to stand alone against an empire that, while militarily weakened, still could draw upon enormous resources and manpower, but could not even rely upon the neutrality of its fellow Christian states. In 1669, the Republic finally surrendered Candia and the island of Crete passed into Ottoman hands.

The hands into which it passed, however, were not the sultan's. Mehmed IV (1648–87) was no more assertive a ruler than his immediate predecessors had been, and in his first years the revolving-door government of the previous few decades persisted and even intensified. In September 1656, however, it ended abruptly when the imperial mother Turhan, desperate because of a renewed and effective Venetian blockade of the Dardanelles, appointed as grand vizier the octogenarian Köprülü Mehmed, who probably had been taken as a *devşirme* boy and had had a long and not very illustrious career in the imperial household.

Mehmed Pasha soon acquired a reputation for mercilessly expunging the corruption that ostensibly suffused the Ottoman administration. According to hearsay, he did so by having killed as many as 4,000 administrators and powerful persons. His role in this bloody purge certainly was vital. Nevertheless, there is some evidence that the sultan already had embarked upon such a policy and deserves some credit (or blame) for the eradication of corrupt statesmen as well as the reforms that followed. The English ambassador, Sir Thomas Bendysh, for example, reported four months before the Köprülü appointment that the young sultan had just ordered the chief customs collector executed,

> And finding his people noway disturbed thereat, takes heart, and every day goes disguised about the city with only one servant appearing with him, and where he sees any injustice done, or any violation made of his orders in selling, buying, or exchanging money, he immediately chops off their heads having his Executioner to that purpose not far off.[45]

Whether it was the sultan or the grand vizier who tightened the reins of government, it was the latter who received the credit. Furthermore, it was under Mehmed Pasha's son, Köprülü Fazıl Ahmed, that the empire finally finished the conquest of Crete in 1669, and under Ahmed Pasha's cousin, Kara Mustafa, that revitalized Ottoman armies in 1683 invested Vienna for one last time.

In short, during the second half of the seventeenth century and into the early eighteenth century – and in the most palpable illustration of the rise of pasha households – the Köprülü clan became the wealthiest and most powerful of Ottoman families. This adjustment from monarchal to vizierial governance was perceptible in many facets of Ottoman life, but displayed itself most plainly in public works. In Izmir, for example, Mehmed Pasha in 1658 or 1659 ordered the construction of a castle, Sancakburnu Kalesi, intended to supervise shipping, and in the 1670s Ahmed Pasha helped finance in the same town the building of an aqueduct, a *khan*, a covered marketplace, public baths, and a customs shed. The Köprülü association with Crete after 1669 was even more visible and absolute. For its conquest, Ahmed Pasha granted himself much of the best land on the island, and he rather than the sultan supervised its integration into the Ottoman world.[46] Under this family, then, the Ottoman polity lost some of its despotic nature; in its place, a form of familial oligarchy emerged.

The Ottoman Empire and the making of Europe

In most spheres, the Ottoman Empire was more a part of Europe in the seventeenth century than it had been in the sixteenth. This movement toward a European norm (and in some ways as we have seen, the passage was toward an Ottoman norm) derived in part simply from a decline in fear. The Veneto-Ottoman war over Crete, even more than the earlier Habsburg–Ottoman ones over Hungary, made it clear that this Islamic

---

[45] Bodleian Library, Rawlinson MS A.38, p. 179.
[46] Greene, *A shared world*, pp. 27–32.

30 Not only their costumes, but also their very postures mark the western Europeans in this opulent reception, for they sit on chairs in a semi-circle and face their vizieral hosts who are reclined on divans. In the center background are a quotation from the Qur'an, two imperial signatures (*tuğras*), and the shadowy figure of the sultan observing the get-together through a latticed casement. D'Ohsson, *Tableau général de l'Empire othoman*, vol. III, after p. 454.

state no longer posed a significant military threat to the rising states of western Europe. Nor were the gazes of these states any longer fixed primarily upon the Mediterranean world, for they had now become aware of the enormous opportunities to exploit the worlds of eastern Asia and the Americas.

Fear of the Ottomans also had had its stereotypical and irrational elements. These began to dissipate in the late sixteenth and early seventeenth centuries as clichéd understandings of the "terrible Turk" in northern Europe began to break down through the dissemination of particulars about Ottoman society. In earlier decades, Italians had secured considerable information about the Ottomans through the settlements of Genoese, Venetians, and others in the empire and the reports of *baili* and other official appointees in Istanbul and elsewhere. The writings of Italian political philosophers such as Guicciardini and Macchiavelli, for example, encompass thoughtful reflections on the Ottoman state and society. Their data must have come from such informants.

As more and more northern Europeans visited the Ottoman domains, they also gained more profound insight into that world. The personal experiences of such sojourners as John Sanderson, George Sandys, Robert Bargrave, Thomas Bendysh, the Chevalier de la Croix, Jean de Thevenot, and Paul Rycaut, distributed across northern Europe through their writings, helped not only to diminish irrational fears of the Ottomans as a civilization of the "other," but also to integrate that empire more securely into an emerging Europe. Although it is difficult to ascertain how generally these writings were read, it is certain that this diffusion of information occurred in various ways.[47] Some of these travelers, such as John Sanderson and George Sandys, recorded their experiences in the travel books that Richard Hakluyt, Samuel Purchas, and others began publishing. Others, such as Thomas Bendysh and Paul Rycaut, did so in letters and political analyses that were meant for heads of companies and states and sometimes found their way into print.

These men (and until Lady Mary Wortley Montague in the eighteenth century, such writers were virtually always men) were not social scientists or historians. They wrote rather as diplomats, clergymen, classicists, and travelers. Their positions helped delineate their audiences; their perspectives in important ways colored their appreciation of the worlds they observed. Some wrote exclusively about classical Greek and Roman sites; others exhibited interest only in Christian Ottomans; still others analyzed the Ottoman military and political system in order to praise or condemn it. With few exceptions, however, these travelers shared with many of today's tourists an absolute disinterest in contemporary indigenous peoples and societies.

By the last decades of the seventeenth century, the Ottoman Empire was as integrated into Europe as it would ever be. Earlier, it had been

---

[47] On this process as applied especially to east Asia, see Donald F. Lach and Edwin J. Van Kley, *Asia in the making of Europe* (Chicago, 1994), *passim*.

perceived as too much the belligerent outsider for Christendom to integrate the empire into its political, economic, and social body. Later, as the "sick man of Europe" (a phrase that does suggest at least its geographic and political acceptance as a part of Europe) it was to become supposedly too weak to be taken seriously, and the empire lost much of its autonomy as the "Great Powers" acted their disputes upon it. The Europe of Louis XIV and Charles II, however, considered the Ottomans – as friend or foe – along with the other states of Europe in their diplomatic, commercial, and military policies. This was an Ottoman Europe almost as much as it was a Venetian or Habsburg one.

8   Conclusion. The Greater Western World

It is never easy to explain the genesis of a state. Why did one people succeed over another? How did a particular family fashion a monarchy? What factors allowed one army to defeat another? Why did one ethnic, linguistic, or cultural group learn to dominate another? In fact, there is never a single or even a best explanation for state building, the details of which, always deemed critical, differ according to individual and group identity and prejudices. For example, the rich and sophisticated ancient Persian Empire represented barbaric despotism to Herodotus and other historians of ancient Greece, and the "manifest destiny" of Americans or the "white man's burden" of Englishmen were mere brutality and bad luck to the native American or the Irish. Indeed, the histories of state formation, while always having some basis in fact, often are constructed according to later desires and constitute the very core of state or national identity.

The story of the foundation of the Ottoman polity is no exception. There is little evidence to back the accepted versions of the lineage of the House of Osman as ancient and highborn or the reputations of Osman, Orhan, and Murad as astute politicians and fierce warriors. Indeed, in terms of concrete documentation, there is no certainty that the dynasty was even ethnically Turkish. It could as easily have been of Arab, Persian, or even French as of Turkoman extraction (although common sense and circumstantial evidence do bespeak a central-Asian origin). Since identities are historical and social constructs, however, one can argue that what is historically most significant in this case, as in others, is not whether Osman actually swept out of Central Asia, or whether his first language was Turkic, Indo-European, or Semitic, but that those who came later understood him to have done certain things and acted in certain ways. In other words, a central tenet of Ottoman identity was that the dynasty came out of Central Asia, an essential aspect of identity in the Republic of Turkey is that Osman was Turkish, and an imperative in other Ottoman successor states' perceptions of self is that Ottoman rulers were Turkish – as *they* emphatically are not.

Common sense also suggests that although Ottoman lineage (at least in its male line) may have been Turkic, the ideological and political shape of the Ottoman emirate owed a great deal to Persia, the Arab lands, the Byzantine Empire, and Italian city-states. After all, during its early centuries the polity drew upon the civilizations of the Middle East and Islam. Furthermore, it not only abutted Byzantium, but also was entangled physically with that Greek Orthodox state, and its emirs quickly established commercial relations with both Genoa and Venice. Living in such middle grounds, the Ottomans proved adept at learning about and borrowing from Christendom and its institutions. Ottoman brides and concubines often came from European states and dynasties, the polity's bureaucracy and administration owed much to Byzantine sources, and its commercial and economic policies were built upon Genoese and Venetian models. If an early fifteenth-century concept of Europe as a civilizational entity had existed, this state surely would have had a place in it.

Of course, "Europe" as a unifying notion did not exist in the early modern world and religion remained a potent divide between the Christian and Islamic ecumenes. Indeed, the conquest of Constantinople in 1453 merely magnified an Ottoman sense of destiny even as it deepened the Christian world's dread of and aversion toward this new-sprung Islamic state. In other words, the conquest dampened any nascent psychological or physical sense of integration into a greater European world that economic and social dealings and marital intimacy may have induced. Nevertheless, even this perceived disaster for Christendom in some ways inspired accommodation. The conquest certainly legitimized Ottoman claims as a successor to Rome. It also filled a vacuum at the empire's core and obliged the governments of all merchants plying the eastern Mediterranean seas to conclude commercial and political alliances with this Islamic state and establish settlements in its domains. Italians were the first to do so, with the Genoese colony in Galata negotiating a treaty even before Constantinople had fallen and the Venetians speeding a representative to negotiate commercial agreements as soon as the Senate received the news. In subsequent decades, the French, English, Dutch and others followed the Italian lead.

Such treaties established ground rules by which foreigners and their governments could not only communicate with the Ottoman state but also learn first-hand about Ottoman society. During the sixteenth and early seventeenth centuries, several European states posted diplomats in Istanbul even as factories boasting consuls, clergymen, and merchants established themselves in other Ottoman cities such as Cairo, Aleppo, and Izmir. Venetian, French, English, Dutch, and other sojourners not only soon became part of these cities' topographies, but also communicated their experiences and impressions to their governments and peoples back home. Such contacts helped shrink the ideological chasm between the Christian and Islamic worlds and made the empire seem less exotic and terrible.

Despite the Ottoman insistence that their state also had the right to set up such outposts in other European principalities, these western European settlements were not much reciprocated. Shipwrecked and captive Turks sometimes made their ways to the streets of London, Paris, and Genoa in the early modern period, as did the occasional emissary. Nevertheless, with the exception of a small *fondaco* that Ottoman Muslims founded in late sixteenth-century Venice, no Muslim Ottoman quarters existed in any foreign European cities before the eighteenth century. Consequently, although citizens of Ottoman port cities were on familiar terms with both subject and foreign Christians, only those few western Europeans who ventured into the empire had met Ottoman Muslims who were not either slaves, captives, or extraordinary ambassadors. Furthermore, this lopsided familiarity meant that although many Ottomans knew individual foreigners personally, few had first-hand experience of the civilizations that had produced them. Similarly, even though the Ottoman government learned a great deal about the West by way of emissaries, renegades, merchants, and missionaries, the Ottoman public probably knew far less about other European polities and societies than those societies knew of the Ottomans. As a result, our understanding of early modern interactions between the Ottoman Empire and the rest of Europe derives principally from non-Ottoman sources.

Partly because of such lopsided documentation, historians long have envisaged the sixteenth-century Ottoman Empire, and especially the period during which Süleyman the Magnificent governed (1520–66), as splendid. During this "Golden Age," it often is observed, the empire reached its "natural" frontiers in the Balkan, Mediterranean, and Middle Eastern worlds. The Ottomans also realized both land- and sea-based military dominance over their foes, and exercised "despotic" control over their far-flung provinces. Most importantly, it is claimed, the Empire's societal and governmental institutions attained a pristine flawlessness from which they could only degenerate. In short, many scholars have conceptualized Süleyman's regime as an ideal toward which earlier Ottomans had striven and which later Ottomans, perhaps inevitably, had corrupted.

Not only did Süleyman's own descendants accept this model, but Ottoman chroniclers also helped perpetuate it, and it has much to recommend it, for those institutions that historians usually cite to exemplify it – the janissary corps, the *timar* system, the codified legal edifice, the imperial household – did work particularly well during his reign. Nevertheless, accepting this model is like admiring the façade of a medieval church without inspecting its interior. Not only was the Ottoman Empire far too complex to be incapsulated in a few institutions, but also already in Süleyman's time some formative organizations were in "decline" or had been jettisoned entirely and others had not yet even appeared. Even those most often cited as typically and uniquely Ottoman never achieved the perfect form that later ages assigned them. During the Süleymanic age as always they were everchanging, permeable, and transitory.

Just as Ottoman institutions were never immutable, so did Ottoman relations with the rest of Europe never become fixed. An elastic association with the Byzantine Empire and other states had distinguished Ottoman international relations during the fourteenth and early fifteenth centuries. By the mid fifteenth century, however, that Greek Orthodox behemoth had expired. After 1453 the Ottoman Empire confronted Catholic Europe directly, in both the Balkan Peninsula and the Mediterranean Sea. This intrusion dismayed and disrupted all Catholic states, but particularly those such as Poland, Hungary, and Venice that now shared frontiers with the Islamic giant.

Ottoman advances westward probably influenced and transformed the Republic of St. Mark more than any other of those Catholic principalities that had survived the initial onslaught. For Venice now not only shared a frontier with the Ottomans and had to acquire grains, spices, and other goods from Ottoman port towns, but also had to adjust to the gradual loss of the seaborne commercial empire that the city-state had painstakingly raised in the eastern Mediterranean over the previous several centuries. Beginning in 1453 with the conquest of Constantinople and ending over 200 years later with the taking of Venetian Crete in 1669, the Ottoman Empire slowly consumed the Venetian Empire until, east of the Adriatic, the city-state possessed only a few small islands.

If in the late fifteenth century the Venetian Empire had confronted the Ottomans as a military equal, by the turn of the century it could no longer compete even on the seas. Furthermore, within decades the city-state would be willing to fight only in coalition with other more potent and zealous powers, and even then it skirmished only reluctantly, for with each engagement its frontiers and resources shrank as it lost a host of colonies, including Negroponte, Lepanto, and Cyprus. By the mid seventeenth century, Venice could no longer rely upon even the neutrality of other Christian states, as the example of Crete proves. Here, Dutch, English, and French ships all helped provision and transport Ottoman troops, thereby directly contributing to the Venetian loss of that island.

Remarkably, Ottoman–Venetian relations did not collapse as a result of these humiliating losses. Rather, they became richer and more complex as Venice learned to replace empire with commerce, power with diplomacy. Through its ability to adjust, the Serenissima proved a key actor in the integration of the Ottoman Empire into the rest of Europe. As a frontier state nestled between Christian and Islamic Europe, Venice itself became a kind of middle ground; it had to adapt to survive. Its subjects sojourned in Ottoman Istanbul, Negroponte, Lepanto, and Cyprus as merchants. Here they learned Ottoman ways, disseminating this knowledge throughout western Europe, and helped sustain Venice's economic power despite its loss of empire.

The city-state's tenuous situation vis-à-vis the Ottomans also helped spur its leaders to form their celebrated diplomatic corps. Astute resident agents settled in Istanbul, Aleppo, Alexandria, and other Ottoman cities to learn how best to negotiate and live with this new leviathan. Not only did other European states eventually follow the Venetian lead, but also the Venetians applied the diplomatic forms that they mastered in Ottoman domains first to their relations with other Italian states and subsequently to the rest of Europe. These archetypes proved vital in the development of early modern diplomacy.

The structure of Ottoman society also evolved as the empire drove deeper into Europe and adapted itself to the acquisition of millions of Christian and Jewish subjects and the arrival of thousands of visitors from Europe. Ottoman accommodation considerably facilitated economic, diplomatic, religious, and even civilizational couplings. Indeed, an important element in Ottoman expansion was the state and society's ability to learn from European civilizations and adapt to European mores. It was as much a reflection of Ottoman flexibility as western European inquisitiveness that the frontiers between the Christian and Islamic civilizations began to break down during the Ottoman classical age, long before Western imperialism forced the issue. Not that the ideological walls were crumbling. Not only did these remain as a barrier between East and West, but also new ones were raised within Europe itself as in the sixteenth century the Christian ecumene shattered. Rather, religious faith itself was ebbing as a primary societal identifier, to be replaced by other constructs in which the Ottomans could more comfortably, if eventually quite negatively, be situated.

In part it was Ottoman elasticity that allowed the empire to insert itself into the European world of the sixteenth and seventeenth century. The government was fully aware that it no longer could dictate its place in the early modern European world order, and that it more and more had to bargain with equal or even more powerful states. The causes for this transformation may have been partially internal. In the late sixteenth century, the Ottoman state simultaneously became more bureaucratized and less centralized. The result was a diffusion of power that complicated the ability of the sultan's government to control and focus its military manpower. By the mid seventeenth century, the Ottomans found it difficult to defeat even the Venetians, much less the Habsburgs or the Safavids. Negotiation and even concession more and more marked Ottoman policy in the state's relations with the rest of Europe.

Nevertheless, changes in the balance of power in Europe also stimulated Ottoman integration. The fragmentation of first Italy and subsequently the rest of Europe destroyed even the semblance of a Christian cohesion and replaced it with princes and despots who paid little more than lip service to the idea of a religious ecumene. Fast on the heels of this emergence of secular politics was the development of principles to serve it in the form of Protestantism, which accomplished ideologically what the Renaissance had done politically. By the seventeenth century, not only had non-Ottoman Europe become more able to accommodate religious and political difference, but martial achievements by the Habsburg Empire, the Republic of Venice, and Dutch and English pirates against the Ottoman military machine had considerably reduced the rest of Europe's dread of this large domain.

Furthermore, western Europe's geographic horizons were broadening at the very time that its fear of the Ottomans was receding. Whereas, in the fifteenth century, the states of the Mediterranean and Atlantic seaboards had concentrated their commerce and proselytizing on the East, by the sixteenth century the Americas constituted a tempting distraction, and by the middle of the seventeenth century the principal focus of Atlantic seaboard states had shifted across the western seas. In this light, Cromwell's decision in 1655 to send a fleet to the Caribbean rather than the Mediterranean marked a vital shift that has often been dated much earlier.

In their studies of European expansion and imperialism, historians have tended to neglect the Middle East and concentrate on the Americas and East Asia. This emphasis, however, is in part the product of hindsight. Until the mid seventeenth century most western European societies continued to bestow more money and manpower upon the Mediterranean world than upon either the Far West or the Far East. It is probable, for example, that in the early seventeenth century there were more Englishmen and Frenchmen settled in the Ottoman Empire than in the Americas, and that the Dutch, English, and French Levant companies generated more revenue than did their sister East Indies or American companies. From about this time, however, migration to and income from the Americas accelerated, and revenue from Indian and Moluccan textiles and spices began to outstrip revenue from Mediterranean sources.

Consequently, the Greater European World of the late seventeenth century took on a new shape. No longer were the Mediterranean seas at its center, no longer were the states of Europe focused upon the southeastern margin of the landmass, and no longer was the Ottoman Empire a major player among them. Instead, Europe's hub had moved to the northwest, the gazes of its most powerful states had become fixed upon the Americas and East Asia, and the Ottoman Empire had become a second-tier power among them. By the mid seventeenth century, this Islamic state was no longer feared (although a few admired its social and religious variety). Instead, it was regarded as one among many polities. The empire again was to become a threat to the rest of Europe in the modern era, but the peril then would come less from strength than from weakness. Whereas one of the great concerns of early modern Europe had been how to comprehend, contain, borrow from, and incorporate an always grand, constantly transforming, and sometimes aggressive Ottoman polity, the "Eastern Question" of the eighteenth and nineteenth centuries swirled around a different issue: whether and how to shore up this same entity. Ultimately, it was allowed agonizingly and ignobly to fall to pieces.

In the period between the sixteenth and eighteenth centuries, then, the Ottoman Empire existed briefly as a full and active member of a concert of European states. Nevertheless, it did not, as it probably could not, follow a course parallel to the emerging imperial powers of the modern world. In the eighteenth and nineteenth centuries, Britain, France, and Prussia led in developing the political, economic, and social institutions that would engender the modern nation state; neither Venice, the Habsburgs, the Ottomans, nor any other Mediterranean power succeeded in effectively following their leads. The Ottomans in particular faced many obstacles to the processes of modernization, democratization, constitutional self-governance, centralization, and industrialization that characterized the rise of the European nation states and produced in them feelings of societal commonality and citizenship. France, for example, learned to construct an identity for many (but not all) of its people based upon a sense of shared language, shared religion, shared government, shared history, and shared borders. By 1800, most inhabitants of France saw their Frenchness as the essence of their identities. The peoples of the Ottoman Empire, however, never developed a comparable Ottoman identity. They spoke a plethora of languages; they espoused several religions; their sense of governance was diffused not only by patriarchal and rabbinic authority and power but also by French, Russian, and British determination to regulate Ottoman treatment of Catholic, Orthodox, and Protestant Ottoman subjects; their sense of past was utterly diverse; and their borders were more and more blurred and malleable because of the insistence of foreign powers on commercial, political, and missionary access. Such manifold barriers to the creation of a national identity proved too many to overcome. The empire in the eighteenth century became a second-tier power. By the nineteenth century, many statesmen considered it no power at all, but merely a potential problem.

Perhaps even more indicative of the empire's tumble than the Western-inspired political and social reorganization upon which the Ottoman government embarked especially after 1839, was the Anglo-Ottoman Commercial Convention of 1838. This agreement not only declared that "all rights, privileges, and immunities which have been conferred on the subjects or ships of Great Britain by the existing Capitulations and Treaties, are confirmed now and for ever," but also stipulated that "the subjects of Her Britannic Majesty, or their agents, shall be permitted to purchase at all places in the Ottoman Dominions . . . all articles, without any exception whatsoever."[1] This accord stripped the Ottoman government of control over the movement of goods across its own borders and granted British traders free access to Ottoman products and Ottoman markets. In other words, it provided a legal framework for British economic imperialism, deprived the Ottomans of economic autonomy and thereby detached the empire from the European concert of nations, and, at least in the opinion of many, not only turned it into a British dependency but also made it a target for colonization. One Englishman writing in 1887 could dream of a future in which "the vast plains and fertile slopes [of western Anatolia] shall have become tenanted by an improving race of scientific farmers [he had in mind Scotsmen] unprejudiced by the agricultural legends and superstitions of past ages [he had in mind Turks]."[2] Such comments emphasize that, by the mid nineteenth century, early modern European attitudes of both dread toward and appreciation of the Ottoman Empire had been thoroughly undermined and transformed.

---

[1] In Charles Issawi (ed.), *The economic history of the Middle East, 1800–1914: a book of readings* (Chicago, 1982), p. 39.
[2] William Cochran, *Pen and pencil* (London, 1887), p. 211.

Glossary

This glossary includes those Ottoman Turkish words that occur more than once in the text. They alone are italicized.

abode of Islam: lands controlled by Islamic governments
abode of the Covenant: lands ruled by non-Islamic governments, but paying tribute to Islamic states
abode of war: lands controlled by non-Islamic governments
alum: metal used as a clarifier or purifier in various trades, especially in the tanning industry; important in early modern Mediterranean commerce
apostasy: repudiation of a faith, usually to embrace another
Ashkenazim: German Jews; that community of Jews whose vernacular and customs reflected centuries of settlement in German lands
askeri: Ottoman ruling elite, administrative, military, and religious
bailo: envoy or ambassador; often specifically referring to a Venetian or Dubrovnikan representative in Istanbul
bertone: sailing ship of a type developed in the early modern period and used especially by Atlantic seaboard states
bey: honorific title; Ottoman military commander
bostancı: member of the imperial guards, powerful particularly in the city of Istanbul
cacophony: many dissonant voices or viewpoints
cadastral survey: measurement of land for purposes of taxation and, in the Ottoman case, for division among the Ottoman *sipahi* (q.v.)
caique: small, oared vessel used to transport people or goods over short distances
caliph: successor to the Prophet Muhammed; often titular ruler over the community of Muslims

capitulations: commercial agreements, usually between the Ottomans and foreign governments

catechism: a book summarizing the essentials of a particular faith

çavuş: an Ottoman pursuivant or messenger, often granted extraordinary authority on a particular issue

cizye: annual head tax taken from non-Muslim subjects in an Islamic state

concubine: woman living with a man without being married; female slave in an imperial or wealthy household

converso: a convert; often refers to a reluctant convert in Iberia during and after the Christian reconquest

corvée: forced labor as a form of taxation; usually associated with serfdom

damad: husband of an imperial Ottoman princess; son-in-law

devşirme: method by which usually Christian Ottoman boys were "tithed" into imperial service

diaspora: scattering from its historical location of a religious or ethnic group

Doge: elected leader of government in Venice

dragoman: translator and interpreter in the Ottoman Empire

ducat: a gold coin; formerly were several types including the Venetian and the Spanish

ecumene: region where the principal faith claims universality

emir: ruler of a small state; prince or governor in the Middle East

entrepôt: place, usually a city, where goods are exchanged and transferred

eschatological: concerned with last things, such as death or the end of the world

Eurocentrism: belief in the political, economic, and intellectual superiority of European civilization

exogamy: marriage outside of a particular family, society, or group

extraterritoriality: exemption from legal jurisdiction; right to live in a foreign land according to one's own laws

fetva: a written opinion by a religious authority in Islam

fondaco: place in a Mediterranean port city where an alien community, usually of merchants, lives and trades

Franks: term for western Europeans in the Islamic Middle East; associated with crusading and other armies

fratricide: killing one's siblings

gaza: warfare on behalf of Islam

gazi: a Muslim warrior who is fighting for his faith

grand vizier: most important imperial minister of state in the early modern Ottoman world

hajj: pilgrimage, usually to Mecca; one of the five "pillars" of Islam

harem: area of house reserved for the family; sultan's household

Hasidim: sect of Jewish mystics founded in eighteenth-century Poland

hegemony: situation in which one state dominates over others

heterodoxy: having religious beliefs that a particular faith does not accept as orthodox

hierocracy: government by a clergy or religious elite

hinterland: lands contiguous to a town or city, from which it draws its food

historiography: historical literature and its interpretation

imam: prayer leader in Islam, often in an official or governmental post; successor to Muhammed in Shi'ism (q.v.)

inquisition: Catholic tribunal authorized and instructed to ferret out heresy

Interregnum: period between monarchs, often of turmoil

isthmus: a sliver of land connecting two larger land masses

janissary corps: Ottoman infantry army, consisting at first of the sultan's slaves or servants and subsequently more generally recruited

kadi: religious judge or municipal commissioner in Islamic states

kadizadeli: member of an Islamic reformist movement in the seventeenth-century Ottoman Empire

kanun: sultanic law, in the Ottoman Empire used to complement and at times replace Islamic law

kapıkulu: anyone who is a servant of the sultan

kapudanpaşa: Commander of the Ottoman fleet; member of the imperial divan

Karaite: Jewish sect that accepts only the Torah as religious law and repudiates all Talmudic commentaries

khan: an often fortified resting place for merchants and other travelers

Latin: the Catholic church, especially in contrast to the Greek Orthodox church

latitudinarianism: favoring freedom of thought; act of pushing the limits of religious orthodoxy

Levant: Syrian or eastern-Mediterranean coastal regions

lingua franca: hybrid language, principally Italian but mixing other languages and used for communication in the early modern eastern Mediterranean

Lurianic Kabbalah: form of Jewish mysticism formulated by Isaac Luria and popularized in the seventeenth century

marrano: Spanish-Jewish convert to Catholicism; derogatory term for a crypto-Jew

Maskalim: Jewish intellectuals who carried the ideas of the Enlightenment to eastern Europe in the nineteenth century

medrese: Islamic religious school

millet: a non-Muslim community in the Ottoman Empire; before the nineteenth century, the term was used loosely

monotheism: belief in a single God; usually refers to Judaism, Christianity, and Islam

oligarchy: rule by a few, a faction, or a small group of families

Orientalism: the idea that Western scholars long have studied and constructed the East or "Orient" in Western terms and using Western models to maintain Western hegemony

Ottomancentrism: viewing the world from the perspective of the Ottoman state, society, interests, and history

padishah: monarch; sultan

pasha: military commander; Ottoman high statesman

pastoralist: herdsman, especially of sheep

patois: particular language of a special class or region; substandard speech

Patriarch: spiritual and political leader in the Greek Orthodox, Armenian, and other eastern Christian religions

pax ottomanica: "Ottoman peace"; region under Ottoman control within which commerce and travel were relatively secure

Phanariot: group of Greek Orthodox Ottomans associated with the district in Istanbul known as Fener; rose to economic and political prominence in the eighteenth century

polygyny: the taking of more than one wife at once

primogeniture: system by which the firstborn child (usually son) inherits wealth and/or status

proselytization: conversion, or endeavor to convince others to convert to one's faith

reaya: flock; subjects of the Ottoman Empire who are not part of the ruling elite

Romaniot: that part of the Ottoman-Jewish community whose ancestors had lived in the Byzantine Empire

Sephardim: Spanish Jews; Jews involved in the Iberian diaspora (q.v.) of the late fifteenth and sixteenth centuries

Serenissima: the state of Venice

şeyhülislam: highest religious functionary in the Ottoman state; a political appointment whose possessor sat on the Imperial Divan

shamanism: religion in which good and evil spirits are believed to infuse nature and can be called upon by priests

shariah: Islamic law; usually based in the Qur'an, the pronouncements of Muhammed (*hadith*), and the mores of the community of believers during Muhammed's lifetime (*umma*)

shaykh: a religious leader, often associated with Sufism (q.v.)

Shi'ism: branch of Islamic belief, considered heretical by the Ottomans, that believed that blood descendants of Muhammed should lead the community of Muslims

signory: group of signors who constituted the Venetian government

sipahi: an Ottoman cavalryman and provincial administrator

Sublime Porte: Ottoman government; associated with the grand vizier (q.v.) and his bureaucracy

suet: animal fat used in cooking and making tallow for candles

Sufism: Islamic mysticism; many versions usually associated with particular holy men

sumptuary: restricting personal behavior or dress in accordance with religious or moral codes

Sunnism: leading branch of Islamic belief, espoused by the Ottoman state; often juxtaposed with Shi'ism (q.v.)

syncretism: combination into new forms of differing systems of belief or customs

taife: any group or community

tekke: Sufi house of worship and communal gathering place

Templars: a militant crusading order founded in twelfth-century Jerusalem

theosophy: religious philosophy based upon mystical insight

Turkoman: nomadic peoples from Central Asia and speaking a Turkic language

ulema: masters of Islamic jurisprudence

unigeniture: system by which a single child (usually son) inherits wealth and/or status

valide sultan: mother of the Ottoman sultan; often a towering political presence in the late sixteenth and seventeenth centuries

vizier: Ottoman statesman, especially one with a seat on the Imperial Divan

zimmi: non-Muslim subject in an Islamic polity

Suggestions for further reading

Although this book's notes occasionally employ non-English-language texts, the works cited below are limited to the English language. My decision to do so does not disavow the richness of French, German, Italian, or especially Turkish literature. The selection rather is based upon the question of audience and constitutes a suggestion that the exclusion of the Ottoman Empire from European history is as much ideological as linguistic or because of a lack of accessible materials. The exhaustive body of English-language texts enables the interested historian to incorporate this empire fully into the Greater European World.

GENERAL TEXTS

The most important reference work for Ottoman terms remains *The encyclopaedia of Islam*, new edn (Leiden, 1960–), which is now available in an excellent CD-Rom edition. Entries that the reader may find particularly useful include "ghulām," "Imtiyāzāt," "Istanbul," and "Maktu^{c}." There are several English-language surveys of early modern Ottoman history. The most thorough and reliable remains Halil İnalcık, *The Ottoman Empire: the classical age, 1300–1600*, trans. Norman Itzkowitz and Colin Imber (London, 1973). A briefer introduction that covers much the same ground is Norman Itzkowitz, *Ottoman Empire and Islamic tradition* (Chicago, 1972). Justin McCarthy also offers a readable survey that perhaps over-stresses the Turkishness of the Ottomans in *The Ottoman Turks: an introductory history to 1923* (Harlow, Essex, 1997). Its lack of notes and bibliography also limits its value. The advanced student might profitably consult the exhaustive state-of-the-profession survey by Halil İnalcık with Donald Quataert, *An economic and social history of the Ottoman Empire, 1300–1914* (Cambridge, 1994). Suraiya Faroqhi presents a fascinating look at Ottoman society and its material bases in *Subjects of the sultan: culture and daily life in the Ottoman Empire* (London, 2000). A text that, while focusing on the late empire also includes concise summary chapters on the early modern Ottoman world, is Donald Quataert, *The Ottoman Empire, 1700–1922* (Cambridge, 2000).

On the specific problem of the Ottoman Empire's connection to Europe, see Paul Coles, *The Ottoman impact on Europe* (New York, 1968), which is limited because of its view of the empire as a parasite. Cemal Kafadar, "The Ottomans and Europe," in *Handbook of European history, 1400–1600*, Vol. I: *Structures and assertions*, ed. Thomas A Brady, Jr., Heiko A. Oberman, and James D. Tracy (Grand Rapids, MI, 1994), pp. 589–635, constitutes an extended abstract toward a more balanced treatment. Andrew Wheatcroft, *The Ottomans: dissolving images* (New York, 1993) is intriguing, but idiosyncratic and not always reliable. The highly popular Jason Goodwin, *Lords of the horizons: a history of the Ottoman Empire* (London, 1998) is entertaining, but problematic because of inaccuracies and flights of fancy. Those interested in the Ottoman legacy to the Middle East and the Balkans should turn to L. Carl Brown (ed.), *Imperial legacy: the Ottoman imprint on the Balkans and the Middle East* (New York, 1996).

There are several "framing" texts that, while not specifically about the Ottomans, are theoretically and conceptually essential. Donald Lach and Edwin Van Kley's multivolume *Asia in the making of Europe* (Chicago, 1965–93) remains central for any study of how European expansion influenced Europe itself. Any examination of the ideological relationship between western Europe and the rest of the world must begin with Edward Said, *Orientalism* (New York, 1978). A good complement to this study is Thierry Hentsch, *Imagining the Middle East*, trans. Fred A. Reed (Montreal, 1992), which traces the specific concepts of Islam and the Middle East from the ancient through the modern European worlds. Anglo-Indian relations are particularly well studied by both historians and literary critics, on which see Jyotsna G. Singh, *Colonial narratives, cultural dialogues: "discoveries" of India in the languages of colonialism* (London and New York, 1996). For a study that persuasively explores the influence of gender roles in both Islamic and Christian societies, see Carol L. Delaney, *Abraham on trial* (Princeton, 1998). An entire issue of *Past and Present* (137[1992]) is devoted to an attempt to define how Europe has been envisioned historically. The specific Ottoman case is presented in M. E. Yapp, "Europe in the Turkish mirror," *Past and Present* 137(1992): 134–55. The theoretical construct of nations and nationalisms, which has so obscured Ottoman history, is ably thrashed out in Benedict Anderson, *Imagined communities: reflections on the origin and spread of nationalism* (London, 1983).

FOUNDATIONS OF EMPIRE

The student of Ottoman beginnings should read Cemal Kafadar, *Between two worlds: the construction of the Ottoman state* (Berkeley and Los Angeles, 1995), which, while largely expository, not only lays out and elegantly critiques both Ottoman and modern theses of Ottoman origins, but also presents a middle-ground thesis of its own. A good discussion of the religious diversity that fed into Ottoman beginnings is Ahmet Karamustafa, *God's unruly friends: dervish groups in the Islamic later middle period, 1200–1550* (Salt Lake City, 1994). Some of the works that have contributed to our understanding of (and confusions about) the early Ottoman world are Herbert A. Gibbons, *The foundation of the Ottoman Empire* (Oxford, 1916); Fuat M. Köprülü, *The origins of the Ottoman Empire*, trans. and ed. Gary Leiser (Albany, NY, 1992); Paul Wittek, *The rise of the Ottoman Empire* (London, 1938); and Rudi P. Lindner, *Nomads and Ottomans in medieval Anatolia* (Bloomington, IN, 1983). A revealing critique of both Wittek's writings and the historiography of this topic is Colin Heywood, "Wittek and the Austrian tradition," *Journal of the Royal Asiatic Society* (1988): 7–25. Colin Imber presents a strong summary of Ottoman imaginings of the past in "Ideals and legitimation in early Ottoman history," in *Süleyman the Magnificent and his age: the Ottoman Empire in the early modern world*, ed. Metin Kunt and Christine Woodhead (Harlow, 1995), pp. 138–53.

Colin Heywood examines the idea of an Ottoman frontier in "The frontier in Ottoman history: old ideas and new myths," in *Frontiers in question: Eurasian borderlands, 700–1700*, ed. Daniel Power and Naomi Standen (London, 1999), pp. 228–50. He does not, however, consider the valuable writings on the American frontier that post-date Frederick Jackson Turner, such as Richard White, *The middle ground: Indians, empires, and republics in the Great Lakes region, 1650–1815* (Cambridge, 1989), which examines the idea of frontiers as "middle grounds." For the specific frontier created by the Crusades in Syria as a model for the Byzantine/Turkoman frontier in Anatolia, see Amin Maalouf's ingenious *The Crusades through Arab eyes* (New York, 1984) and Tariq Ali's fictionalized diary by a Jewish scribe, *The book of Saladin: a novel* (New York, 1999). An important source for such treatments is Usamah Ibn-Munidh, *An Arab-Syrian gentleman and warrior in the period of the Crusades*, trans. Philip K. Hitti (Princeton, 1987). On the specific Anatolian background to Ottoman expansion, see Speros Vryonis, *The decline of medieval Hellenism in Asia Minor and the process of Islamization from the eleventh through the fifteenth century* (Berkeley, 1971). Also useful if dated on this topic is Fuat M. Köprülü, *Islam in Anatolia after the Turkish invasion*

(Prolegomena), trans. Gary Leiser (Salt Lake City, 1994). The specific case of the roots of the Ottoman sultanate is discussed in Halil İnalcık, "The Ottoman succession and its relation to the Turkish concept of sovereignty," in *The Middle East and the Balkans under the Ottoman Empire: essays on economy and society* (Bloomington, IN, 1993), pp. 37–69.

THE OTTOMAN GOVERNMENT AND EUROPE

There are several studies of European perceptions of the early modern Ottomans. Among the most important are Clarence Rouillard, *The Turk in French history, thought and literature (1520–1660)* (Paris, 1938), and Robert Schwoebel, *The shadow of the crescent: the Renaissance image of the Turk, 1453–1517* (Nieuwkoop, 1967). Three recent discussions of European attitudes toward the "Turk" are Lucette Valensi, *The birth of the despot: Venice and the Sublime Porte*, trans. Arthur Denner (Ithaca, NY and London, 1993); Christine Woodhead, "'The present terrour of the world?' Contemporary views of the Ottoman Empire *c.* 1600," *History* 72(1987): 20–37; and Aslı Çırakman, "From tyranny to despotism: the Enlightenment's unenlightened image of the Turks," *International Journal of Middle East Studies* 33.1(2000): 49–68. Bernard Lewis attempts to reverse these views, looking at how the Islamic world imagined the western European one, in *The Muslim discovery of Europe* (New York, 1982). Martin Luther's "On war against the Turk, 1528," in *Luther's works*, Vol. XLVI, *The Christian in society, III* (Philadelphia, 1967), pp. 155–205, is perhaps the most accessible of the many early modern religious pamphlets written in Christian Europe about and against the Ottoman Empire. The most essential positive treatment of the Ottoman polity is interspersed throughout Jean Bodin, *The six bookes of a commonweale*, ed. Kenneth Douglas McRae (Cambridge, 1962). There has been much written on Christian Europe's understanding of the Ottoman world. The thoroughness with which the Ottomans knew Christian Europe remains open to debate. Three studies that attack this question from very different angles are Thomas Goodrich's *The Ottoman Turks and the new world* (Wiesbaden, 1990); the novelist Roderick Conway Morris's *Jem: memoirs of an Ottoman secret agent* (New York, 1988); and Virginia Aksan's *An Ottoman statesman in war and peace: Ahmed Resmi Efendi, 1700–1783* (Leiden, 1995).

There is now an excellent study of Ottoman methods of warfare: Rhoads Murphey, *Ottoman warfare, 1500–1800* (Rutgers, NY, 1999). Caroline Finkel examines a particular campaign in *The administration of warfare: the Ottoman military campaigns in Hungary, 1593–1606* (Vienna, 1987). The classic study on the process of Ottoman conquest and integration is Halil İnalcık, "Ottoman methods of conquest," *Studia Islamica* 2(1954): 112–22. A specific example of the process is the same author's "Ottoman policy and administration in Cyprus after the conquest," reprinted in *The Ottoman Empire, conquest, organization and economy* (London, 1978), article 8. For the specific case of Istanbul, see Steven Runciman, *The fall of Constantinople, 1453* (Cambridge, 1991); and Halil İnalcık, "The policy of Mehmed II toward the Greek population of Istanbul and the Byzantine buildings of the city," *Dumbarton Oaks Papers* 23(1970): 213–49. Extant Byzantine as well as Ottoman buildings are discussed in Hilary Sumner-Boyd and John Freely, *Strolling through Istanbul* (Istanbul, 1972). On Ottoman Istanbul there are several recent works. A popular treatment is John Freely, *Istanbul: the imperial city* (London, 1996). Somewhat more sophisticated but still quite accessible is Philip Mansel, *Constantinople: city of the world's desire, 1453–1924* (New York, 1995). Edhem Eldem, "Istanbul: from imperial to peripheral capital," in *The Ottoman city between East and West: Aleppo, Izmir, and Istanbul* (Cambridge, 1999), is a stimulating and reliable survey of the city by a scholar comfortable with both Ottoman and western sources. On the social and political context of the sultan's palace itself, far and away the best study is Gülru Necipoğlu, *Architecture, ceremonial and power: the Topkapı palace in the fifteenth and sixteenth centuries* (Cambridge, MA, 1991). A delightful and gossipy if not always accurate text is Godfrey Goodwin, *Topkapi palace: an illustrated guide to its life and personalities* (London, 2000).

EARLY MODERN OTTOMAN GOVERNMENT AND SOCIETY

The period of Süleyman's reign has received considerable attention. Metin Kunt and Christine Woodhead (eds.), *Süleyman the Magnificent and his age: the Ottoman empire in the early modern world* (Harlow, 1995) is filled with strong essays. Especially useful in this collection is Woodhead's "Perspectives on Süleyman," pp. 164–90. On Islamic and sultanic law, see Colin Imber, *Ebu's-su'ud: the islamic legal tradition* (Stanford, CA, 1997), and on the particular topic of Süleyman's contribution to the codification of Ottoman law, see Halil İnalcık, "Suleiman the lawgiver and Ottoman law," *Archivum Ottomanicum* 1(1969): 105–38. A fascinating study of this sultan's attempt to glorify himself in the context of the European world is Gülru Necipoğlu, "Süleyman the Magnificent and the representation of power in the context of Ottoman-Habsburg-Papal rivalry," *Art Bulletin* 71.3(1989): 401–27; and for his endeavor to do so through public buildings, see Aptullah Kuran, *Sinan the Grand Old Master of Ottoman architecture* (Washington, DC and Istanbul, 1987). A good introduction to Ottoman poetry is Walter Andrews, *Poetry's voice, society's song: Ottoman lyric poetry* (Seattle, WA, 1985); many translations of such poetry are in Walter Andrews, *et al.*, *Ottoman lyric poetry: an anthology* (Austin, TX, 1997).

A revealing work on the sultan and his household is Leslie Peirce, *The imperial harem: women and sovereignty in the Ottoman Empire* (Oxford, 1993). For a narrative of that period on gender relations in other elite households, see Evliya Çelebi, *The intimate life of an Ottoman statesman: Melek Ahmed Pasha (1588–1661)*, intro. and trans. Robert Dankoff, historical comm. Rhoads Murphey (Albany, NY, 1991). On elite careers, see in general İ. Metin Kunt, "Ethnic-regional (*cins*) solidarity in the seventeenth-century Ottoman establishment," *International Journal of Middle East Studies* 5(1974): 233–39; and, for a particular case, Cornell H. Fleischer, *Bureaucrat and intellectual in the Ottoman Empire: the historian Mustafa Âli (1541–1600)* (Princeton, NJ, 1986). The early chapters of Ehud R. Toledano, *Slavery and abolition in the Ottoman Middle East* (Seattle, WA, 1998) constitute a concise introduction to Ottoman slavery. A thorough discussion of the end to Ottoman slavery is Y. Hakan Erdem, *Slavery in the Ottoman Empire and its demise* (Oxford, 1997).

The seventeenth-century crisis, and especially its social aspects, has received much attention in recent years. An organizing model that may apply to Ottoman decentralization is presented in Frederic C. Lane, "The economic consequences of organized violence," *Journal of Economic History* 18(1958): 401–17. Suraiya Faroqhi's "Crisis and change, 1590–1699," in *An economic and social history of the Ottoman Empire, 1300–1914*, ed. Halil İnalcık, with Donald Quataert (Cambridge, 1994), pp. 411–636, is a good place to start for the Ottoman case. This summation should be complemented by Halil İnalcık, "Military and fiscal transformation in the Ottoman Empire, 1600–1700," *Archivum Ottomanicum* 6(1980): 283–337; the many articles by Ronald Jennings, particularly his "Urban population in Anatolia in the sixteenth century: a study of Kayseri, Karaman, Amasya, Trabzon, and Erzerum," *International Journal of Middle East Studies* 7(1976): 229–58; and his "Kadi, court and legal procedure in seventeenth-century Ottoman Kayseri," *Studia Islamica* 48(1978): 133–72; Şevket Pamuk, "The price revolution in the Ottoman Empire reconsidered," *International Journal of Middle East Studies* 33.1(2001): 68–89; as well as Suraiya Faroqhi's *Towns and townsmen of Ottoman Anatolia: trade, crafts and food production in an urban setting, 1520–1650* (Cambridge, 1984). A sociological model that links provincial unrest and the state apparatus is Karen Barkey, *Bandits and bureaucrats: the Ottoman route to state centralization* (Ithaca, NY and London, 1994).

A study of society and commerce in a particular city is Daniel Goffman, *Izmir and the Levantine world, 1550–1650* (Seattle, WA, 1990); religious unrest is covered in Madeline C. Zilfi, *The politics of piety: the Ottoman ulema in the postclassical age (1600–1800)* (Minneapolis, 1988). Financial innovations, with profound implications for the earlier periods, are persuasively analyzed in Ariel Salzmann, "An *ancien regime* revisited: privatization and political economy in the eighteenth century Ottoman Empire," *Politics and Society* 21.4(1993): 393–423. A fascinating examination of the ideas of "distance" and "travel" in the early modern Ottoman world is Kurt W. Treptow, "Distance and communications in southeastern Europe, 1593–1612," *East European Quarterly* 24.4(1991): 475–82.

There are several strong critiques of the Ottoman decline paradigm. One that focuses on Ottoman observers is Douglas Howard, "Ottoman historiography and the literature of 'decline' of the sixteenth and seventeenth centuries," *Journal of Asian History* 22(1988): 52–77. A second that highlights the Ottoman bureaucracy and treasury is Linda T. Darling, *Revenue raising and legitimacy: tax collection and finance administration in the Ottoman Empire, 1560–1660* (Leiden and New York, 1996). A concise summary and critique of the debate, which does not do away with the concept entirely but argues that decline set in much later than usually presumed, is in Quataert, *Ottoman Empire*.

THE COMPETITION FOR THE EASTERN MEDITERRANEAN

One should begin a study of the sixteenth-century Mediterranean seas with Fernand Braudel's sweeping and still stimulating *The Mediterranean and the Mediterranean world in the age of Philip II*, trans. Sian Reynolds, 2 vols. (New York, 1972). A definitive work on Byzantine–Venetian relations is Donald M. Nicol, *Byzantium and Venice: a study in diplomatic and cultural relations* (Cambridge, 1988). Kenneth M. Setton, meanwhile, thoroughly studies relations between the papacy and the Ottomans in his *The papacy and the Levant (1204–1571)*, 4 vols. (Philadelphia, 1974). General studies on Venice include Frederic C. Lane, *Venice: a maritime republic* (Baltimore, 1973), which remains the best English-language survey of Venetian history; while William H. McNeill, *Venice: the hinge of Europe, 1081–1797* (Chicago and London, 1974), is an impressive attempt to show Venice as a great disseminator of ideas. One may complement *Venice* with William H. McNeill's companion volume, *Europe's steppe frontier, 1500–1800* (Chicago and London, 1964), and, less engagingly but more from the Ottoman perspective, C. Max Kortepeter, *Ottoman imperialism during the Reformation: Europe and the Caucasus* (New York, 1972).

Andrew C. Hess persuasively and with poise examines the far western Ottoman borders in *The forgotten frontier: a history of the sixteenth-century Ibero-African frontier* (Chicago and London, 1978); Palmira Brummett, *Ottoman seapower and Levantine diplomacy in the Age of Discovery* (Albany, NY, 1994) imaginatively examines Venetian–Ottoman–Mamluk–Safavid relations at a specific point in time; and John Francis Guilmartin, Jr., *Gunpowder and galleys: changing technology and Mediterranean warfare at sea in the sixteenth century* (Cambridge, 1974), persuasively and significantly liberates the early modern Mediterranean world from the Mahanian model of naval warfare. The commercial impact of the Portuguese movement into Asia is traced in Niels Steensgaard, *The Asian trade revolution of the seventeenth century* (Chicago, 1974); the specific Ottoman–Portuguese confrontation in the Red Sea and Indian Ocean is dealt with in Salih Özbaran, "Ottoman naval policy in the south," in *Süleyman the Magnificent*, pp. 55–70; and the pivotal naval battle at Lepanto is lucidly studied in Andrew C. Hess, "The Battle of Lepanto and its place in Mediterranean history," *Past and Present* 57(1972): 53–73.

Two charming and eloquent, if profoundly orientalist, introductions, especially to the topography of Venice and its empire, are Jan Morris, *The world of Venice* (Orlando, FLA, 1993), and her *The Venetian Empire: a sea voyage* (London, 1990). On Venetian Cyprus, the classic study remains Sir George Hill, *A history of Cyprus*, Vol. III: *The Frankish period, 1432–1571* (Cambridge, 1948), but one must balance this account with Halil İnalcık, "Ottoman policy and administration in Cyprus after the conquest," in *The Ottoman Empire: conquest, organization and economy* (London, 1978), article 8. Ronald C. Jennings, *Christians and Muslims in Ottoman Cyprus and the Mediterranean world, 1571–1640* (New York, 1993), studies early Ottoman Cyprus. Seventeenth-century Habsburg–Ottoman–Venetian relations, with exhaustive attention given to war over Crete, are thoroughly and carefully examined in Kenneth Setton, *Venice, Austria, and the Turks in the seventeenth century* (Philadelphia, 1991). The consequences of the Ottoman–Venetian Cretan War, with particular attention to the Catholic – Greek Orthodox – Muslim nexus, is the topic of Molly Greene, *A shared world: Christians and Muslims in the early modern Mediterranean* (Princeton, 2000). The best study of Ottoman economic policy and its influence on the Mediterranean world remains Halil İnalcık, "Capital formation in the Ottoman Empire," *Journal of Economic History* 19(1969): 97–140.

Piracy played a consequential role in inter-societal relations in the Mediterranean basin, as Peter Lamborn Wilson, *Pirate utopias: Moorish corsairs and European renegadoes* (Brooklyn, NY, 1995) argues. Several fine books exist on this subject, including Alberto Tenenti, *Piracy and the decline of Venice, 1580–1615*, trans. Janet Pullan and Brian Pullan (Berkeley and Los Angeles, 1967); Catherine Wendy Bracewell, *The Uskoks of Senj: piracy, banditry, and holy war in the sixteenth-century Adriatic* (Ithaca, NY, 1992); and C. Lloyd, *English corsairs on the Barbary coast* (London, 1981).

On the early modern Mediterranean world as a cultural middle ground that rivaled the American colonies, see Nabil Matar's important and provocative *Turks, Moors, and Englishmen in the Age of Discovery* (New York, 1999). An account of the early English presence in the empire, which includes many of the most important sources on that settlement, is Susan A. Skilliter, *William Harborne and the trade with Turkey, 1578–1582: a documentary study of the first Anglo-Ottoman relations* (London, 1977). A. H. de Groot, *The Ottoman Empire and the Dutch Republic: a history of the earliest diplomatic relations, 1610–1630* (Leiden, 1978), accomplishes much the same thing for the Dutch case. A comparative study of the role of Ottoman cities in the Mediterranean world is Edhem Eldem, Daniel Goffman, and Bruce Masters, *The Ottoman city between East and West: Aleppo, Izmir, and Istanbul* (Cambridge, 1999), and a case study is Bruce Masters, *The origins of western economic dominance in the Middle East: mercantilism and the Islamic economy in Aleppo, 1600–1750* (New York, 1988).

NON-MUSLIM OTTOMANS AND EUROPE

On political formations that linked the Ottoman Empire to the rest of Europe, see, for Dubrovnik, Francis W. Carter, *Dubrovnik (Ragusa): a classic city-state* (London, 1972); and, for Chios, Philip P. Argenti, *Chius Vincta or the occupation of Chios by the Turks (1566) and their administration of the island (1566–1912)* (Cambridge, 1941). Philip D. Curtin, *Cross-cultural trade in world history* (Cambridge, 1984), eloquently frames the study of Armenian, western European, and other communal trading networks. The fundamental work for the specific case of Jews in commerce in the Islamic world is S. D. Goitein, *Mediterranean society: an abridgment in one volume*, ed. Jacob Lassner (Berkeley, CA, 2000); but see also Amitav Ghosh, *In an antique land: history in the guise of a traveler's tale* (New York, 1992), for a stimulating if eccentric treatment.

The most thorough treatment of non-Muslim groups in the Ottoman world, including several provocative articles on the *millet* system, is Benjamin Braude and Bernard Lewis (eds.), *Christians and Jews in the Ottoman Empire*, 2 vols. (New York, 1982). One may supplement this work with Michael Ursinus, "Millet," *Encyclopedia of Islam*, 2nd edn (Leiden: Brill, 1962–); and Daniel Goffman, "Ottoman *millets* in the early seventeenth century," *New Perspectives on Turkey* 11 (1994): 135–58.

On the tangled question of Jewish relations with hegemonic religions, both Christian and Muslim, Mark R. Cohen, *Under crescent and cross: the Jews in the middle ages* (Princeton, 1994), is responsible and readable, while the most accessible works on the specific Ottoman case are Bernard Lewis, *The Jews of Islam* (Princeton, 1984); and Avigdor Levy, *The Sephardim in the Ottoman Empire* (Princeton, 1992). An inspiring case study of Mediterranean commerce is Benjamin Arbel, *Trading nations: Jews and Venetians in the early modern eastern Mediterranean* (Leiden, 1995); much of the raw data for my imagined biography of Kubad Çavuş, pieces of which preface each chapter of this book, derives from Arbel's work. For an examination of an Ottoman settlement in a Christian city, see Cemal Kafadar, "A death in Venice (1575): Anatolian Muslim merchants trading in the Serenissima," *Journal of Turkish Studies* 10(1986): 191–218.

The case of the Ottoman Balkans remains shadowy, but has received some attention in recent years. Its history has been particularly prey to the subjective ruminations of nationalist agendas. Two good corrective essays for the Yugoslavian region in particular are Mark Pinson (ed.), *The Muslims of Bosnia-Herzegovina: their historic development from the middle ages to the dissolution of Yugoslavia* (Cambridge, MA, 1993); and Robert Donia and John Fine, *Bosnia and Hercegovina* (New York, 1995).

THE ALIEN IN OTTOMAN SOCIETY

Despite recent attention to the Ottoman place in the "world economy," surprisingly little has been done to examine the alien in early modern Ottoman society. This lacuna derives in large part from the historiography's persistent Eurocentric thrust. Volumes such as Alfred Wood, *The history of the Levant Company* (Cambridge, 1935), and Sonia Anderson, *An English consul in Turkey: Paul Rycaut at Smyrna, 1667–1678* (Oxford, 1989), both of which ably and exhaustively discuss western Europeans in Ottoman domains, do so almost exclusively from a western European perspective and through English sources. Garrett Mattingly, *Renaissance diplomacy* (Boston, 1955), is another good example of Eurocentric partiality. This classic text traces the rise of modern diplomacy exclusively through Italy and Christian nation states. Niels Steensgaard has done much to ascertain the administrative structure of foreign merchant communities in his "Consuls and nations in the Levant from 1570 to 1650," *Scandinavian Economic History Review* 15(1967): 143–62. J. G. A. Pocock presents a revisionist agenda for examining the English encounter with others in "British history: a plea for a new subject," *Journal of Modern History* 4(1975): 601–24. An attempt to implement some aspects of this agenda is Daniel Goffman, *Britons in the Ottoman Empire, 1642–60* (Seattle, 1998).

OTTOMAN STUDIES AND SOURCES

There are countless published sources on European observers of the Ottoman world. One of the most astute of such witnesses was O. G. de Busbecq, on which see *Ogier Ghiselin de Busbecq: Imperial ambassador at Constantinople* (Oxford, 1968). A second is found in Konstantin Mihailovich, *Memoirs of a janissary* (Ann Arbor, 1975). Quite different but equally important is Robert Bargrave, *The travel diary of Robert Bargrave*, ed. Michael G. Brennan (London, 1999). Also fascinating is Lady Mary Wortley Montague, *The Turkish Embassy letters*, intro. Anita Desai (London, 1993).

While the publication of Ottoman documents has become quite an industry in Turkey, there are unfortunately few such collections available in English, especially for the earliest period. Any investigation into Ottoman sources, though, should begin with Suraiya Faroqhi's *Approaching Ottoman history: an introduction to the sources* (Cambridge, 1999), which constitutes an exhaustive discussion of Ottoman holdings in many libraries and archives. Bernard Lewis (ed. and trans.), *Islam from the Prophet Muhammad to the Capture of Constantinople*, 2 vols. (Oxford, 1987), contains a number of sources from the formative years of the Ottoman polity. More specific studies include Lewis V. Thomas's work on one of the most important seventeenth-century Ottoman chroniclers, *A study of Naima*, ed. Norman Itzkowitz (New York, 1971); Bernard Lewis's *Notes and documents from the Turkish archives: a contribution to the history of the Jews in the Ottoman Empire* (Jerusalem, 1952), which looks at a specific topic through the lens of the central Ottoman archives; Yvonne Seng's examination of kadi court records, "The şer'iye sicilleri of the Istanbul müftülüğü as a source for the study of everyday life," *Turkish Studies Association Bulletin* 15.2(1991): 307–25; and Daniel Goffman's discussion of the "registers of foreigners" in *Izmir and the Levantine world*, pp. 147–54.

Among studies that discuss the difficulties of dealing with particular Ottoman sources are Heath Lowry, "The Ottoman *tahrir-defterleri* as a source for social and economic history: pitfalls and limitations," *Türkische Wirtschafts- und Sozialgeschichte von 1071 bis 1920* (Wiesbaden, 1995), pp. 183–96; and Rifa'at Ali Abu-El-Haj, *Formation of the modern state: the Ottoman Empire, sixteenth to eighteenth centuries* (Albany, NY, 1992). Rifa'at's book also is a severe critique of the state of Ottoman studies, as is Halil Berktay and Suraiya Faroqhi, *New approaches to the state and peasant in Ottoman history* (London, 1992). Şevket Pamuk has attacked the complicated issue of Ottoman money in *A Monetary History of the Ottoman Empire* (Cambridge, 2000); and Jane Hathaway has recently dealt with the hoary matter of Ottoman periodization in "Problems of periodization in Ottoman history: the fifteenth through the eighteenth centuries," *Turkish Studies Association Bulletin* 20.2(1996): 25–31.

Index

NEW APPROACHES TO EUROPEAN HISTORY

13 ROGER CHICKERING   Imperial Germany and the Great War, 1914–1918
0 521 56148 5 hardback
0 521 56754 8 paperback

14 W. R. WARD   Christianity under the Ancien Régime, 1648–1789
0 521 55361 X hardback
0 521 55672 4 paperback

15 SIMON DIXON   The Modernisation of Russia 1676–1825
0 521 37100 7 hardback
0 521 37961 X paperback

16 MARY LINDEMANN   Medicine and Society in Early Modern Europe
0 521 41254 4 hardback
0 521 42354 6 paperback

17 DONALD QUATAERT   The Ottoman Empire, 1700–1922
0 521 63328 1 hardback
0 521 63360 5 paperback

18 REX A. WADE   The Russian Revolution, 1917
0 521 41548 9 hardback
0 521 42565 4 paperback

19 JAMES R. FARR   Artisans in Europe, 1300–1914
0 521 41888 7 hardback
0 521 42934 X paperback

20 MERRY E. WIESNER   Women and Gender in Early Modern Europe Second
Edition
0 521 77105 6 hardback
0 521 77822 0 paperback

21 CHARLES W. INGRAO   The Habsburg Monarchy 1618–1815 Second Edition
0 521 78034 9 hardback
0 521 78505 7 paperback

22 JULIUS R. RUFF   Violence in Early Modern Europe
0 521 59119 8 hardback
0 521 59894 X paperback

23 JAMES VAN HORN MELTON   The Rise of the Public in Enlightenment Europe
0 521 46573 7 hardback
0 521 46969 4 paperback

24 DANIEL GOFFMAN   The Ottoman Empire and Early Modern Europe
0 521 45280 5 hardback
0 521 45908 7 paperback